THE PRINCIPAL PARTS
OF THE BAVLI'S DISCOURSE
A Preliminary Taxonomy

SOUTH FLORIDA STUDIES IN THE HISTORY OF JUDAISM

Edited by
Jacob Neusner
William Scott Green, James Strange
Darrell J. Fasching, Sara Mandell

Number 53
The Principal Parts of the Bavli's Discourse
A Preliminary Taxonomy

by
Jacob Neusner

THE PRINCIPAL PARTS OF THE BAVLI'S DISCOURSE

A Preliminary Taxonomy

MISHNAH COMMENTARY, SOURCES, TRADITIONS, AND AGGLUTINATIVE MISCELLANIES

by
Jacob Neusner

THE PRINCIPAL PARTS
OF THE BAVLI'S DISCOURSE
A Preliminary Taxonomy

©1992
University of South Florida

Publication of this book was made possible by a grant from the Tisch Family
Foundation, New York City. The University of South Florida acknowledges
with thanks this important support for its scholarly projects.

Library of Congress Cataloging in Publication Data

Neusner, Jacob, 1932-
    The principal parts of the Bavli's discourse : a preliminary
    taxonomy : Mishnah commentary, sources, traditions, and
    agglutinative miscellanies / by Jacob Neusner.
    p.   cm. — (South Florida studies in the history of Judaism ;
    no. 53)
    Includes index.
    ISBN 1-55540-750-1
    1. Talmud—Criticism, Redaction. 2. Mishnah—Criticism,
interpretation, etc. 3. Talmud—Sources. I. Title. II. Series:
South Florida studies in the history of Judaism ; 53.
BM503.6.N486   1992
296.1'25066—dc20   92-25795
                                                    CIP

Printed in the United States of America
on acid-free paper

Table of Contents

Preface

In a series of free-standing monographs, I have been solving, piece by piece, the literary puzzle presented by the Talmud of Babylonia. In the present work of *haute vulgarisation*, I set forth my principal results on the types of compositions of which the document is made up, with some further comments, at the end, on how the Bavli's framers imposed their own program upon most of the compositions and composites from which they drew. The principal monographs that I summarize here are as follows (in the order of their composition and appearance):

The Bavli's Primary Discourse. Mishnah Commentary, Its Rhetorical Paradigms and Their Theological Implications in the Talmud of Babylonia Tractate Moed Qatan (Atlanta, 1992: Scholars Press for South Florida Studies in the History of Judaism).

Sources and Traditions. Types of Composition in the Talmud of Babylonia (Atlanta, 1992: Scholars Press for South Florida Studies in the History of Judaism).

The Bavli's Massive Miscellanies. The Problem of Agglutinative Discourse in the Talmud of Babylona (Atlanta, 1992: Scholars Press for South Florida Studies in the History of Judaism).

How the Bavli Shaped Rabbinic Discourse (Atlanta, 1991: Scholars Press for South Florida Studies in the History of Judaism).

Other monographs to which reference is made in the four chapters before us are epitomized in context.

The project at hand gains in importance for my larger project of providing an accurate and detailed description of the Bavli as a piece of writing. This monograph therefore forms one of the final pieces of a large puzzle on which I have been working for some years, and on which I shall continue to work for several years more: the complete description of the Bavli, from a fresh translation, the first analytical one ever, onward through a clear and comprehensive account of what the document is and how its authors or authorship accomplished their goals. In the work at hand, five now-completed writings form the foundation of this one.

They are [1] *The Rules of Composition of the Talmud of Babylonia. The Cogency of the Bavli's Composite* (Atlanta, 1991: Scholars Press for South Florida Studies in the History of Judaism), which led directly to, [2], *The Bavli's One Voice: Types and Forms of Analytical Discourse and Their Fixed Order of Appearance* (Atlanta, 1991: Scholars Press for South Florida Studies in the History of Judaism); [3], *The Bavli's Massive Miscellanies. The Problem of Agglutinative Discourse in the Talmud of Babylonia* (Atlanta, 1992: Scholars Press for South Florida Studies in the History of Judaism); [4], *Sources and Traditions. Types of Compositions in the Talmud of Babylonia* (Atlanta, 1992: Scholars Press for South Florida Studies in the History of Judaism); and [5] *The Law Behind the Laws. The Bavli's Essential Discourse* (Atlanta, 1992: Scholars Press for South Florida Studies in the History of Judaism).

[1] *Rules of Composition* identified for me the units of analytical consequence in the Bavli, showing me the main beams of the document's composition as distinct from its subordinate and merely amplificatory compositions. All further work of description of the Bavli began in the simple observations of that monograph, which defined for me the largest whole units of analytical inquiry. In the present work, I replicate the same method by identifying what I conceive to be the composites, and, within them, the compositions that form the principal parts of said composites. I further indicate how the various compositions relate to the work of Mishnah commentary, or of elaborating Mishnah commentary. The method laid out in *Rules of Composition*, and the results of that book, therefore form the basis for the analytical processes of this one; and the various visual means of showing what's what – indenting secondary materials, centering free-standing compilations, for instance – show in a very striking way how the Bavli works and what its authorship means to accomplish, not only in a general way, but, in detail, over and over again.

[2] In *The Bavli's One Voice* I have shown that the Bavli is made up of materials intended to serve as a commentary to the Mishnah; the principal type of writing that the framers of the Bavli produced on their own account is exegetical and analytical. That was not a conclusion, only an initial observation. For if the Bavli really is a commentary to the Mishnah, then I had to attend to the varieties of materials utilized in that commentary. This required attention, first, to the anomalous components of the document, namely, the fairly large-scale composites that in no way appear to take shape around the tasks of the exposition of the Bavli. So I turned first of all to the exceptional materials, which, though small in proportion to the whole, challenge any description of the Bavli as a rather well-crafted and sturdily composed, systematic explanation and expansion of what is found in the Mishnah. The present work follows up on *The Bavli's One Voice*, refining its judgment as to the character, as

Mishnah commentary, of nearly the whole of the Bavli. I aim ultimately at being able to say what I conceive to be the Bavli's one statement. But I am far from reaching that goal.

[3] In *The Bavli's Massive Miscellanies*, further, I was able to demonstrate that the Bavli's other type of composite, the one that is formulated not as an analytical, propositional, or even syllogistic Mishnah commentary, conformed to rules entirely familiar to us within the framework of the Bavli's own editorial program. What I did not anticipate was that the miscellanies, though massive, in no way emerged as miscellaneous at all; their principles of conglomeration and agglutination proved only to differ from those that operate in the main composites of the Bavli. The results of that study are apparent here, in my treatment of a number of rather large composites, in no way formed in response to the Mishnah's statements and propositions, or even, in any concrete way, its themes.

[4] Once I had worked my way around the fringes of the document, it was time to return to my original theory on the description of the writing, refining the rather gross claim that in its definitive literary structure the Bavli is a commentary to the Mishnah. That leaves open the issue of the compositions that are used in the formation of what I called those "massive miscellanies." In *Sources and Tradition* I addressed the problem of classifying the components of those "massive miscellanies" (which of course are not at all miscellaneous), and the result set the stage for the present work and its forthcoming companion. In *Sources and Traditions* my purpose was to identify types of writings, in a sample of tractates, that serve some editorial program and context other than the Bavli's. This book of course complements that one in obvious ways.

[5] It was in that setting that I realized the Bavli derives much of its intellectual power from a kind of writing that I had treated only tangentially, and never in a systematic way. In *The Law Behind the Laws: The Bavli's Essential Discourse,* I turned to one side of the Bavli's essential discourse, Mishnah commentary that transcends and unites the Mishnah's rules into a composition of another order altogether. What I realized is that most of these essential discourses begin in the work of Mishnah commentary and turn out not so much to transcend as to extend that work of exegesis. That is why I found it necessary, in this companion work, to identify and classify the Bavli's main entries: its commentary to the Mishnah in the most conventional sense of the genre, commentary – that is to say, the Bavli's primary discourse – its commentary to the Mishnah. Here, then, I set forth what I conceive to be the paramount and ubiquitous kind of discourse of the Talmud of Babylonia, which is, very simply, the exegetical program of the Bavli: *the*

questions repeatedly asked by the authors of the Bavli's Mishnah exegetical compositions, and by the framers of the Bavli's Mishnah exegetical composites; and what is at stake in the repeated proof of the propositions set forth in answer to those questions.

I express my genuine pleasure at the opportunity for a life of learning through both teaching and scholarly inquiry that is afforded to me by the University of South Florida. I express thanks to my University for its generous support of my scholarly work. I also thank my colleagues in the Department of Religious Studies for not only friendship but intellectual stimulus. As always, I talked over my ideas with Professor William Scott Green, University of Rochester, and found in his responses important guidance for my own thinking.

JACOB NEUSNER

Distinguished Research Professor of Religious Studies
UNIVERSITY OF SOUTH FLORIDA
Tampa, St. Petersburg, Sarasota, Lakeland, Fort Myers

735 Fourteenth Avenue Northeast
St. Petersburg, Florida 33701-1413 USA

1

Mishnah Commentary

The Bavli, a.k.a. the Talmud of Babylonia, in form and substance presents a commentary to the Mishnah, and, to a markedly lesser degree, Scripture as well. From 80 percent to 99 percent of the composites of the tractates of the Bavli – depending on the tractate – focus upon the work of Mishnah exegesis. The taxonomy of Mishnah commentary, for a significant sample of the document, is worked out here: a catalogue of the types of exegetical compositions and composites that accomplish the paramount goal of explaining the sense and meaning of the Mishnah. I treat in particular the manner in which the Talmud of Babylonia proposes, in Bavli-tractate Moed Qatan, to read Mishnah-tractate Moed Qatan. Defining in detail what the sages of the Bavli did, and how they did it, imparts immediacy and concreteness to the general description of their writing as "a commentary to the Mishnah." Not only so, but by showing how most of the Bavli's composites, as well as the larger part of the composites formed into those composites, form a commentary to the Mishnah or a secondary expansion of commentary to the Mishnah, I provide in highly graphic form a clear picture of the structure of the document as a commentary, covering also secondary elaboration of its own commentaries. My method is familiar.

I. The Talmud of Babylonia: A Commentary to the Mishnah

For the most part, the Talmud of Babylonia is a commentary to the Mishnah. Let me start by giving a simple example of what characterizes the initial phase of nearly every sustained composite of the Bavli: a commentary to the Mishnah. This is what I mean by Mishnah commentary:

Mishnah-Tractate Baba Qamma
3:1

    A.   He who leaves a jug in the public domain,

    B.   and someone else came along and stumbled on it and broke it –

    C.   [the one who broke it] is exempt.

    D.   And if [the one who broke it] was injured by it, the owner of the barrel is liable [to pay damages for] his injury.

I.1   A.   *How come the framer of the passage refers, to begin with, to a jug but then concludes with reference to a* **barrel**? *And so, too, we have learned in another passage in the Mishnah:* **This one comes along with his barrel, and that one comes along with his beam – [if] the jar of this one was broken by the beam of that one, [the owner of the beam] is exempt.** *How come the framer of the passage refers, to begin with, to a* **barrel** *but then concludes with reference to a* **jug**? *And so, too, we have learned in the Mishnah:* **This one is coming along with his barrel of wine, and that one is coming along with his jug of honey – the jug of honey cracked, and this one poured out his wine and saved the honey in his jar – he has a claim only for his wages** [M. B.Q. 10:4A-E]. *How come the framer of the passage refers, to begin with, to a* **barrel** *but then concludes with reference to a* **jug**?

      B.   Said R. Hisda, "Well, as a matter of fact, there really is no difference between a jar and a barrel."

      C.   *So what is the practical difference between the usages?*

      D.   It has to do with buying and selling.

      E.   *How can we imagine such a case? If it is in a place in which a jug is not called a barrel, nor a barrel a jug, for in such a case, the two terms are kept distinct!*

      F.   *The distinction is required for a place in which most of the people call a jug a jug and a barrel a barrel, but some call a barrel a jug and some call a jug a barrel. What might you then have supposed? That we follow the majority usage? [27B] So we are informed that that is not the case, for in disputes over monetary transactions, we do not follow the majority usage.*

All that we have here is an investigation of the linguistic properties of the Mishnah paragraph that is cited. The framer of the anonymous writing notes that a variety of other passages seem to vary word choices in a somewhat odd way. The point of insistence – the document is carefully drafted, the writers do not forget what they were talking about, so when they change words in the middle of a stream of thought, it is purposeful – constitutes an exegetical point, pure and simple.

The foregoing exemplifies Mishnah commentary as a process of clarification. But commentators in the Bavli stand not only within the framework of the Mishnah, aiming at the explanation of what it says. They also take a stance outside of that framework, and propose to challenge its statements or their implications. To understand precisely what the Bavli means by a commentary to the Mishnah, we have therefore to begin with the clear picture that the Bavli asks the questions of not only the teacher, standing inside the document and looking outward, but also of the reader, located outside the document and looking inward. In what follows, then, the stance of the commentator now is external to the text, and the commentator wants to know why the Mishnah finds self-evident what is not necessarily obvious to all parties:

1:7-8/I.1

A. *So if it's* **an occasion of rejoicing for the groom,** *what's so bad about that?*

B. Said R. Judah said Samuel, and so said R. Eleazar said R. Oshaia, and some say, said R. Eleazar said R. Hanina, "The consideration is that one occasion of rejoicing should not be joined with another such occasion."

C. Rabbah bar R. Huna said, "It is because he neglects the rejoicing of the festival to engage in rejoicing over his wife."

D. Said Abbayye to R. Joseph, "This statement that has been said by Rabbah bar R. Huna belongs to Rab, for said R. Daniel bar Qattina said Rab, 'How on the basis of Scripture do we know that people may not take wives on the intermediate days of the festival? As it is said, "You shall rejoice in your feast" (Deut. 16:14), meaning, in your feast – not in your new wife.'"

E. Ulla said, "It is because it is excess trouble."

F. R. Isaac Nappaha said, "It is because one will neglect the requirement of being fruitful and multiplying" [if people postponed weddings until festivals, they might somehow diminish the occasion for procreation, which is the first obligation]."

G. *An objection was raised:* All those of whom they have said that they are forbidden to wed on the festival **[9A]** are permitted to wed on the eve of the festival. *Now this poses a problem to the explanations of all the cited authorities!*

H. *There is no problem from the perspective of him who has said,* "The consideration is that one occasion of rejoicing should not be joined with another such occasion," *for the main rejoicing of the wedding is only a single day.*

I. *And from the perspective of him who has said,* "It is because it is excess trouble," *the principal bother lasts only one day.*

J. *And from the perspective of him who has said,* "It is because one will neglect the requirement of being fruitful and multiplying," *for merely one day someone will not postpone the obligation for any considerable length of time.*

What is important in understanding the nature of commentary in the Bavli is the dual stance of the commentator: inside and outside.

Now to generalize on the basis of the cases before us: what I mean by a commentary is a piece of writing that depends for its program – topics to be treated, coherence and cogency, alike – upon some other writing. We know the difference between a base text and a commentary because the base text will be cogent in its own terms, and the commentary will make sense only in relationship to the base text. And we know the difference between the one and the other because a commentary's author will always signal the text, for example, by citing a phrase or by a clear allusion, and will further identify what he then proposes to contribute. Commentaries may take a variety of forms, but the mark of them all will be the same: they make sense only by appeal to, in the context of, some piece of writing outside of themselves. But that common trait among them all scarcely exhausts the program that a commentary will undertake – or even define it. One type of commentary will follow a quite well-defined program of questions, another will promiscuously comment on this, that, and the other thing, without ever suggesting that the commentator has a systematic inquiry in mind. And, it goes without saying, the range of issues subject to comment – philological, historical, aesthetic, not to mention theological – can be limited only by the number of texts deemed by an author or compiler to deserve a commentary.

These somewhat abstract and general remarks may forthwith be given concrete exemplification in a passage that, in my view, forms an archetype of the Bavli's commentary to the Mishnah. Let us rapidly examine it, identify its paramount traits, and turn to the question of how we shall then define, for the Bavli overall, the repertoire and program that dictated to its authors of compositions and compilers of composites precisely the task they were to undertake. Since this exercise in definition and classification pertains to Bavli-tractate Moed Qatan, I take my exemplary definition from the opening lines of that tractate. To explain what follows: the Mishnah paragraphs are cited in boldface type, and whenever they recur, it is in the same form.

1:1

A. **They water an irrigated field on the intermediate days of a festival and in the Seventh Year,**

B. **whether from a spring that first flows at that time, or from a spring that does not first flow at that time.**

I.1   A. **[They water an irrigated field on the intermediate days of a festival and in the Seventh Year, whether from a spring that first flows at that time, or from a spring that does not first flow at that time:]** *Since it is explicitly stated that they may water from a spring that flows for the first time, which may damage the soil by erosion [making necessary immediate repair of the damage during the intermediate days of the festival], is it necessary to specify that they may water from a spring that does not first flow at that time, which is not going to cause erosion?*

The question that our commentary asks at the outset concerns the language of the Mishnah, and the specific issue is whether the Mishnah's framer has repeated himself or has told us something that, absent his articulation of the point, we might not have discerned on our own. That is what precipitates the question before us.

B. *One may say that it is necessary to include both the latter and the former, for if the Tannaite framer had given the rule only covering a spring that first flows on the intermediate days of the festival, it is in that case in particular in which it is permitted to work on an irrigated field, but not for a rain-watered field, because the water is going to cause erosion, but in the case of a spring that does not first flow on the intermediate days, which is unlikely to cause erosion, I might have said that even a rain-watered field may be watered. So he tells us that there is no distinction between a spring that flows for the first time and one that does not flow for the first time. The rule is the same for both: an irrigated plot may be watered from it, but a rain-watered plot may not be watered from [either a new or an available spring].*

The second comment on the Mishnah is equally interested in the formulation of the Mishnah, but it is now concerned with the meanings of words and phrases.

I.2   A. *And on what basis is it inferred that the meaning of the words "irrigated field" is, a thirsty field [which has to be irrigated]?*
       B. *It is in line with that which is written:* "When you were faint and weary" (Deut. 25:18), *and the Hebrew word for weary is represented in Aramaic by the word that means, "exhausted."*
       C. *And how do we know that the words translated rain-watered field refers to a fucked field?*
       D. "For as a man has sexual relations with a maiden, so shall your sons be as husbands unto you" (Isa. 62:5), *and the word in Aramaic is rendered, "Behold, as a boy fucks a girl, so your sons shall get laid in your midst."*

Our third comment wishes to identify the authority behind the rule of our Mishnah, which is to say, who stands behind a premise that is implicit and formative?

I.3   A. *Who is the Tannaite authority who takes the position that work on the intermediate days of a festival is permitted if it is to prevent loss, but if it is to add to gain it is not permitted, and, further, even to prevent loss, really heavy labor is forbidden?*
       B. *Said R. Huna, "It is R. Eliezer b. Jacob, for we have learned in the Mishnah:* R. Eliezer b. Jacob says, 'They lead water from one tree to another, on condition that one not water the entire field. Seeds which have not been watered before the festival one should not water on the intermediate days of the festival' [M. 1:3]."
       C. *Well, I might concede that there is a representation of R. Eliezer's position that he prohibits work to add to one's gain, but have you heard a tradition that he disallows work in a situation in which otherwise loss will result?*
       D. *Rather, said R. Pappa, "Who is the authority behind this rule? It is R. Judah, for it has been taught on Tannaite authority:* 'From a spring that first flows on the intermediate days of a festival they irrigate even a rain-watered field,' the words of R. Meir. And sages say, 'They irrigate from it only a field that depends upon irrigation, which has gone dry.' R. Eleazar b. Azariah says, "Not this nor that, [but

they do not irrigate a field from it (namely, a field the spring of which has gone dry) even in the case of an irrigated field]' [T. M.Q. 1:1A-C]. Even further, said R. Judah, 'A person should not clean out a water channel and with the dredging on the intermediate days of a festival water his garden or seed bed.'"

E. *Now what is the meaning of "that has gone dry"? If you say that it really has dried up, then what is going to be accomplished by watering it?*

F. *Said Abbayye, "The point is that this former water source has gone dry and another has just emerged."*

G. **R. Eleazar b. Azariah says, "Not this nor that":** *There is no difference between the case of an old spring that has gone dry or that has not gone dry; in any event a spring that has just flowed may not be utilized on the intermediate days of the festival.*

H. *And how do you know [that it is Judah in particular who takes the position that work on the intermediate days of a festival is permitted if it is to prevent loss, but if it is to add to gain it is not permitted, and, further, even to prevent loss, really heavy labor is forbidden]? Perhaps R. Judah takes the position that he does, that is, that it is permitted to use the water for an irrigated field but not for a field that depends on rain, only in the case of a spring that has just now begun to flow, [2B] since it may cause erosion, but a spring that has not just now begun to flow and will not cause erosion might be permitted for use even on a field that depends on rain?*

I. *If so, then in accord with which authority will you assign our Mishnah paragraph? For in fact, in R. Judah's view, there is no distinction between a spring that has just now flowed and one that has not just now flowed; in either case, an irrigated field may be watered, one that depends on rain may not. And the reason that the passage specifies the spring that has just now flowed is only to show the extent to which R. Meir was prepared to go, even a spring that has just now flowed may be used, and that is, even for a field that depends upon rain.*

With these three comments, the work of Mishnah commentary has come to a conclusion. We now turn to a problem that concerns the theme of our Mishnah's rule, and the point of intersection with the Mishnah will be explicit: the paragraph of the Mishnah at hand will contribute a fact toward the solution of the problem, and that will show us a deeper dimension of our Mishnah's rule. Hence while not a commentary to the Mishnah in any formal sense, what follows is a secondary expansion of what the Mishnah says: a making explicit of what is implicit.

I.4   A. *It has been stated:*

B. He who on the Sabbath weeds a field or waters his seedlings — *on what count is he to be admonished [not to do so]?*

C. Rabbah said, "On the count of ploughing."

D. R. Joseph said, "On the count of sowing."

E. *Said Rabbah, "It is more reasonable to see matters as I do. For what is the purpose of ploughing, if not to loosen the soil, and, here, too, he loosens the soil."*

F. *Said R. Joseph, "It is more reasonable to see matters as I do. For what is the purpose of sowing? It is to make produce sprout up. And here, too, he makes produce sprout up."*

G. *Said Abbayye to Rabbah, "There is a problem in your position, and there also is a problem in the position of R. Joseph.*

H. *"There is a problem in your position: Does this act come only under the classification of ploughing and not sowing?*

I. *"And there also is a problem in the position of R. Joseph: Does this act come only under the classification of sowing and not ploughing?*

J. *"And should you say that in any place in which an act may be classified under two taxa, one is subject to liability on only one count, has not R.* Kahana said, 'If one pruned his tree but requires the wood for fuel, he is liable on two counts, one on the count of planting, the other on the count of harvesting'?"

K. *That's a problem.*

L. Objected R. Joseph to Rabbah, **"He who weeds or covers with dirt diverse seeds is flogged. R. Aqiba says, 'Also one who preserves them'** [T. Kil. 1:15A-B]. *Now from my perspective, in that I hold that one is liable on the count of sowing, that explains the penalty, since sowing is forbidden in connection with mixed seeds in the vineyard; but from your perspective, in that you say that the count is ploughing, is there any prohibition of ploughing in connection with mixed seeds?"*

M. *He said to him, "The count is that he has preserved them."*

N. *"But lo, since the concluding clause states,* **R. Aqiba says, 'Also one who preserves them,'** *it must follow that the initial Tannaite authority maintains that the count for sanction is not that of preserving the crop of mixed seeds!"*

O. *"The whole of the statement represents the position of R. Aqiba, and the sense of the passage is to explain the operative consideration, specifically: What is the reason that* **he who weeds or covers with dirt diverse seeds is flogged?** *It is because one is thereby preserving them, since* **R. Aqiba says, 'Also one who preserves them.'"**

P. *What is the basis in Scripture for the position of R. Aqiba?*

Q. *It is in line with that which has been taught on Tannaite authority:*

R. "You shall not sow your field with two kinds of seed" (Lev. 19:19) —

S. I know only that sowing is forbidden. How do we know that preserving the sown seed is forbidden?

T. Scripture says, "Mixed seeds in your field not....," [meaning: It is the mixing of seeds that is emphatically forbidden, and you may have no share by your action in producing such a situation (Lazarus)].

So what we **are** given are three clear citations and explanations of the language of the Mishnah, followed by a composition that is a comment of a different order. If, as I maintain, the Bavli is a commentary on the Mishnah, then we should anticipate that some systematic program has told compilers what comes first and what follows. A preliminary thesis then will suggest that first comes attention to the wording of the passage, followed by inquiry into its implications and the authorities who will endorse the implicit meanings, and, at the end, a more subtle and wide-ranging reflection of some depth.

Enough has been said to define the work before us. We now work our way through a single tractate and ask, line by line, about the purpose of a given statement, meaning, a whole and complete unit of thought. Since, the very form of the document dictates, the initial, and precipitating, purpose of all compositions and many composites is the exegesis of the Mishnah, on the strength of our survey, we catalogue the types of Mishnah commentary set forth by the authors of the Bavli's tractate, Moed Qatan, organized around the Mishnah's tractate of the same name.

II. Agglutinative Miscellanies and the Mishnah

Since I claim that the Bavli is a commentary to the Mishnah, I also account, systematically, for compositions and even entire composites that are not written in response to the statements of the Mishnah but that stand on their own, forming coherent statements out of all relationship to the Mishnah. I indent what I conceive to be secondary expansions of prior materials. Indented material is not Mishnah commentary; but it is always tacked on to complement Mishnah commentary, or to supplement a theme introduced by the Mishnah's statement or by the Bavli's Mishnah commentary. Not uncommonly I refer to a passage as (a) talmud; by this I mean a sustained, rigorous exegesis of a given text. Thus "a talmud to a Tosefta passage" is not much different from "a talmud to a Mishnah passage," namely, a sustained exegesis of the prior text, amplifying detail, proposing propositions and testing them.

Mishnah-tractate Moed Qatan
1:1

A.   They water an irrigated field on the intermediate days of a festival and in the Seventh Year,

B.   whether from a spring that first flows at that time, or from a spring that does not first flow at that time.

C.   But they do not water [an irrigated field] with (1) collected rain water, or (2) water from a swape well.

D.   And they do not dig channels around vines.

1:2

A.   R. Eleazar b. Azariah says, "They do not make a new water channel on the intermediate days of a festival or in the Seventh Year."

B.   And sages say, "They make a new water channel in the Seventh Year, and they repair damaged ones on the intermediate days of a festival."

    C.   **They repair damaged waterways in the public domain and dig them out.**
    D.   **They repair roads, streets, and water pools.**
    E.   **And they (1) do all public needs, (2) mark off graves, and (3) go forth [to give warning] against Diverse Kinds.**

We commence with a proof that, while the Mishnah covers a variety of cases, it is not verbose or repetitious, because each case makes its own point and therefore has to be set forth in its own terms.

I.1   A.   **[They water an irrigated field on the intermediate days of a festival and in the Seventh Year, whether from a spring that first flows at that time, or from a spring that does not first flow at that time:]** *Since it is explicitly stated that they may water from a spring that flows for the first time, which may damage the soil by erosion [making necessary immediate repair of the damage during the intermediate days of the festival], is it necessary to specify that they may water from a spring that does not first flow at that time, which is not going to cause erosion?*

    B.   *One may say that it is necessary to include both the latter and the former, for if the Tannaite framer had given the rule only covering a spring that first flows on the intermediate days of the festival, it is in that case in particular in which it is permitted to work on an irrigated field, but not for a rain-watered field, because the water is going to cause erosion, but in the case of a spring that does not first flow on the intermediate days, which is unlikely to cause erosion, I might have said that even a rain-watered field may be watered. So he tells us that there is no distinction between a spring that flows for the first time and one that does not flow for the first time. The rule is the same for both: an irrigated plot may be watered from it, but a rain-watered plot may not be watered from [either a new or an available spring].*

The comment is to be classified as criticism of the formulation of the Mishnah, with the intent of proving that the Mishnah does not repeat itself. We now proceed to another Mishnah commentary, this one on the language of the Mishnah, the meanings of its word choices:

I.2   A.   *And on what basis is it inferred that the meaning of the words "irrigated field" is, a thirsty field [which has to be irrigated]?*

    B.   *It is in line with that which is written: "When you were faint and weary" (Deut. 25:18), and the Hebrew word for weary is represented in Aramaic by the word that means, "exhausted."*

    C.   *And how do we know that the words translated rain-watered field refers to a fucked field?*

    D.   **"For as a man has sexual relations with a maiden, so shall your sons be as husbands unto you"** (Isa. 62:5), *and the word in Aramaic is rendered, "Behold, as a boy fucks a girl, so your sons shall get laid in your midst."*

The foregoing forms a standard talmudic inquiry: what do words mean? The answer will ordinarily derive from the lexical evidence of Scripture.

I.3   A.   *Who is the Tannaite authority who takes the position that work on the intermediate days of a festival is permitted if it is to prevent loss, but if it is to add to gain it is not permitted, and, further, even to prevent loss, really heavy labor is forbidden?*

        B.   *Said R. Huna, "It is R. Eliezer b. Jacob, for we have learned in the Mishnah:* **R. Eliezer b. Jacob says, 'They lead water from one tree to another, on condition that one not water the entire field. Seeds which have not been watered before the festival one should not water on the intermediate days of the festival'** *[M. 1:3]."*

        C.   *Well, I might concede that there is a representation of R. Eliezer's position that he prohibits work to add to one's gain, but have you heard a tradition that he disallows work in a situation in which otherwise loss will result?*

        D.   *Rather, said R. Pappa, "Who is the authority behind this rule? It is R. Judah, for it has been taught on Tannaite authority:* **'From a spring that first flows on the intermediate days of a festival they irrigate even a rain-watered field,'** *the words of R. Meir. And sages say,* **'They irrigate from it only a field that depends upon irrigation, which has gone dry.'** *R. Eleazar b. Azariah says,* **"Not this nor that, [but they do not irrigate a field from it (namely, a field the spring of which has gone dry) even in the case of an irrigated field]'** *[T. M.Q. 1:1A-C]. Even further, said R. Judah,* **'A person should not clean out a water channel and with the dredging on the intermediate days of a festival water his garden or seed bed.'"**

        E.   *Now what is the meaning of "that has gone dry"? If you say that it really has dried up, then what is going to be accomplished by watering it?*

        F.   *Said Abbayye, "The point is that this former water source has gone dry and another has just emerged."*

        G.   **R. Eleazar b. Azariah says, "Not this nor that":** *There is no difference between the case of an old spring that has gone dry or that has not gone dry, in any event a spring that has just flowed may not be utilized on the intermediate days of the festival.*

        H.   *And how do you know [that it is Judah in particular who takes the position that work on the intermediate days of a festival is permitted if it is to prevent loss, but if it is to add to gain it is not permitted, and, further, even to prevent loss, really heavy labor is forbidden]? Perhaps R. Judah takes the position that he does, that is, that it is permitted to use the water for an irrigated field but not for a field that depends on rain, only in the case of a spring that has just now begun to flow, [2B] since it may cause erosion, but a spring that has not just now begun to flow and will not cause erosion might be permitted for use even on a field that depends on rain?*

        I.   *If so, then in accord with which authority will you assign our Mishnah paragraph? For in fact, in R. Judah's view, there is no distinction between a spring that has just now flowed and one that has not just now flowed; in either case, an irrigated field may be watered; one that depends on rain may not. And the reason that the passage specifies the spring that has just now flowed is only to show the extent to which R. Meir was prepared to go, even a spring that has just now flowed may be used, and that is, even for a field that depends upon rain.*

Yet another standard inquiry raises the question of authority: Who stands behind a rule, or who does not concur with a rule? Is the authority behind the rule consistent in applying the same principle to other cases? and similar matters.

What follows is not Mishnah commentary in particular, but the rule of the Mishnah is refined through the presentation of secondary and derivative questions. I indent this passage and what follows to show that it is not Mishnah commentary in the simple sense operative until this point, but it also is not utterly unrelated to the exposition of the rule of the Mishnah. I do not catalogue as Mishnah commentary entries that address the theme and principle of the Mishnah, but that stand entirely on their own foundations and do not require for intelligibility an allusion to or citation of the Mishnah's language. In my *Bavli's One Voice*, I classified such items as amplification of the Mishnah, which they are, but I do not regard them as commentary in the same way as the foregoing items form commentaries to a prior document.

I.4   A.   *It has been stated:*

          B.   He who on the Sabbath weeds a field or waters his seedlings – *on what count is he to be admonished [not to do so]?*

          C.   Rabbah said, "On the count of ploughing."

          D.   R. Joseph said, "On the count of sowing."

          E.   *Said Rabbah, "It is more reasonable to see matters as I do. For what is the purpose of ploughing, if not to loosen the soil, and, here, too, he loosens the soil."*

          F.   *Said R. Joseph, "It is more reasonable to see matters as I do. For what is the purpose of sowing? It is to make produce sprout up. And here, too, he makes produce sprout up."*

          G.   *Said Abbayye to Rabbah, "There is a problem in your position, and there also is a problem in the position of R. Joseph.*

          H.   *"There is a problem in your position: Does this act come only under the classification of ploughing and not sowing?*

          I.   *"And there also is a problem in the position of R. Joseph: Does this act come only under the classification of sowing and not ploughing?*

          J.   *"And should you say that in any place in which an act may be classified under two taxa, one is subject to liability on only one count, has not R. Kahana said, 'If one pruned his tree but requires the wood for fuel, he is liable on two counts, one on the count of planting, the other on the count of harvesting'?"*

          K.   *That's a problem.*

I.5   A.   Objected R. Joseph to Rabbah, "**He who weeds or covers with dirt diverse seeds is flogged. R. Aqiba says, 'Also one who preserves them' [T. Kil. 1:15A-B].** *Now from my perspective, in that I hold that one is liable on the count of sowing, that explains the penalty, since sowing is forbidden in connection with mixed seeds in the vineyard; but from your perspective, in that you say that the count is ploughing, is there any prohibition of ploughing in connection with mixed seeds?"*

          B.   *He said to him, "The count is that he has preserved them."*

C.   *"But lo, since the concluding clause states,* **R. Aqiba says, 'Also one who preserves them,'** *it must follow that the initial Tannaite authority maintains that the count for sanction is not that of preserving the crop of mixed seeds!"*

D.   *"The whole of the statement represents the position of R. Aqiba, and the sense of the passage is to explain the operative consideration, specifically: What is the reason that* **he who weeds or covers with dirt diverse seeds is flogged?** *It is because one is thereby preserving them, since* **R. Aqiba says, 'Also one who preserves them.'"**

E.   *What is the basis in Scripture for the position of R. Aqiba?*

F.   *It is in line with that which has been taught on Tannaite authority:*

G.   "You shall not sow your field with two kinds of seed" (Lev. 19:19) –

H.   I know only that sowing is forbidden. How do we know that preserving the sown seed is forbidden?

I.   Scripture says, "Mixed seeds in your field not....," [meaning: it is the mixing of seeds that is emphatically forbidden, and you may have no share by your action in producing such a situation (Lazarus)].

II.1   A.   *We have learned in the Mishnah:* **They water an irrigated field on the intermediate days of a festival and in the Seventh Year.**

B.   [With respect to the inclusion of **in the Seventh Year:**] *Now there is no difficulty understanding the rule concerning the intermediate days of the festival, which pertains to a situation in which there is substantial loss, on account of which rabbis have permitted irrigation. But as to the Seventh Year, whether one holds that watering is classified as sowing or that watering is classified as ploughing, is it permitted either to sow or to plough in the Sabbatical Year [that it should be permitted to water the field]?*

C.   Said Abbayye, "It is concerning the Seventh Year at this time that the rule speaks, and the rule represents the position of Rabbi."

D.   *For it has been taught on Tannaite authority:*

E.   Rabbi says, "'This is the manner of release: release [by every creditor of that which he has lent his neighbor' (Deut. 15:2) – it is of two different acts of release that Scripture speaks, one, the release of lands, the other, the release of debts. When you release lands you release debts, and when you do not release lands, you do not release debts." [The prohibition of agricultural labor in the Seventh Year now that the Temple is destroyed is merely by reason of rabbinical authority, and that prohibition is not enforced where loss is involved (Lazarus).]

F.   *Raba said, "You may even maintain that the rule before us represents the position of rabbis [vis-à-vis Rabbi].* It is the generative categories of labor that the All-Merciful has prohibited, [3A] but the subsidiary classes of labor have not been forbidden. For it is written, 'But in the Seventh Year shall be a Sabbath of solemn rest for the land...you shall neither sow your field nor prune your vineyard. That which grows of itself of your harvest you shall not reap and the grapes of your undressed vine you shall not gather' (Lev. 25:4-5). *Since pruning falls within the generative category of sowing, and grape gathering falls within the generative category of reaping, for what concrete legal purpose did the All-Merciful make written reference to these items?*

> *It is to present the inference that it is to these particular derivative classes of generative categories of labor that liability pertains, but to all others, there is no liability."*

G. *So they don't, don't they? But has it not been taught on Tannaite authority:*

H. ["The Lord said to Moses on Mount Sinai, Say to the people of Israel, When you come into the land which I give you, the land shall keep a Sabbath to the Lord. Six years you shall sow your field, and six years you shall prune your vineyard and gather in its fruits; but in the Seventh Year there shall be a Sabbath of solemn rest for the land, a Sabbath to the Lord; you shall not sow your field or prune your vineyard. What grows of itself in your harvest you shall not reap, and the grapes of your undressed vine you shall not gather; it shall be a year of solemn rest for the land. The Sabbath of the land shall provide food for you, for yourself and for your male and female slaves and for your hired servant and the sojourner who lives with you; for your cattle also and for the beasts that are in your land all its yield shall be for food" (Lev. 25:1-7):] "You shall not sow your field or prune your vineyard":

I. The Torah forbids me only to sow or prune,

J. And how do we know that farmers may not fertilize, prune trees, smoke the leaves, or cover roots over with powder for fertilizer?

K. Scripture says, "Your field you shall not...." – no manner of work in your field, no manner of work in your vineyard, shall you do.

L. And how do we know that farmers may not trim trees or nip off dry shoots?

M. Scripture says, "Your field you shall not...." – no manner of work in your field, no manner of work in your vineyard, shall you do.

N. And how do we know that one may not manure, remove stones, dust the flower of sulphur, or fumigate?

O. Scripture says, "Your field you shall not...." – no manner of work in your field, no manner of work in your vineyard, shall you do.

P. Since Scripture says, "you shall not sow your field or prune your vineyard,"

Q. might one suppose that the farmer also may not hoe under the olive trees, fill in the holes under the olive trees, or dig between one tree and the next?

R. Scripture says, "You shall not sow your field or prune your vineyard" –

S. sowing and pruning were subject to the general prohibition of field labor. Why then were they singled out?

T. It was to build an analogy through them, as follows:

U. What is distinctive in sowing and pruning is that they are forms of labor carried on on the ground or on a tree.

V. So I know that subject to the prohibition are also other forms of labor that are carried on on the ground or on a tree, [excluding from the prohibition, therefore, the types of labor listed] [Sifra CCXLV:I.3-6].

W. *What we have here is a rule made by rabbinical authority, for which support is adduced from Scripture.*

Here is an instance in which scriptural bases for the rules of the Mishnah
are set forth; there are many forms in which this exegetical staple will be
set forth. What follows sets forth a secondary exposition of the
foregoing, and for that reason is indented here.

II.2 A. *And is it permitted to stir the soil under an olive tree in the
Seventh Year? Has it not been taught on Tannaite authority:*

B. Now it is permitted to hoe [in the Seventh Year]?

C. And has it not been taught on Tannaite authority:

D. "But the Seventh Year you shall let [the land] rest and lie
still" (Ex. 23:11).

E. "You shall let it rest" from hoeing,

F. "and lie still" from having stones removed.

G. Said R. Uqba bar Hama, "There are two kinds of hoeing.
In one kind one closes up the holes [around the roots of a
tree], and in the other, he aerates the soil [around the roots
of a tree].

H. "Aerating the soil is forbidden, closing up the holes is
permitted [since the former serves the roots of the tree, the
latter merely protects the tree]."

The next entry forms a secondary development of the foregoing, so is
further indented. This allows us to see how the Mishnah forms the
principal element of the Bavli's program, with secondary expansion and
tertiary amplification of Mishnah commentary making up an important
part of the whole. At the same time, we also note that the Bavli's
composites, as we have seen them to this point, simply explain the
Mishnah or explain the explanation.

II.3 A. *It has been stated:*

B. He who ploughs in the Seventh Year –

C. R. Yohanan and R. Eleazar –

D. One said, "He is flogged."

E. The other said, "He is not flogged."

F. *May we say that the dispute concerns that which R. Abin
said R. Ilaa said, for* said R. Abin said R. Ilaa, "In any
passage in which you find a generalization concerning
an affirmative action, followed by a qualification
expressing a negative commandment, people are not
to construct on that basis an argument resting on the
notion of a general proposition followed by a concrete
exemplification only the substance of the concrete
exemplification." [Freedman, *Sanhedrin*, p. 777-78,
n. 8: The rule in such a case is: the general
proposition includes only what is enumerated in the
particular specification. But when one is thrown into
the form of a positive command and the other stated
as a negative injunction this does not apply.]

G. *By this theory of what is at issue, one who says he is flogged does not concur with what R. Abin said R. Ilai said, and one who said, "He is not flogged," concurs with what R. Abin said.* [Lazarus: The general rule in positive terms: "The land shall keep a Sabbath..." (Lev. 25:2-5); the particulars in negative terms, "You shall neither sow..." (Lev. 25:4-5); the general rule again in positive form, "It shall be a year of solemn rest...." Then the particulars are considered typical as illustrations, serving to include in the general rule all such items as are similar to the particulars. If the particulars are typical of the general rule, one who does any of these would break the law. In the case of the former, he takes sowing, pruning, reaping, and gleaning as typical illustrative instances, and ploughing is covered and is punishable. In the case of the latter, ploughing is not included among the forbidden processes and is not punishable.]

H. *No, all parties reject the position stated by R. Abin in R. Ilai's name. One who says he is flogged has no problems anyhow.*

I. *The one who says he is not flogged may reply in this way:*

J. *Since pruning falls within the generative category of sowing, and grape gathering falls within the generative category of reaping, for what concrete legal purpose did the All-Merciful make written reference to these items? It is to present the inference that it is to these particular derivative classes of generative categories of labor that liability pertains, but to all others, there is no liability."*

K. *So they don't, don't they? But has it not been taught on Tannaite authority:*

L. ["The Lord said to Moses on Mount Sinai, Say to the people of Israel, When you come into the land which I give you, the land shall keep a Sabbath to the Lord. Six years you shall sow your field, and six years you shall prune your vineyard and gather in its fruits; but in the Seventh Year there shall be a Sabbath of solemn rest for the land, a Sabbath to the Lord; you shall not sow your field or prune your vineyard. What grows of itself in your harvest you shall not reap, and the grapes of your undressed vine you shall not gather; it shall be a year of solemn rest for the land. The Sabbath of the land shall provide food for you, for yourself and for your male and female slaves and for your hired servant and the sojourner who lives with you; for your cattle also and for the beasts that are in your land all its yield shall be for food" (Lev. 25:1-7):] "You shall not sow your field or prune your vineyard":

M. The Torah forbids me only to sow or prune,

N.	And how do we know that farmers may not fertilize, prune trees, smoke the leaves or cover roots over with powder for fertilizer?
O.	Scripture says, "Your field you shall not...." – no manner of work in your field, no manner of work in your vineyard, shall you do.
P.	And how do we know that farmers may not trim trees or nip off dry shoots?
Q.	Scripture says, "Your field you shall not...." – no manner of work in your field, no manner of work in your vineyard, shall you do.
R.	And how do we know that one may not manure, remove stones, dust the flower of sulphur, or fumigate?
S.	Scripture says, "Your field you shall not...." – no manner of work in your field, no manner of work in your vineyard, shall you do.
T.	Since Scripture says, "You shall not sow your field or prune your vineyard,"
U.	might one suppose that the farmer also may not hoe under the olive trees, fill in the holes under the olive trees, or dig between one tree and the next?
V.	Scripture says, "You shall not sow your field or prune your vineyard" –
W.	sowing and pruning were subject to the general prohibition of field labor. Why then were they singled out?
X.	It was to build an analogy through them, as follows:
Y.	What is distinctive in sowing and pruning is that they are forms of labor carried on on the ground or on a tree.
Z.	So I know that subject to the prohibition are also other forms of labor that are carried on on the ground or on a tree, [excluding from the prohibition, therefore, the types of labor listed] [Sifra CCXLV:I.3-6].
AA.	*What we have here is a rule made by rabbinical authority, for which support is adduced from Scripture.*

What follows carries forward the prior item.

II.4	A.	[3B] *When R. Dimi came, he said, "Might one suppose that one is flogged even for doing so during the additional time that has been added to the Seventh Year [fore and aft]? But the discussion resolved in favor of exempting one who worked during the addition to the Seventh Year."*

B.
But I don't know what is this "discussion" and to what reference is made under the category, "addition"!

C.
R. Eleazar said, "Reference is made to ploughing, and this is the sense of the statement: Might one suppose that one is flogged on account of ploughing in the Seventh Year? For that conclusion would derive from a reading of the relevant verses under the principle of a generalization followed by a particularization of the foregoing followed by another generalization. And the discussion resolved in favor of exempting one who worked during the addition to the Seventh Year in the following way: If the flogging were in order, then what is the sense of the many particularizations that the text contains?"

D.
R. Yohanan said, "Reference is made to the days that sages added to the Seventh Year prior to the advent of the New Year that marks the commencement of the Seventh Year proper, *and this is the sense of the statement: Might one suppose that one is flogged on account of ploughing on the days that sages added to the Seventh Year prior to the advent of the New Year that marks the commencement of the Seventh Year proper? For that conclusion would derive from the following: 'In ploughing time and in* reaping time you shall rest' (Ex. 34:21). *And the discussion resolved in favor of exempting one who did so," as we shall have to explain below.*

II.5   A.
To what is reference made in the allusion to the days that sages added to the Seventh Year prior to the advent of the New Year that marks the commencement of the Seventh Year proper?

B.
That is in line with what we have learned in the Mishnah: Until what time do they plough an orchard during the year preceding the Sabbatical Year? The House of Shammai say, "As long as [the ploughing] continues to benefit the produce [of the Sixth Year. Until that year's fruit ripens and is harvested]." But the House of Hillel say, "Until Pentecost." And the opinion of the one is close to the opinion of the other [M. Sheb. 1:1]. Until what time do they plough in a field of grain (lit.: a white field) during the year preceding the Sabbatical Year? Until the moisture [in the ground] is gone As long as people plough in order to plant chatemelons and gourds. Said R. Simeon,

"You have put the law into the hands of each individual. Rather, [one may plough] in a field of grain until Passover [when Israelites offer the first sheaf of new grain at the Temple; cf. Lev. 23:10] and [one may plough] in an orchard until Pentecost [when they present the first fruits] [M. Sheb. 2:1].

C.   And said R. Simeon b. Pazzi said R. Joshua b. Levi in the name of Bar Qappara, "Rabban Gamaliel and his court took a vote concerning these two spells and annulled them." [It was permitted to till down to the New Year itself (Lazarus).]

D.   *Said R. Zira to R. Abbahu, and some say, R. Simeon b. Laqish to R. Yohanan, "How could Rabban Gamaliel and his court have annulled an ordinance made by the House of Shammai and the House of Hillel? And lo, we have learned in the Mishnah:* [And why do they record the opinion of an individual along with that of the majority, since the law follows the opinion of the majority? So that, if a court should prefer the opinion of the individual, it may decide to rely upon it.] For a court has not got the power to nullify the opinion of another court unless it is greater than it in wisdom and in numbers. [If] it was greater than the other in wisdom but not in numbers, in numbers but not in wisdom, it has not got the power to nullify its opinion – unless it is greater than it in both wisdom and numbers [M. Ed. 1:5]*!"*

E.   *For a moment he was stupefied, but then he said to him, "I say, this is what they stipulated among themselves: whoever wants to nullify the rule may come along and nullify it."*

F.   *Well, did that measure really belong to them? Was it not a law revealed by God to Moses at Mount Sinai? For that is in line with what R. Assi said R. Yohanan said in the name of R. Nehunia of the Valley of Bet Hauran,* "The rules covering ten saplings, [As regards ten saplings which are spread out within a seah space – they plough the entire seah space for the saplings' sake until the New Year of the Sabbatical Year] [M. Sheb. 1:6A-B], the willow [carried around the altar during the festival], and the water-offering are laws revealed to Moses at Sinai."

G. *Said R. Isaac, "When we received as a tradition the law adding additional restricted time to the Seventh Year as a law revealed to Moses at Sinai, it was only concerning the thirty days prior to the New Year. The House of Shammai and Hillel came along and ordained that work should cease from Passover [for the grain field] and from Pentecost [for an orchard], and, at the same time, they made the stipulation with regard to what they said that, whoever might afterward come along and want to nullify those spells of restricted time may come along and nullify them."*

H. *But are these specified spells of time merely law? Are they not based in fact on explicit verses of Scripture? For has it not been taught on Tannaite authority:*

I. "Six days you shall work but on the seventh day you shall rest, in ploughing time and in harvest you shall rest" (Ex. 34:21) [whatever the need, ploughing and reaping may not be done on the Sabbath or the Sabbatical Year] –

J. R. Aqiba says, "The reference to ploughing and reaping is not required to indicate that these actions are forbidden in the Sabbatical Year itself, for that is explicitly covered when Scripture says, 'neither shall you sow your field or prune your vineyard (Lev. 25:4-5). Rather, the purpose is to impose the restriction of ploughing even in the year prior to the Sabbatical Year [4A] when the effect of the ploughing will extend into the Sabbatical Year, and it is to restrict harvesting produce partly grown in the Sabbatical Year but reaped in the year following the Sabbatical Year."

K. R. Ishmael says, "Just as ploughing is optional, so reaping is optional. Excluded from the prohibition of work on the Sabbath then is the reaping of the first sheaf of barley for the sheaf to be waved, which is a religious duty [and may be done on the Sabbath]."

L. *Rather, said R. Nahman bar Isaac, "When the law was handed on as a tradition [concerning the time prior to the Seventh Year], this concerned permitting tilling to benefit saplings, while the cited verses of Scripture concern prohibiting tilling around old trees."*

M. *Well, if it was necessary to appeal to a traditional law to allow tilling around saplings up to the advent of the New Year, is it not self-evident that*

		doing so around old trees is going to be forbidden?
	N.	*Rather, when the traditional law was handed down as a prohibition, it was required only from the view of R. Ishmael, while the verses of Scripture form the basis of the position of R. Aqiba.*
II.6	A.	*R. Yohanan said, Rabban Gamaliel and his court nullified the restrictions on the authority of the Torah."*
	B.	*What is the scriptural basis for their position?*
	C.	*They formed a verbal analogy based on the use of the word "Sabbath" with reverence to both the Seventh Year, called the Sabbatical Year, and also the Sabbath of Creation, along these lines:*
	D.	Just as in the case of the Sabbath of Creation, prohibitions pertain to the holy day but not to the time beforehand or afterward, so in the case of the Seventh Year, prohibitions pertain to the year but not to the time beforehand or afterward.
	E.	*Objected R. Ashi, "On the view of one who maintains that the restriction is a traditional law, can an argument based on verbal analogy come along and nullify a traditional law? And if one says that it is based on a verse of Scripture, along these same lines, can an argument formed of a verbal analogy come along and nullify the result of the reading of a verse of Scripture?"*
	F.	*Rather, said R. Ashi, "Rabban Gamaliel and his court adopted the reasoning of R. Ishmael, who said, 'The prohibitions of tilling on the spell prior to the actual advent of the Seventh Year derives from a traditional law. And to what span of time did that traditional law pertain? It was during the time that the Temple was standing, just as the rule of the water libation [which likewise derived from a traditional law] pertained only during the time that the Temple was standing. But when the Temple is no longer standing, the law received by tradition does not apply.'"*

Now we return to the amplification of the Mishnah, starting a new clause; there is no continuity between the foregoing and what follows. What holds the whole together is the Mishnah, only that. That fact once more underlines the character of the Bavli as Mishnah commentary, however wide-ranging and even meandering; and it further shows us how the Bavli holds together all of its materials only by referring back to a prior, exterior document, not by an effort – however contrived – at showing the linkage between one principal unit of discourse and those that come fore and aft. We further note that, once we do turn to the Mishnah, we start all over again; nothing from the foregoing compositions and composites is required to grasp a single line of what now follows.

III.1   A.   **But they do not water [an irrigated field] with (1) collected rain water, or (2) water from a swape well:**

        B.   *There is no trouble in understanding why water from a swape well should not be used, since watering in that way involves heavy labor. But what objection can there be to using collected rain water, since what heavy labor can possibly be involved in irrigating with rain water?*

        C.   *Said R. Ilaa said R. Yohanan, "It is a precautionary decree, on account of the possibility of the farmer's going on to make use of water from a swape well."*

        D.   R. Ashi said, "Rain water itself can be as hard to draw as the water of a swape well."

        E.   *At issue between them is what R. Zira said. For said R. Zira said Rabbah bar Jeremiah said Samuel, "From irrigation streams that draw water from ponds it is permitted to irrigate on the intermediate days of the festival." One authority [Ashi] concurs with the position of R. Zira, and the other authority does not concur with the position of R. Zira.*

The foregoing represents an explanation of how the Mishnah's several examples cohere; we explain an unanticipated ruling.

III.2   A.   Reverting to the body of the foregoing: said R. Zira said Rabbah bar Jeremiah said Samuel, "From irrigation streams that draw water from ponds it is permitted to irrigate on the intermediate days of the festival."

        B.   *Objected R. Jeremiah to R. Zira, "* **But they do not water [an irrigated field] with collected rain water, or water from a swape well."**

        C.   *He said to him, "Jeremiah my son, the pools in Babylonia are like water that never languishes."*

For the purpose of the present inquiry into the characteristics of the Bavli's Mishnah commentary, we shall not deal with Tannaite complements to the Mishnah, for example, originating in the Tosefta, that, on their own, do not fall into the category of commentary. My definition of commentary then limits our interest to what clearly cites or alludes to the Mishnah's statements and clarifies them in some important way.

Topically relevant materials formulated on Tannaite authority but not clearly serving as amplification of the Mishnah in particular in a broad and maximalist definition may be seen as Mishnah commentary, and in my *Mishnah's One Voice* I do regard Toseftan and other Tannaite restatement of rules pertinent to the Mishnah's rules as Mishnah exegesis. But for the present purpose, a parallel Tannaite formulation of a rule must be bypassed, unless it clearly relates to, and means to expand and refine, a rule of the Mishnah or the secondary implications thereof, for example, a more complex case, clarification of how a rule of the Mishnah applies (or does not apply), and similar matters. So while the following is of interest in study of the law of the Mishnah, it is not Mishnah commentary. I indent the item to indicate that it is attached to the foregoing but not continuous with it. In work of mine on the Tosefta, in various works, summarized by *The Tosefta: Its Structure and Its Sources* (Atlanta, 1986: Scholars Press for Brown Judaic Studies), I have shown in great detail how most of the Tosefta serves to amplify statements in the Mishnah, whether the Mishnah's language is quoted or merely alluded to; only a small proportion of the Tosefta is fully and exhaustively understood without reference to the Mishnah's counterpart statements. We now see that other materials formulated like Tosefta's statements, and marked with the same sigla (for example, "It has been taught on Tannaite authority" and the like) stand in the same relationship of dependency.

III.3	A.	*Our rabbis have taught on Tannaite authority:*
	B.	Ditches and pools that were filled with water on the eve of the festival may not be used for irrigation on the intermediate days of the festival. But if an irrigation ditch passes between them, they may be used.
	C.	Said R. Pappa, "But that is so only if the greater part of that field derives its water from that irrigation ditch."
	D.	R. Ashi said, "Even though the greater part of that field does not derive its water from that irrigation ditch, *since the water flows continuously, the owner concludes, although the field does not get enough water one day, it will get enough two or three days later [and he will not undertake heavy labor during the intermediate days of the festival].*"
III.4	A.	*Our rabbis have taught on Tannaite authority:*
	B.	**A pool that gets a trickle of water from an irrigated field higher up may be used for watering another field. [R. Simeon b. Menassia says, "Two pools, one above the other – one should not draw water from the lower to water the upper, but he may draw water from the upper to water the lower one. R. Simeon b. Eleazar says, "A furrow, part of which is low and part high – one should not draw water from the lower part for the upper part and irrigate it. But he may draw water from the upper part for the lower part and irrigate by that means" [T. M.Q. 1:1F-I].**
	C.	[With reference to the statement, **A pool that gets a trickle of water from an irrigated field higher up may be used for watering another field,**] *but lo, will it not give out?*
	D.	Said R. Jeremiah, "In any event at this moment it is still trickling."

E. Said Abbayye, "The rule applies only so long as the first spring has not languished." [Lazarus: But once the trickling has ceased, the pool has lost its supply and becomes like a swape well or stored rain likely to entail exertion.]

III.5 A. *It has been taught on Tannaite authority:*

B. **R. Simeon b. Menassia says, "Two pools, one above the other – one should not draw water from the lower to water the upper, but he may draw water from the upper to water the lower one.**

C. **R. Simeon b. Eleazar says, "A furrow, part of which is low and part high – one should not draw water from the lower part for the upper part and irrigate it. But he may draw water from the upper part for the lower part and irrigate by that means" [T. M.Q. 1:1F-I].**

III.6 A. *Our rabbis have taught on Tannaite authority:*

B. They may raise up water by buckets from a well during the festival week for vegetables so as to eat them. But if it is only to improve their appearance, it is forbidden to do so.

III.7 A. *Rabina and Rabbah Tosefaah were going along the way. They saw somebody who was drawing buckets of water during the intermediate days of the festival. Said Rabbah Tosefaah to Rabina, "So let's go and excommunicate theat man."*

B. *He said to him, "But has it not been taught on Tannaite authority They may raise up water by buckets from a well during the festival week for vegetables so as to eat them. But if it is only to improve their appearance, it is forbidden to do so?"*

C. *He said to him, "Do you really think that the meaning of 'raise up' means raise up water? What is the real meaning of 'raise up'? [4B] It is to pull out vegetables. That meaning of the word is in line with what we have learned in the Mishnah: "He who thins [using the word at hand] grape vines, just as he [is allowed] to thin his own [produce, the normal clusters], so may he thin [the defective clusters] which belong to the poor," the words of R. Judah. R. Meir says, "He is permitted to thin his own [produce], but he is not permitted [to thin produce] which belongs to the poor" [M. Peah 7:5]."*

D. *He said to him, "But has it not been taught on Tannaite authority: They may raise up water by buckets from a well during the festival week for vegetables so as to eat them?"*

E. *He said to him, "So if that has been taught on Tannaite authority, that is what has been taught [and no more discussion]."*

Once more we revert to the Mishnah, and once more we commence afresh, now with the explanation of the meanings of words and phrases.

IV.1 A. **And they do not dig channels around vines:**

B. *What are "channels"?*

C. *Said R. Judah, "They are little hollows."*

D. *So, too, it has been taught on Tannaite authority:*

E.   **What are channels dug around a tree? These are ditches dug around the roots of trees [T. M.Q. 1:2B-C].** They hoe lightly around the roots of olives and vines.

F.   *Is that so? But did not R. Judah permit the sons of Bar Zittai to make little hollows in their vineyards?*

G.   *That's no problem, the statement of our Mishnah speaks of fresh ones, R. Judah's to established ones.*

V.1   A.   **R. Eleazar b. Azariah says, "They do not make a new water channel on the intermediate days of a festival or in the Seventh Year." And sages say, "They make a new water channel in the Seventh Year, and they repair damaged ones on the intermediate days of a festival":**

B.   *There is no problem with respect to the prohibition concerning the intermediate days of a festival, since the operative consideration is that this is heavy labor, but why ever not make a channel in the Seventh Year?*

C.   R. Zira and R. Abba b. Mamel differ on the matter –

D.   One said, "The reason is that the one who digs appears to be hoeing."

E.   And the other said, "The reason is that he looks as though he is preparing the banks for sowing."

F.   *So what's at stake?*

G.   *At issue is when water comes along immediately. From the perspective of him who has said, "The reason is that he looks as though he is preparing the banks for sowing," it is still objectionable. But from the perspective of him who has said, "The reason is that the one who digs appears to be hoeing," there is no objection.*

H.   *But should not the one who objects for the reason that it looks as though he is spading also object that he looks as though he is preparing the bank for seed?*

I.   *Rather, this is what's at stake between the two explanations: it would involve a case in which he takes what is in the trench and tosses it out. From the perspective of him who says, "The reason is that he looks as though he is preparing the banks for sowing," there is no objection; but from the perspective of him who says, "The reason is that the one who digs appears to be hoeing," it is still subject to an objection.*

J.   *But from the perspective of him who says that he appears to be preparing the sides for seed, would he not also admit that he seems to be hoeing?*

K.   *Not really, for one who hoes, as soon as he takes up a spadeful, he puts it down again in place.*

We proceed to a secondary expansion of the foregoing.

V.2   A.   *Amemar repeated the Mishnah's law along with the reason, The reason is that the one who digs appears to be hoeing, but this presented a problem to him because of a contradiction between two statements of R. Eleazar b. Azariah: "And has R. Eleazar b. Azariah taken the position that any act that looks as if he is hoeing is forbidden? And in contradiction to that position:* **A person places [all] the manure in his possession in [one large] pile. R. Meir forbids [the farmer from doing this] unless he either deepens [the**

> ground by] three [handbreadths] or raises [the ground by] three [handbreadths]. If one had a small amount [of manure already piled up in the field], he continually adds to it. R. Eleazar b. Azariah forbids [the farmer from doing so] unless he either deepens [the ground by] three [handbreadths] or raises [the ground by] three [handbreadths] or unless he places [the manure] on rocky ground [M. Shebiit 3:3D-G]. [Lazarus: Here Eleazar permits digging in the field in the Sabbatical Year to prepare a place for the manure store without concern about giving a wrong impression, such as he had in mind when he prohibited making a water channel.]

B. R. Zira and R. Abba b. Mamel differ on the matter —

C. One said, "The cited passage speaks of a case in which he had the place excavated."

D. And the other said, "The operative consideration is that the manure heap itself shows what his real intention is."

What follows contains no surprises: reversion to a clause of the Mishnah, repetition of an established exegetical program, here: meanings of words and phrases.

VI.1 A. **And they repair damaged ones on the intermediate days of a festival:**

B. *What is the meaning of* "damaged ones"?

C. Said R. Abba, "If one was only a handbreadth deep, he may restore it to a depth of six handbreadths."

VI.2 A. *It is obvious that restoring the channel from a half-handbreadth to three, since there was to begin with hardly any flow of water, is null [and work that is useless]; to deepen it from two handbreadths to the original twelve involves heavy labor and that is not permitted. But what about deepening it from two to seven? Here he deepens it by five handbreadths, from one to six, so here, too, he deepens it by five, two to seven? Or perhaps what is going on here is that he is actually deepening it by an extra handbreadth, so that involves heavy and needless labor and is forbidden?*

B. *The question stands.*

The next entry carries forward the foregoing and draws upon it:

VI.3 A. *Abbayye permitted the people of Harmakh [during the intermediate days of the festival] to clear away the growths obstructing the irrigation ditch.*

B. *R. Jeremiah permitted the people of Sacuta [during the intermediate days of the festival] to dredge a ditch that had been blocked.*

C. *R. Ashi permitted the people of Mata Mehasia to clear obstructions from the Barnis canal, saying, "Since people get their water from it, it is as public domain, and we have learned in the Mishnah:* **And they do all public needs.**

The clarification of the Mishnah now requires us to investigate the implications, for law and principle, of the language of the Mishnah. The close reading of the Mishnah's formulation is what generates the problem that will be discussed.

VII.1   A.   **[5A] They repair damaged waterways in the public domain and dig them out:**

B.   *Repairing is all right, but not digging afresh.*

C.   Said R. Jacob said R. Yohanan, "They have taught this rule only when the public has no need of the waterways, but if the public needs them, then it is permitted even to dig afresh."

D.   *But if the public needs them, is it permitted to do that work? And has it not been taught on Tannaite authority:* Cisterns, pits, and caverns that belong to private property may be cleaned out, and, it goes without saying, those that belong to the public; but cisterns, pits, and caverns belonging to the public may not be dug, and all the more so those of a private person? *Does this not address a case in which the public has need of these facilities?*

E.   *No, it addresses a case in which the public has no need of those facilities.*

F.   *Along these same lines with respect to a private party, where the private person has no need of the facility, is repairing allowed? And has it not been taught on Tannaite authority:* As to cisterns, pits, and caverns of a private person, they collect water in them but they may not be cleaned out, nor may their cracks be plastered; but as to those belonging to the public, they may be cleaned out and their cracks may be plastered?

G.   *Now what is the point here? It is when a private person has need of the facility. And in that case, in regard to what is required for public use, where the public has need of it the same rule pertains? And where the public has need of the facility, is it forbidden to dig? Has it not been taught on Tannaite authority:* As to cisterns, pits, and caverns belonging to a private person, they collect water in them and clean them out, but they may not plaster their cracks nor put scourings into them to fill cracks; as to those serving the public, they may dig them to begin with and plaster them with cement?

H.   *So the initial formulation poses a contradiction.*

I.   *This is how to iron out the difficulty:* They may clean out wells, ditches, or caverns of a private person, when the private party requires the facility, and, it goes without saying, those that belong to the public *when the public requires use of the facility, in which case even digging them out is permitted.* But they may not dig out wells, ditches, or caverns belonging to the public when the public does not require use of the facility, and, it goes without saying, those belonging to a private party. *When the private party does not require using them, then even cleaning them out is forbidden.*

J.   *Said R. Ashi, "A close reading of our Mishnah paragraph yields the same result:* **And they do all public needs.** *Now what is encompassed within the augmentative formulation,* **all?** *Is it not to encompass, also, digging?"*

K.   *Not at all, it is to encompass what is covered in that which has been taught on Tannaite authority:* **On the fifteenth day of Adar agents of the court go forth and dig cisterns, wells, and caves. And they repair immersion pools and water channels. Every immersion pool that** contains forty seahs of water is suitable for receiving further drawn water if need be, and to every immersion pool that does not contain forty seahs of water they lead a water course and complete its volume to the measure of forty seahs of water that has not been drawn so that it is suitable to receive further drawn water if need be [T. Sheq. 1:1]. And how on the basis of Scripture do we know that if they did not go forth and carry out all these duties, that any blood that is shed there is credited by Scripture as though they had shed it? Scripture states, "And so blood be upon you" (Deut. 19:10).

L. *Lo, in point of fact the framer of the Mishnah has covered these matters explicitly:* **They repair roads, streets, and water pools. And they do all public needs!** *what is encompassed within the augmentative formulation,* **all?** *Is it not to encompass, also, digging?*

M. *Yes, that's the proof!*

The following item cites further language of the Mishnah and adduces scriptural foundations for the Mishnah's rule:

VIII.1 A. **Mark off graves:**

B. Said R. Simeon b. Pazzi, "Whence do we find an indication in Scripture that it is required to mark off graves? Scripture states, 'And when they pass through the land and one sees a man's bone, then shall he set up a sign by it' (Ezek. 29:15)."

C. *Said Rabina to R. Ashi, "So before Ezekiel made that point, how did we know it?"*

D. *Said R. Ashi to Rabina, "So until Ezekiel came along and made that statement, how did we know the correct rule?"*

E. *"According to your reasoning, when R. Hisda made his statement, 'This matter we have not learned from the Torah of our lord, Moses, but from the teachings of Ezekiel b. Buzi we have learned it, "No alien, uncircumcised in heart and uncircumcised in flesh, shall enter my sanctuary" (Ezek. 44:9)' – until Ezekiel came along and made that statement, how did we know the correct rule? Rather, it is a tradition that was handed on, and Ezekiel came along and supplied it with support from Scripture. Here, too, it is a tradition that was handed on, and Ezekiel came along and supplied it with support from Scripture."*

VIII.2 A. *R. Abbahu said, "It derives from the following: 'And he shall cry, unclean, unclean' (Lev. 13:45) – the uncleanness affecting him cries out for him and says, 'Keep away.'"*

B. And so said R. Uzziel, grandson of Rabbah, "'...the uncleanness affecting him cries out for him and says, 'Keep away.'"

C. *But does that verse serve the specified purpose? It is in point of fact required in line with that which has been taught on Tannaite authority:*

D. "And he shall cry, unclean, unclean" (Lev. 13:45) – one has to publicize his pain in public, so that the public may seek for mercy on his behalf.

E. *If that were the case, then Scripture can as well have written,* "Unclean he shall cry out." *Why say,* "Unclean, unclean"? *It is to yield both points.*

VIII.3   A.   *Abbayye said, "It derives from the following: 'And do not put a stumbling block before the blind' (Lev. 19:14)."*
         B.   *R. Pappa said, "It derives from the following: 'And he will say, Cast you up, cast you up, clear the way' (Isa. 57:14)."*
         C.   *R. Hinena said, "It derives from the following: 'Take up the stumbling block out of the way of my people' (Isa. 57:14)."*
         D.   *R. Joshua b. R. Idi said, "It derives from the following: 'And you shall show them the way in which they must walk' (Ex. 18:20)."*
         E.   *Mar Zutra said, "It derives from the following: 'And you shall separate the children of Israel from their uncleanness' (Lev. 15:31)."*
         F.   *R. Ashi said, "It derives from the following: 'And they shall have charge of my charge' (Lev. 22:9), meaning, protect my charge [the priesthood]."*
         G.   *Rabina said, "It derives from the following: 'And to him who orders his way will I show the salvation of God' (Ps. 50:23)."*

VIII.4   A.   And R. Joshua b. Levi said, "Whoever properly sets his ways in this world will have the merit of witnessing the salvation of the Holy One, blessed be He,
         B.   "as it is said, 'To him who orders his way I will show the salvation of God' (Ps. 50:23).
         C.   "Do not read 'orders' but 'properly sets' [his] way" [Cohen, *Sotah*, p. 21, n. 6: He calculates the loss incurred in fulfilling a precept against the reward it will bring him.]

VIII.5   A.   *R. Yannai had a disciple who day by day raised tough questions, but on the Sabbaths of festivals did not raise tough questions.*
         B.   *[5B] In his regard he recited the verse, "And to him who orders his way will I show the salvation of God" (Ps. 50:23).*

The next item is already familiar: amplification of the Mishnah by citation and analysis of the Tosefta's counterpart materials.

VIII.6   A.   *Our rabbis have taught on Tannaite authority:*
         B.   **They do not make a mark to indicate the presence of corpse matter that is not bigger in volume than an olive's bulk, nor a human bone that is not bigger than a barley seed, nor any human remains that would not convey uncleanness when under a tent. But they do make a marking to indicate the presence of a spine, skull, or major limb of a skeleton, or the larger part of the small bones.**
         C.   **They make markings not when the matter is certainly known, but only when it is uncertain.**
         D.   **What are cases of uncertainty?**
         E.   **Leafy bowers, jutting ledges, and a grave area.**
         F.   **And they do not make a mark right on the spot of the source of uncleanness, so as not to waste what is unaffected, nor is a mark placed far from the spot, so as not to waste space in the Land of Israel [cf. T. Sheq. 1:5].**
         G.   *But will an olive's bulk of human flesh not convey uncleanness in a tent? Lo, we have learned in the Mishnah:* **These contaminate in the Tent: (1) the corpse, and (2) an olive's bulk [of flesh] from the corpse,**

[and (3) an olive's bulk of corpse dregs, and (4) a ladleful of corpse mould; (5) the backbone, and the skull, and (6) a limb from the corpse, and (7) a limb from the living person on which is an appropriate amount of flesh; (8) a quarter-qab of bones from the larger part of the frame [of the skeleton] or (9) from the larger number; and (10) the larger part of the frame or (11) the larger number of the corpse, even though there is not among them a quarter-qab, are unclean. How much is the "larger number"? One hundred twenty-five] [M. Oh. 2:1]*!*

H.   *Said R. Pappa, "Here we deal with a piece of flesh precisely an olive's bulk in size, since ultimately it will be found lacking.* It is better that on its account food in the status of priestly rations and Holy Things should be burned on its account for a little while, but not for all time."

VIII.7   A.   What are cases of uncertainty? Leafy bowers, jutting ledges, and a grave area:

B.   Leafy bowers: A tree that overshadows the ground near a cemetery.

C.   Jutting ledges: Protruding stones that project from a wall [T. Oh. 9:2].

D.   And a grave area: *That is in line with that which we have learned in the Mishnah:* He who ploughs up the grave – lo, he makes [the field into] a grave area. How much [space] does he make? The length of a furrow of a hundred cubits, [over] a space of four seahs [M. Oh. 17:1A-B].

VIII.8   A.   *So does dirt deriving from a grave area convey uncleanness through overshadowing by a common tent? But did not R.* Judah say Samuel said, "One [who wants to remain uncontaminated by corpse matter] in a *beth haperas [a grave area, an area possibly contaminated by corpse matter]* blows away the earth and goes along his way."

B.   R. Judah bar Ammi in the name of R. Judah said, "A *beth haperas [a grave area, an area possibly contaminated by corpse matter]* that has been trodden down is no longer a source of uncleanness."

C.   Said R. Pappa, "There is no contradiction. The one statement speaks of a field in which the location of a grave has been lost" [so the whole field is a source of uncleanness], and the other speaks of a field in which a grave has been turned up by a plough [which crushes the bones so that they are no longer a source of uncleanness]."

D.   *But is a field in which a grave has been ploughed up even classified as a grave area?*

E.   *Yes indeed, for we have learned in the Mishnah:* There are three kinds of grave areas: [1] He who ploughs up the grave – it may be planted with any kind of tree, but it may not be sown with any kind of seed, except for seed [the plants of which] are cut. And if one uprooted it, one heaps up the threshing floor in it, and sifts – "the grain through two sieves," the words of R. Meir. And sages say, "The grain with two sieves, and the pulse through

> three sieves." And one burns the stubble and the stalks
> [in the grave area]. And it renders unclean through
> contact and through carrying, and it does not render
> unclean through the Tent. [2] A field in the midst of
> which a grave has been lost is sown with any kind of
> seed but is not planted with any kind of tree. And they
> do not preserve trees in it, except for a barren tree, which
> does not produce fruits. And it renders unclean through
> contact and through carrying and through the Tent. [3] A
> field of mourners/tomb niches is not planted, and is not
> sown, but its dust is clean. And they make from it ovens
> for holy [use] [M. Oh. 18:2-4].

What now follows is a talmud to the Tosefta's and other Tannaite
complements to the Mishnah; much of the Bavli is made up of this kind
of talmud – sustained amplification, analysis, secondary inquiry of
various other sorts – to its own Mishnah commentary. I continue to
indent what is an expansion of amplificatory material.

VIII.9   A.   *What is the definition of* **A field of mourners?**

       B.   R. Joshua bar Abba in the name of Ulla said, "It is a field in which they take leave of the dead."

       C.   *And how come [it is classified as a grave area, imparting uncleanness]?*

       D.   Said Abimi, "It is because of the contingency of abandonment by the owners [of the limbs that may have been dropped there when collection was made for secondary burial]."

VIII.10   A.   *And is it not necessary to mark off a field in which a grave has been dug up by a plough? Has it not been taught on Tannaite authority:*

       B.   If one found a field that is marked off as having corpse matter in its midst, and the nature of the uncleanness is not known, if there is a tree in it, one may be sure that a grave has been ploughed up in it. If there is no tree in it, one may be sure that a grave has been lost in it.

       C.   Said R. Judah, "Under what circumstances? When there is available a sage or a disciple, for not everybody is going to be expert in this matter" [T. Ahilot 17:12].

       D.   *Said R. Pappa, "When that passage was repeated on Tannaite authority,* it made reference to a field in which a grave had been lost and which therefore had been marked. If, then, there are trees in the field, that means that a grave had been ploughed up by a plough thereafter; if there are no trees in it, it means a grave has been lost in it."

       E.   *But should we not take account of the possibility that trees are located in the field but the grave lies outside of it? For that would be in line with what Ulla said, "We speak of a* case in which trees are located at the edges of the field," *so here, too,* "We speak of a case in which trees are located at the edges of the field."

F. [6A] *But perhaps the uncleanness is located inside the field and trees are situated outside* [Lazarus: and since corpses are not buried on the road, the grave must be located among the trees and it must have been run over by the plough when the field was tilled for the sake of the trees].

G. *We deal with a case in which the trees were planted irregularly.*

H. *If you prefer, I shall say, "It is in line with what we said earlier:* **Nor is a mark placed far from the spot, so as not to waste space in the Land of Israel."**

VIII.11 A. **Said R. Judah, "Under what circumstances? When there is available a sage or a disciple, for not everybody is going to be expert in this matter":**

B. *Said Abbayye, "That proves that, when a neophyte rabbi is located in a place, all affairs of the place are assigned to his authority."*

VIII.12 A. Said R. Judah, "If one found a stone with a marking, the space under it is deemed to be unclean [with corpse uncleanness]. If there were two such stones, then if there is lime between them, the space between them is deemed unclean. If there is no lime between them, then the space between them is deemed clean."

B. *But is that the case even if there is no mark of ploughing there? And has it not been taught on Tannaite authority:*

C. **If one found a single stone marked off, even though it is not to be kept in that way, he who overshadows it is clean. If one found two of them, if there is a mark of ploughing between them, the space between them is clean, if not, it is unclean** [T. Sheq. 1:5D-E].

D. Said R. Pappa, "Here we deal with a case in which the lime was poured on top of the stones and then spread down on either side. If there is a mark of ploughing between them, the space is clean, *for we assume that the lime that splashed was peeled off by the ploughing; if there is no mark of ploughing, the lime is clearly intended to mark the space between and that space is held to be unclean."*

VIII.13 A. Said R. Assi, "If there is a marking on one side, that side is unclean, the rest of the whole field is clean. If there is marking on two sides, those are unclean, the whole rest of the field is clean; if there was marking on three sides, those are unclean, but the whole rest of the field is clean. If there is a marking on four boundaries, they are then held to be the marks of what is clean, but the entire field inside is unclean."

B. **"For a master has said, Nor is a mark placed far from the spot, so as not to waste space in the Land of Israel."**

We now compare a rule of the Mishnah with an intersecting one, showing that the two do not contradict one another.

IX.1   A.   **And go forth [to give warning] against Diverse Kinds:**
        B.   *But in fact in the intermediate days of a festival do we go about to inspect whether or not there are mixed seeds in a field? But there is the following contradiction:* **On the first day of Adar they make public announcement concerning [payment of] sheqel dues and concerning the sowing of mixed seeds [Lev. 19:19, Deut. 22:9]. On the fifteenth day of that month they read the Megillah [Scroll of Esther] in walled cities. And they repair the paths, roads, and immersion pools. And they carry out all public needs. And they mark off the graves. And they go forth [to inspect the fields] on account of mixed seeds [M. Sheq. 1:1]***!*
        C.   R. Eleazar and R. Yosé bar Hanina –
        D.   One said, "The latter refers to the crops that ripen earlier [in mid-Adar], the other, of late ripening crops [and our Mishnah paragraph has a further inspection, now in mid-Nisan, during the intermediate days of the festival of Passover]."
        E.   And the other said, "In the one case [in Adar] they go out to inspect the condition of grain fields, in the other, vegetable patches."
        F.   Said R. Assi said R. Yohanan, "The rule pertains only in a case in which the sprouts are not yet recognizable [earlier on]; but where it is possible to discern the character of the sprouts early on, they went forth to inspect the situation earlier."

We proceed to a talmud for the foregoing.

IX.2   A.   *What makes the festival week special that we go out at that time for the purpose at hand?*
        B.   *Said R. Jacob said R. Yohanan, "It is at that time labor is cheap with us [since there is no demand for labor during the intermediate days of the festival]."*
        C.   *Said R. Zebid, and some say, R. Mesharshayya, "That leads to the inference that, when we pay them, we pay them out of the heave-offering taken up from the sheqel-chamber. For if you should imagine that the owners of the fields are paid, what difference does it make to us? Pay whatever the workers ask [and don't try to hire workers at a time when wages are low, since the householders are going to have to shell out]!"*
IX.3   A.   How much [constitutes a mixture of seeds]?
        B.   Said R. Samuel bar Isaac, "It is in line with that which we have learned in the Mishnah: [Concerning] every seah [of one kind of seeds] which contains [6B] a quarter [-qab] of another kind – he shall lessen [the quantity of seeds of the other kind, so that those seeds form less than a quarter-qab] [M. Kil. 2:1A]."
        C.   *But has it not been taught on Tannaite authority:* They ordained that they should declare ownerless the crop of the entire field?
        D.   *There is no contradiction, the Mishnah rule describes how things were done before the ordinance, the latter tells us how things were done afterward, in line with what has been taught on Tannaite*

> *authority:* At first they would uproot the crops and throw them in front of their cattle, but the householders were delighted on two counts, first, that they weeded their fields for them, second, they threw the crop to the cattle. So they ordained that they should uproot the forbidden crop and throw it in the road. So the householders were still delighted, because the court then took care of weeding their field. So in the end they ordained that they should declare ownerless the crop of the entire field.

Now to review the entirety of the foregoing. **I.1** raises a fundamental question of Mishnah exegesis. No. 2 proceeds to explain the meanings of words. No. 3 asks a third routine question of Mishnah exegesis. Nos. 4-5 pursue their own interests, and the composite is included here because of the point of intersection with our Mishnah; this is then an appendix. **II.1** raises the obvious exegetical question concerning a detail of the Mishnah. No. 2 footnotes the foregoing. No. 3 then provides a further composition for this thematic anthology on the general theme of work done or not done in the Seventh Year. Nos. 4-6 continue No. 3. **III.1** asks an obvious question in clarifying the principle of the Mishnah's rule. No. 2 footnotes the foregoing. Nos. 3, 4, 5, 6+7 provide an anthological supplement, principally deriving from the Tosefta, to the theme of the Mishnah. **IV.1** engages in a simple exercise of Mishnah exegesis. **V.1** asks a question invited by the point of the Mishnah's rule. No. 2 clarifies the foregoing explanation. **VI.1** explains the meaning of the language of the Mishnah, and No. 2 then builds on the facts given in No. 1. No. 3 then provides case reports on how the law at hand is applied. **VII.1** investigates the implications of the rule of the Mishnah in light of other Tannaite formulations on the subject. **VIII.1, 2, 3** ask the familiar question of the scriptural basis for a rule of the Mishnah. No. 4 is tacked on to the foregoing by reason of the shared prooftext. No. 5 is present for the same reason. The Mishnah's theme then accounts for the inclusion of the Tannaite appendix that follows, Nos. 6, 7-13, which is hardly required except for a complete presentation of the topic. **IX.1** investigates the implications of the framing of the Mishnah's rule and harmonizes them with other rulings. No. 2 continues the exposition of the Mishnah's rule. No. 3 then turns to the theme at hand.

1:3

A. R. Eliezer b. Jacob says, "They lead water from one tree to another,

B. "on condition that one not water the entire field.

C. "Seeds which have not been watered before the festival one should not water on the intermediate days of the festival."

D. And sages permit in this case and in that.

We begin with an example of how the Bavli will ask about the way in which the law is realized, here meaning, the conditions under which the Mishnah's statement applies:

I.1   A.   **[On condition that one not water the entire field:]** Said R. Judah, "If the field's soil is clay, he may water it."

       B.   *So, too, it has been taught on Tannaite authority:*

       C.   When they made the rule that it is forbidden to irrigate on the intermediate days of a festival, they made that statement only concerning seed that had not drunk before the festival; but as to seed that had been watered before the festival, they may be watered during the intermediate days of the festival; and if the soil of the field was clay, it is permitted to water it. And a bare field [without a crop at that time] is not watered during the festival week. But sages permit doing so in both cases [where seeds were not watered, watering a bare field].

       D.   *Said Rabina, "That statement leads to the inference that it is permitted to hand sprinkle a vegetable patch during the intermediate days of a festival. For in the case of a bare field, why is it permitted to do so? It is because that renders the soil fit to be sown or planted, and here, too, that is permitted."*

Next comes a Tannaite complement to the Mishnah's rule. This will be investigated in the same way in which that of the Mishnah is worked out. We want to know how two Tannaite formulations cohere, and whether or not they contradict; if they do, then we shall try to show the rational basis for the conflict, for example, two different authorities; two conflicting principles, each brought into play under circumstances particular to itself; and the like.

I.2   A.   *Our rabbis have taught on Tannaite authority:*

       B.   They sprinkle water on a field of grain in the Seventh Year but not during the intermediate days of a festival.

       C.   *But lo, it has been taught on Tannaite authority:*

       D.   It is permitted to sprinkle a grain field both in the Seventh Year and in the intermediate days of the festival?

       E.   *Said R. Huna, "There is no contradiction, the one speaks for R. Eliezer b. Jacob* [**R. Eliezer b. Jacob says, 'They lead water from one tree to another, on condition that one not water the entire field. Seeds which have not been watered before the festival one should not water on the intermediate days of the festival'**], *the other, rabbis."*

I.3   A.   *It has been further taught on Tannaite authority:*

       B.   A field of grain may be sprinkled on the even of the Seventh Year so that the greens may sprout in the Seventh Year; and not only so, but they may sprinkle a field of grain in the Seventh Year so that the greens may sprout in the year after the Seventh Year.

I.1 clarifies the application of the Mishnah's rule. Nos. 2, 3 deal with the subsidiary issue of the Seventh Year, which is not addressed in our Mishnah paragraph.

1:4

    A.   They hunt moles and mice in a tree-planted field and in a field of grain,

    B.   in the usual manner,

    C.   on the intermediate days of a festival and in the Seventh Year.

    D.   And sages say [R. Judah], "[They do so] in a tree-planted field in the normal manner, and in a grain field not in the normal manner."

    E.   They [may only] block up a breach in the intermediate days of a festival.

    F.   And in the Seventh Year, one builds it in the normal way.

Our starting point presents no surprises: explaining the words used in the Mishnah. Where the Bavli proposes to investigate the language or sources (for example, in the Written Torah) of the Scripture, that inquiry will always stand at the head of the presentation of the Mishnah paragraph at hand. There is a clear order of business, first, language and sources and authorities, second, inquiry into issues of conflict and harmonization, and, third, investigation of secondary issues raised by the Mishnah's rule but not required for the clear re-presentation of that rule. As to the items of the first of the three categories of Mishnah commentary, I see no fixed order, though, in general, we shall expect the matter of the source of the Mishnah, in Scripture, to come first; then the clarification of the Mishnah's language; then any other items on the order of business for a given paragraph of the Mishnah; and, finally, Tannaite amplification of the Mishnah's rule or extension of its theme to other matters altogether. After translating nineteen Bavli tractates, I cannot point to a single passage in which the Mishnah is first complemented with Tannaite materials and only then analyzed as to its language and sources and authority; but in a document of the dimensions of this one, it is easier to say what we find than what we do not find.

I.1   A.   *What is the definition of* **moles**?

       B.   Said R. Judah, "It is a creature without eyes."

       C.   *Said Raba bar Ishmael, and some say, R. Yemar bar Shelamayya, "What is the pertinent verse of Scripture? 'Let them be as a snail that melts and passes away, like the young mole that has not seen the sun' (Ps. 58:9)."*

Now comes the Tannaite complement, this one adding to the Mishnah's rule, then itself amplified in exactly the same manner as is the Mishnah itself.

I.2   A.   *Our rabbis have taught on Tannaite authority:*
          B.   Moles and mice may be trapped in a grain field and in an orchard
               in the ordinary way, and ants' holes may be destroyed. How are
               they destroyed?   Rabban Simeon b. Gamaliel says, "They get
               earth from one hole and put it into another and the ants strangle
               each other" [T. M.Q. 1:5].
          C.   *Said R. Yemar bar Shelamayya in the name of Abbayye, "And that is the
               case only if the nests are located on opposite sides of the river, if there is no
               bridge, if there is not even a plank, if there is not even a rope."*
          D.   [7A] How far apart must they be?
          E.   Up to a parasang.

The next clause of the Mishnah is amplified by Tannaite complements;
these are not merely congruent to the Mishnah but allude to and explain
its language.

II.1   A.   And R. Judah says, "[They do so] in a tree-planted field in the
               normal manner, and in a grain field not in the normal manner":
          B.   *Our rabbis have taught on Tannaite authority:*
          C.   What is the usual way? He digs a hole and suspends a trap in it.
               What is the unusual way? He drives in a stake or strikes it with a
               pick and crushes the dirt underneath [T. M.Q. 1:4A-B].
II.2   A.   *It has been taught on Tannaite authority:*
          B.   R. Simeon b. Eleazar says, "When they spoke of a grain field in
               which it was not to be done in the normal manner, reference was
               made to a grain field near town. But as to a grain field near an
               orchard, even doing it in the normal way is permitted, lest the
               pests come out of the grain field and destroy the orchard" [T.
               M.Q. 1:4C-D].

Another form of explanation of the Mishnah, and the simplest, will be to
answer a question left open by the Mishnah and urgent for the
explanation of the Mishnah's rule: commentary in its simplest form.

III.1   A.   They block up a breach in the intermediate days of a festival.
               And in the Seventh Year, one builds it in the normal way:
          B.   How is the breach blocked up?
          C.   *Said R. Joseph, "With* [Lazarus:] *a hurdle made of twigs and daphne
               stakes."*
          D.   *In a Tannaite statement it was set forth:* One piles up pebbles but does
               not hold them down with mortar.
III.2   A.   Said R. Hisda, "This rule has been taught only of a wall around a
               vegetable patch, but as to a wall around a courtyard, one may build
               it up in the normal way."
          B.   *May we say that the following supports his position:* As to a wall that is
               hanging over into public domain, they may tear it down and
               rebuild it in the usual way, because it is a public nuisance [T.
               1:7A-B]?
          C.   *Well, that does not necessarily sustain the proposition, for that case bears a
               stated reason, namely,* because it is a public nuisance.
          D.   *And there are those who present matters in this way:*

E. *Come and take note:* **As to a wall that is hanging over into public domain, they may tear it down and rebuild it in the usual way, because it is a public nuisance [T. 1:7A-B]**, *so if it is a public nuisance, that may be done, but if not, it may not be done. Then may we say that this forms a refutation of the position of R. Hisda?*

F. *R. Hisda may say to you, "There one may both tear down the wall and rebuild it, here one may build the wall but not tear it down."*

G. *So in that case, too, maybe one should tear down the wall but not rebuild it?*

H. *If so, one will just give up and not tear it down at all!*

I. *Said R. Ashi, "A careful reading of the Mishnah yields that same result:* **And in the Seventh Year, one builds it in the normal way. Now what is the point of saying he may block up the breach.** *If it is the wall of his courtyard, this hardly requires explicit articulation. So it can only be a breach in his garden wall, even though it might appear that he is doing it to safeguard his crop."*

J. *That leads to the proposed inference.*

I.1 clarifies a word choice in the Mishnah. No. 2 then complements the Mishnah with a Tannaite addition. II.1, 2 do the same. III.1 answers a question of Mishnah exegesis. No. 2 explains the application of the Mishnah's rule.

1:5A-B

A. R. Meir says, "They examine marks of the presence of the skin ailment [to begin with] to provide a lenient ruling but not to provide a strict ruling."

B. And sages say, "Neither to provide a lenient ruling nor to provide a strict ruling."

The Tannaite complement to the Mishnah paragraph in fact forms a commentary upon it. We have a restatement of matters in the Mishnah, now with a consideration of how matters are to be worked out in practice: Rabbi's statement of his judgment.

I.1   A. *It has been taught on Tannaite authority:*

      B. R. Meir says, "They examine marks of the presence of the skin ailment [to begin with] to provide a lenient ruling but not to provide a strict ruling."

      C. R. Yosé says, "Neither to provide a lenient ruling nor to provide a strict ruling, for if you undertake a ruling in his case so as to present a lenient ruling, you will have also to provide the stringent ruling if it is called for."

      D. Said Rabbi, "The opinion of R. Meir makes more sense in the case of one who is merely shut up for inspection, and the opinion of R. Yosé makes more sense in the case of one who is certified as unclean" [T. M.Q. 1:8].

A secondary expansion of the Tannaite complement to the Mishnah now gets under way:

I.2   A.   *Said Raba, "In the case of someone who is now assumed to be clean, all parties concur that he is not subject to an examination at all during the intermediate days of the festival. In the case of someone who has been shut up for the first week, all parties concur that he is examined. Where there is a disagreement, it concerns [7B] one who has been shut up for a second span of time.*

        B.   *"One authority [Meir] takes the view that we leave the decision to the priest's discretion, so that if the person is clean, he declares him clean, but if he looks unclean, the priest shuts his mouth, while the other authority invokes the verse, 'this is the law of the plague and the skin ailment, to make a pronouncement of clean or unclean' (Lev. 13:59), [meaning, without dissimulation]."*

I.3   A.   The master has said: **"The opinion of R. Meir makes more sense in the case of one who is merely shut up for inspection, and the opinion of R. Yosé makes more sense in the case of one who is certified as unclean"**:

        B.   *But has not the opposite been taught on Tannaite authority?*

        C.   *It represents a conflict of Tannaite statements in respect to the position of Rabbi. One authority takes the view that having company is preferable to the victim, the other, having the company of his wife is preferable to him.* [Lazarus: Meir has confirmed patient in mind and holds, "Inspect him now to mitigate his plight; if he is still a leper, he loses nothing; if he is found cured, he can at once get back to town, even though he has to part from his wife for seven days, he does not mind, since he wants to get back to his buddies. Yosé has in mind a second shutting up and says there should be no inspection, for if he is found a leper, he is then confirmed as such and isolated from everybody except his wife.]

        D.   *Is that to say that sexual relations [in Rabbi's view] are permitted to a person who is confirmed unclean with the skin ailment?*

        E.   *Yes indeed, for so it has been taught on Tannaite authority:*

        F.   **"And he will dwell outside his tent" (Lev. 14:8) –**

        G.   **He is prohibited from having sexual relations, for "His tent" (Lev. 14:8) – his tent means only his wife, as it is said, "Return to your tents" (2 Kgs. 15:1) [Sifra CL:I.4].**

        H.   **R. Judah says, "'And after he is cleaned they shall reckon for him seven days' (Ezek. 44:26) – that is while he is counting seven clean days, but not while he is confirmed as unclean with the skin ailment."**

        I.   **R. Yosé b. R. Judah says, "If he is prohibited during the days of his counting, all the more so is he to be prohibited during the days when he is completely unclean."**

        J.   **Said R. Hiyya, "I said before Rabbi, 'You have taught us, our lord, that Jothan was born to Uzziah [2 Kgs. 15:5]** only during the days when he was certified unclean'" [T. Neg. 8:6].

K. He said to him, "Yeah, that's just what I said."

L. *What is at issue between them?*

M. *R. Yosé b. R. Judah takes the view that the All-Merciful has made it explicit that during the days of his counting out [clean days] ["shall dwell outside his tent,"] and all the more so should he not have sexual relations when he is confirmed as unclean with the skin ailment.*

N. *Rabbi takes the position that what Scripture has articulated is to be taken as fact, and what has not to be explicitly articulated is not to be imputed.*

I.4 A. *Does that position of Raba stated earlier [In the case of someone who is now assumed to be clean, all parties concur that he is not subject to an examination at all during the intermediate days of the festival. In the case of someone who has been shut up for the first week, all parties concur that he is examined. Where there is a disagreement, it concerns One authority [Meir] takes the view that we leave the decision to the priest's discretion, so that if the person is clean, he declares him clean, but if he looks unclean, the priest shuts his mouth, while the other authority invokes the verse, 'this is the law of the plague and the skin ailment, to make a pronouncement of clean or unclean' (Lev. 13:59),] bear the implication that the postponement of a decision on the cultic status of the person depends on the priest's discretion?*

B. *Yes indeed, for so it has been taught on Tannaite authority:*

C. "And on the day" (Lev. 13:14) – there is a day on which you inspect him, and there is a day on which you do not inspect him.

D. In this connection they have said: **A bridegroom on whom a plague appeared – they give him the seven days of the marriage feast [before inspecting him], him, and his house, and his garment. And so with respect to the festival: they give him all the seven days of the festival** [M. Neg. 3:2], the words of R. Judah.

E. Rabbi says, "Lo it says, 'And the priest will command that they empty the house before the priest goes in to see the plague, that all that is in the house not be made unclean' (Lev. 14:36).

F. "If they wait for an optional matter, should they not wait for a required matter?" [Sifra CXXXIV:I.1-2]

G. *What is at issue between them?*

H. Said Abbayye, "The implications of the exegesis of Scripture is what is at issue between them."

I. *And Raba said, "The disposition of an optional matter is what is at issue between them. And R. Judah does not derive the rule from the verse cited by Rabbi [Lev. 14:36], because that is an anomaly, for, in any event, [8A] wood and stone in general do not contract uncleanness, while here they contract uncleanness. Rabbi for his part says that the verse is required [not for the purpose cited by Judah but for another purpose,] for had*

Scripture written, 'and on the day when raw flesh shall be seen in him' alone, I might have supposed that one may postpone inspection only in connection with carrying out a religious duty but not in the case of an optional matter, so the All-Merciful has already said, 'And the priest shall command.' And if the All-Merciful had said only, 'And the priest shall command that they empty the house,' I might have supposed that that is in the case of these matters because uncleanness does not affect a human being, but in a case in which the uncleanness affects a human being, I might have supposed that the priest has to inspect him without delay. So both verses are required."

I.5   A.   *The master has said:* "And on the day" (Lev. 13:14) – there is a day on which you inspect him, and there is a day on which you do not inspect him. *How does the cited verse yield this conclusion?*

B.   *Said Abbayye, "If the verse yielded no such conclusion, the All-Merciful could as well have written, 'on the day.' Why say, 'and on the day'? That yields the conclusion that* there is a day on which you inspect him, and there is a day on which you do not inspect him."

C.   *Raba said, "The whole of the verse is redundant, for otherwise Scripture could have said, 'and when raw flesh is seen in him.' Why add, 'and on a day'? That yields the conclusion that* there is a day on which you inspect him, and there is a day on which you do not inspect him."

D.   *And Abbayye?*

E.   *That is required to indicate,* by day and not by night.

F.   *And how does Raba know that it is to be* by day and not by night?

G.   *He derives that fact from the following:* "According to everything that the priest sees" (Lev. 13:12) [which is to say, by day, when people can see properly].

H.   *And Abbayye?*

I.   *That is required to exclude from the inspection process a priest who is blind in one eye.*

J.   *And does not Raba require the verse to make this point as well?*

K.   *True enough.*

L.   *Then how does he know that it is to be* by day but not by night?

M.   *He derives it from the verse,* "Like as a plague was seen by me in the house" (Lev. 14:35) – by me, not with the help of a lamp.

N.   *And Abbayye?*

O.   *If the rule derived from there, I might have supposed that the restriction applies when the uncleanness does not affect a person's body, but where uncleanness affects the body, I might have supposed that one may inspect it by a lamp. So the original prooftext is the better one.*

I.1 complements the Mishnah's ruling with further relevant data, and Nos. 2, 3, 4 (reverting to No. 2), and 5 form a talmud to the foregoing.

1:5C-G

C. And further did R. Meir say, "[On the intermediate days of the festival] a man may go out and gather the bones of his father and his mother,

D. "because it is a time of rejoicing for him."

E. R. Yosé says, "It is a time of mourning for him."

F. A person may not call for mourning for his deceased,

G. or make a lamentation for him thirty days before a festival.

Our first inquiry concerns the harmony of the law. We see here that the intersecting rule need not occur in another Mishnah paragraph. The item before us is in the same Hebrew as the Mishnah's rule, but does not bear an explicit indicator of Tannaite origin or formulation; the language forms the taxic indicator.

I.1   A. "Because it is a time of rejoicing for him":

      B. *An objection was raised on the basis of the following:*

      C. He who collects the bones of his mother and father for secondary burial – lo, one observes mourning for them all that day. But in the evening he no longer observes mourning for them. And in that connection said R. Hisda, "Even if he had them tied up in a sheet."

      D. *Said Abbayye, "Say the rule as follows: 'Because the rejoicing of the festival affects him.'"*

Clarification of the Mishnah's language forms the purpose of the treatment of the next clause of the Mishnah:

II.1   A. A person may not call for mourning for his deceased:

      B. *What is the sense of* may not call for mourning for his deceased?

      C. *Said Rab, "In the West, when a professional lamenter comes around, people say, 'Let everybody of mournful spirit weep with him.'"*

III.1   A. Or make a lamentation for him thirty days before a festival:

      B. *What distinguishes the spell of* thirty days?

      C. Said R. Kahana said R. Judah said Rab, "There was the case of someone who saved money to go up to Jerusalem for the festival, and the professional mourner came along and stood at the door of his house, and his wife took the money and handed it over to him, so he never got to go up. At that moment they said, a **person may not call for mourning for his deceased, or make a lamentation for him thirty days before a festival.**"

      D. And Samuel said, [8B] "It is because for at least thirty days, the deceased is not put out of mind."

      E. What is at issue between them?

      F. At issue between them is where the professional mourner does it for nothing.

I.1 harmonizes Tannaite rules on the same subject. II.1 clarifies the facts to which the Mishnah's rule makes reference. III.1 explains what is at issue in the rule of the Mishnah.

1:6

A. They do not hew out a tomb niche or tombs on the intermediate days of a festival.
B. But they refashion tomb niches on the intermediate days of a festival.
C. They dig a grave on the intermediate days of a festival,
D. and make a coffin,
E. while the corpse is in the same courtyard.
F. R. Judah prohibits, unless there were boards [already sawn and made ready in advance].

Not surprisingly, we commence with the explanation of the language of the Mishnah:

I.1   A. *What are* **tomb niches** *and what are* **tombs?**
        B. Said R. Judah, "Tomb niches are formed by digging, and tombs are formed by building."
        C. *So, too, it has been taught on Tannaite authority:*
        D. What are tomb niches and what are tombs? Tomb niches are formed by digging, and tombs are formed by building.

We proceed to a secondary amplification of the Mishnah's rule: information required for full comprehension of the Mishnah's statement.

II.1   A. **But they refashion tomb niches on the intermediate days of a festival:**
        B. How do they refashion them?
        C. Said R. Judah, "If it was too long, they may shorten it."
        D. *In a Tannaite formulation it is set forth:* **One makes it broader or longer** [T. M.Q. 1:8A-B].

Once more we address the word choices of the Mishnah.

III.1   A. **They dig a grave on the intermediate days of a festival:**
        B. *What is* **a grave?**
        C. Said R. Judah, "It is a small hollow creek" [Lazarus].
        D. But has it not been taught on Tannaite authority: **...a grave and a small hollow...** [cf. T. M.Q. 1:8C].
        E. {That does not mean they are the same thing, for] said Abbayye, and some say, R. Kahana, "*They relate as do a [Lazarus:] trough and a little trough.*"

The next clause of the Mishnah is amplified by appeal to a Tannaite formulation, external to the Mishnah and entirely cogent with it:

IV.1   A. **And make a coffin, while the corpse is in the same courtyard:**

B. *We have a Tannaite formulation along these same lines in that which our rabbis have taught on Tannaite authority:*
C. They do all that is needed for the deceased, cutting the hair, washing his garment, making a box of boards out of boards that had been cut prior to the festival.
D. Rabban Simeon b. Gamaliel says, "They may even bring lumber and, in the privacy of one's house, cut it to size."

I.1 explains the meaning of words in the Mishnah. II.1 amplifies the sense of the Mishnah's statement. III.1 produces a relevant Tannaite complement.

1:7

A. They do not take wives on the intermediate days of a festival,
B. whether virgins or widows.
C. Nor do they enter into levirate marriage,
D. for it is an occasion of rejoicing for the groom.
E. But one may remarry his divorced wife.
F. And a woman may prepare her wedding adornments on the intermediate days of a festival.
G. R. Judah says, "She should not use lime, since this makes her ugly."

1:8

A. An unskilled person sews in the usual way.
B. But an expert craftsman sews with irregular stitches.
C. They weave the ropes for beds.
D. R. Yosé says, "They [only] tighten them."

Here, the clarification of the Mishnah's rule is substantive, not linguistic. That is to say, the stance of the commentator now is external to the text, and the commentator wants to know why the Mishnah finds self-evident what is not necessarily obvious to all parties:

I.1   A. *So if it's* **an occasion of rejoicing for the groom,** *what's so bad about that?*
B. Said R. Judah said Samuel, and so said R. Eleazar said R. Oshaia, and some say, said R. Eleazar said R. Hanina, "The consideration is that one occasion of rejoicing should not be joined with another such occasion."
C. Rabbah bar R. Huna said, "It is because he neglects the rejoicing of the festival to engage in rejoicing over his wife."
D. Said Abbayye to R. Joseph, "This statement that has been said by Rabbah bar R. Huna belongs to Rab, for said R. Daniel bar Qattina said Rab, 'How on the basis of Scripture do we know that people may not take wives on the intermediate days of the festival? As it is said, "You shall rejoice in your feast" (Deut. 16:14), meaning, in your feast – not in your new wife.'"
E. Ulla said, "It is because it is excess trouble."

F. R. Isaac Nappaha said, "It is because one will neglect the requirement of being fruitful and multiplying" [if people postponed weddings until festivals, they might somehow diminish the occasion for procreation, which is the first obligation]."

G. *An objection was raised:* All those of whom they have said that they are forbidden to wed on the festival **[9A]** are permitted to wed on the eve of the festival. *Now this poses a problem to the explanations of all the cited authorities!*

H. *There is no problem from the perspective of him who has said, "The consideration is that one occasion of rejoicing should not be joined with another such occasion," for the main rejoicing of the wedding is only a single day.*

I. *And from the perspective of him who has said, "It is because it is excess trouble," the principal bother lasts only one day.*

J. *And from the perspective of him who has said, "It is because one will neglect the requirement of being fruitful and multiplying," for merely one day someone will not postpone the obligation for any considerable length of time.*

The foregoing has taken for granted a principle not contained in the Mishnah, and we now find a scriptural basis for not the Mishnah but that ancillary principle:

I.2 A. *And how on the basis of Scripture do we know that* one occasion of rejoicing should not be joined with another such occasion?

B. *It is in line with that which has been written:* "So Solomon made the feast at that time and all Israel with him, a great congregation from the entrance of Hamath to the Brook of Eygpt, before the Lord our God seven days and seven days, even fourteen days" (1 Kgs. 8:65). *Now if it were permitted to join one occasion of rejoicing with another such occasion, he should have postponed the celebration of the consecration of the Temple until the festival and should then have held it for seven days concurrently, for both the festival and the consecration [rather than celebrating the occasions sequentially].*

C. *Well, maybe the rule means only that one should not deliberately postpone a wedding until the festival, but where it just happens to work out that way, we may nonetheless hold the wedding on the festival?*

D. *Well, if that were the case, then he should have left unfinished some small detail of the building of the house of the sanctuary?*

E. *We do not leave over some small detail in the building of the Temple!*

F. *He could have left off a cubit of the scarecrow's parapet!*

G. The scarecrow's parapet was an essential part of the Temple.

H. *Rather, in point of fact the cited formulation of Scripture leaves a redundancy.* For it says "fourteen days," so why go and say also, "Seven days and seven days"? *That yields the simple fact that the two sets of seven days were kept distinct from one another [each marking its own occasion for rejoicing].*

What follows stands on its own feet and can be fully understood without reference to the foregoing. The sole issue is why it has been inserted at all, and the answer is clear as soon as the question is asked, so we have a composition that is used to provide a talmud to a talmud:

I.3   A. Said R. Parnakh said R. Yohanan, "In that year, the Israelites did not observe the Day of Atonement, so they worried, saying, 'Perhaps Israel has become subject to extinction. An echo came forth and said to them, 'You all are singled out for the life of the world to come.'"

B. *What was the exegesis that led them to that concern?*

C. They thought along these lines: "It is a matter a fortiori. For if in the case of the tabernacle, which was sanctified not for all time [but only for an interval], the offering of an individual [presented on the occasion of the consecration of the tabernacle, Num. 7] overrode the restriction of the Sabbath, which ordinarily represents a prohibition the violation of which is penalized by stoning, then in the case of the sanctuary, the sanctification of which is for all time, all the more so should it be permitted to present an offering in behalf of the community and the Day of Atonement, which are subject to the penalty merely of extirpation, all the more so [should it be permitted to present offerings in behalf of the individual]!" *So what were they worried about?*

D. *[Reference is made to the private offerings presented by the heads of the tribes as individuals, Num. 7:] there, in that earlier case, the offerings were presented to meet the requirements of the Most High [since the burnt-offerings and sin-offerings yielded no meat for the people, and the sin-offerings yielded meat only to the male priests], while here the offerings were presented to meet the requirements of common folk [since there were peace-offerings for everybody's pleasure].*

E. *Well, here, too, they could have made the offering, without eating the meat or drinking.*

F. There is no such thing as celebration without eating and drinking.

I.4   A. *And how do we know that the consecration of the tabernacle overrode the restrictions of the Sabbath? Should I say because it is written, "On the first day...on the seventh day so and so offered...," [at Num. 7:12, 18, 42]? But maybe that means only, the seventh day in sequence of offerings [but not the Sabbath]!*

B. Said R. Nahman bar Isaac, "Said Scripture, 'On the day of the eleventh day' (Num. 7:72) – just as a day is consecutive, so all the eleven days were consecutive [encompassing the Sabbath, without skipping]."

C. *But perhaps reference is made to days that ordinarily were suitable for such private offerings?*

    D.   *There is yet another verse of Scripture that pertains: "On the day of the twelfth day" (Num. 7:78) – just as a day is consecutive, so all the twelve days were consecutive [encompassing the Sabbath, without skipping].*

    E.   *But perhaps here, too, reference is made to days that ordinarily were suitable for such private offerings?*

    F.   *If that were the sense, why do I need two distinct verses to make the same point?*

I.5   A.   *And how do we know that the consecration of the tabernacle overrode the restrictions of the Day of Atonement? Should I say because it is written, "...even fourteen days"?*

    B.   *But perhaps reference is made to days that ordinarily were suitable for such private offerings?*

    C.   *We draw a verbal analogy based on the common usage of "day" in that other context.*

I.6   A.   "An echo came forth and said to them, 'You all are singled out for the life of the world to come'":

    B.   How do we know that they were forgiven?

    C.   *It is in line with what Tahalipa taught as a Tannaite statement:*

    D.   "'On the eighth day he sent the people home and they blessed the king and went to their own tents joyful and glad of heart for all the goodness that the Lord had shown to David his servant and to Israel his people' (1 Kgs. 8:66) –

    E.   "'to their own tents': they went and found their wives in a state of cleanness suitable for sexual relations.

    F.   "'joyful': for they had feasted on the splendor of God's presence;

    G.   "'and glad of heart': for the wife of every one of them became pregnant with a male child.

    H.   "'for all the goodness': for an echo came forth and said to them, 'You all are singled out for the life of the world to come.'"

I.7   A.   "To David his servant and to Israel his people":

    B.   *Now there is no problem understanding the reference to Israel, his people, since the sin of violating the Day of Atonement was forgiven them. But what is the meaning of the reference to David his servant?*

    C.   Said R. Judah said Rab, "When Solomon had built the house of the sanctuary, he tried to bring the ark into the house of the Holy of Holies. The gates cleaved to one another. He recited twenty-four prayers [Freedman, p. 734, n. 4: in 2 Chr. 6 words for prayer, supplication, and hymn occur twenty-four times], but was not answered.

    D.   "He said, 'Lift up your heads, O you gates, and be lifted up, you everlasting doors, and the King of glory shall come in. Who is this King of glory? The Lord strong and mighty, the Lord mighty in battle' (Ps. 24:7ff.).

    E.   "And it is further said, 'Lift up your heads, O you gates even lift them up, you everlasting doors' (Ps. 24:7).

    F.   "But he was not answered.

G. "When he said, 'Lord God, turn not away the face of your anointed, remember the mercies of David, your servant' (2 Chr. 6:42), forthwith he was answered.

H. "At that moment the faces of David's enemies turned as black as the bottom of a pot, for all Israel knew that the Holy One, blessed be He, had forgiven him for that sin."

I.8 A. *R. Jonathan b. Asemai and R. Judah, son of proselytes, repeated the Tannaite presentation of the laws of vows at the household of R. Simeon b. Yohai and took their leave of him by night, but the next morning they came, and again they took their leave of him. He said to them, "But did you not take leave of me last night?"*

B. *They said to him, "But did you not take leave of me last night?"*

C. They said to him, "You have taught us, our lord: 'A disciple who takes leave of his master but spends the night in that town has to take leave from him once again, in line with this verse: "On the eighth day he sent the people home and they blessed the king and went to their own tents joyful and glad of heart for all the goodness that the Lord had shown to David his servant and to Israel his people" (1 Kgs. 8:66); and then it is written, "And on the twenty-third day of the seventh month he sent the people away" (2 Chr. 7:10). Thus we learn that a disciple who takes leave of his master but spends the night in that town has to take leave from him once again.'"

I.9 A. *He said to his son, "My son, these men are men of standing. Go to them so that they will bestow their blessing on you."*

B. *He went and found them contrasting verses one against the next, in the following way:* "It is written, 'Balance the path of your feet and let all your ways be established' (Prov. 4:26), and, by contrast, 'Lest you should balance the path of life' (Prov. 5:5). But there is no conflict between the advice of these two verses. The one speaks to a case in which a religious obligation can be carried out through someone else, the latter, a case in which the religious obligation can be carried out only by oneself."

C. *They again went into session and raised questions along these lines:* "It is written, 'Wisdom is more precious than rubies, and all things you can desire are not to be compared to her' (Prov. 3:10), meaning that what Heaven wants of you is comparable to Wisdom [Lazarus: your own affairs and wishes are not comparable to the study of the Torah, but such pursuits as please Heaven are comparable to it], but it is written, 'And all things desirable are not to be compared with Wisdom' (Prov. 8:11), which means that what Heaven demands of you is comparable with her. And again, 'And all things desirable are not to be compared to her' (Prov. 8:12), meaning that even things that Heaven wants of you are not comparable to her [so study of Torah is supreme over all]. But there is no conflict between the advice of these two verses. The one speaks to a case in which a religious obligation can be carried out through someone else, the latter, a case in which the religious obligation can be carried out only by oneself."

D. *They said to him, "What did you want here?"*

E. *He said to them, "Father said to me, 'Go to them so that they may bestow their blessing on you.'"*

F. *They said to him, "May it please God that you sow and not harvest, go in but not go out, go out but not go in; that your house be empty but your inn filled; that your table be upset and you not see a new year."*

G. *When he got home, he said to his father, he said to him, "Not only did they not bless me, but they called down pain upon me!"*

H. *He said to him, "So what did they say to you?"*

I. *"Thus and so did they say to me!"*

J. He said to him, "But all of their statements were blessings:

K. *"'That you sow and not harvest': That you father children and they not die;*

L. *"'Go in but not go out': That you bring home daughters-in-law and your sons not die so that the wives do not have to depart from you;*

M. *"'Go out but not go in': That you give your daughters in marriage and their husbands not die so that your daughters do not have to come back;*

N. *"'That your house be empty but your inn filled': This world is your inn, the other world is home, 'Their grave is their house for ever' (Ps. 49:12), reading not 'their inward thought' but 'their grave is their house for ever, and their dwelling places be for generations.'*

O. *"'That your table be upset': By sons and daughters;*

P. *"'And you not see a new year': Your wife should not die so you do not have to take a new wife."*

I.10 A. *R. Simeon b. Halapta took his leave of Rabbi. Said Rabbi to his son, "Go to him that he may bless you."*

B. *He said to him, "May it please God that you not put anybody to shame nor feel ashamed."*

C. *He came back to his father, who said to him, "What did he say to you?"*

D. *He said to him, "Oh, nothing out of the ordinary."*

E. *He said to him, "What he gave to you was the blessing that the Holy One, blessed be He, bestowed upon Israel two times: 'And you shall eat in plenty and be satisfied and shall praise the name of the Lord your God...and my people shall never be ashamed. And you shall know*

> that I am in the midst of Israel, and that I am the Lord
> your God, and there is none else, and my people shall
> never be ashamed' (Joel 2:26-27)."

We return to the Mishnah, and once more begin with a Tannaite complement to the Mishnah's statement. This one explicitly refers to the Mishnah and is formulated as an explanation of its rule.

II.1 A. **And a woman may prepare her wedding adornments on the intermediate days of a festival:**
    B. *Our rabbis have taught on Tannaite authority:*
    C. What are women's adornments: she may blue her eyes, curl her hair, trim her hair and nails, put on rouge, and some say, shave her sexual organs.

The next entry forms a case in illustration of the foregoing:

II.2 A. R. Hisda's wife made herself up in front of her daughter-in-law.
    B. *In session before R. Hisda, R. Hina bar Hinnena said,* "That rule applies only in the case of a girl. But as to a mature woman, that is not so."
    C. He said to him, "By God! Even your mother, and even your mother's mother, and even if she is ready to fall into the grave!' *For people say, 'At sixty, at six,* [Lazarus:] *The sound of the timbrel makes her nimble.'*"

The treatment of the next clause of the Mishnah follows the plan of the foregoing. We note that a given Mishnah paragraph may be split up into two or more clauses, and then the treatment of each clause in form will be identical with the presentation of the others, for example, if we have a scriptural proof serving clause A, we shall have the same in sequence for clauses B, C, and D of the same Mishnah paragraph; if we have a Tannaite complement to clause A, then the same will be given to the successive clauses. Not only so, but each of these will then be analyzed along the same formal lines, so that a single plan and program will dictate the treatment of successive clauses of the Mishnah paragraph.

III.1 A. **R. Judah says, "She should not use lime, since this makes her ugly":**
    B. *It has been taught on Tannaite authority:*
    C. R. Judah says, "A woman should not put lime on her face on the intermediate days of a festival, since it makes her ugly." But R. Judah concedes that if the lime can be scraped off during the intermediate days of the festival, she may put it on during those same intermediate days, for **even though it is distressing to her now, she will be happy about it later."** [There is therefore a contradiction between the two rulings in Judah's name.]
    D. *But does R. Judah hold this view? And have we not learned in the Mishnah:* **Before the festivals of gentiles for three days it is**

> forbidden to do business with them: (1) to lend anything to them or to borrow anything from them; (2) to lend money to them or to borrow money from them; (3) to repay them or to be repaid by them. R. Judah says, "They accept repayment from them, because it is distressing to him." They said to him, "Even though it is distressing to him now, he will be happy about it later" [M. A.Z. 1:1]?

E.   Said R. Nahman bar Isaac, "Forget about the laws of the intermediate days of the festival, for all of them fall into the category, 'Even though it is distressing to him now, he will be happy about it later.'"

F.   *Rabina said, "As to a gentile, so far as getting repaid is concerned, it is always a source of anguish."*

III.2   A.   Said R. Judah, "Israelite girls who reached puberty before they reach the normal age of maturity in years [twelve years and a day], if they are poor, may put on a lime concoction; if they are rich, they put on fine flour; princesses put on oil of myrrh, as it is said, 'Six months with oil of myrrh' (Est. 2:12)."

III.3   A.   "Six months with oil of myrrh" (Est. 2:12):

        B.   *What is oil of myrrh?*

        C.   R. Huna bar Hiyya said, "It is stacte."

        D.   R. Jeremiah bar Abba said, "It is oil derived from olives not yet a third grown."

III.4   A.   *It has been taught on Tannaite authority:*

        B.   R. Judah says, "[Olives for olive oil] from a manured field refers to olives that are not a third grown. And why is it used for smearing? Because it serves as a depilatory and skin softener."

        C.   Why do they apply it? Because it removes hair and softens the skin.

III.5   A.   *R. Bibi had a daughter with dark skin, on which he put that ointment limb by limb, and this produced for her a husband who had four hundred zuz.*

        B.   *A gentile neighbor also had a daughter with dark skin, on which he put that ointment all at once, so she died.*

        C.   *He said, "Bibi killed my daughter."*

        D.   *Said R. Nahman, "R. Bibi drank beer, so his daughters needed ointments, but we don't drink beer, so our daughters don't need ointments."*

Now come several citations and amplifications of the language of the Mishnah, illustrating the point that a single plan and program, involving even a single formal construction, will address successive, free-standing phrases or clauses or sentences of the Mishnah:

IV.1   A.   **[10A] An unskilled person sews in the usual way:**

        B.   *What is the definition of* an unskilled person?

        C.   At the household of R. Yannai they said, "It is anyone who cannot draw a needleful of stitches all at once."

        D.   R. Yosé bar Hanina said, "It is any that cannot sew an even seam on the hem of his shirt."

V.1   A.   **But an expert craftsman sews with irregular stitches:**

        B.   *What does it mean to* sew with irregular stitches?

C. R. Yohanan said, "Overstepping."
D. *Rabbah bar Samuel said, "Dogs' teeth."*
VI.1 A. **They weave the ropes for beds. R. Yosé says, "They [only] tighten them":**
B. *What defines* **weaving and tightening?**
C. *When R. Dimi came, he said, "There was a dispute on this matter between R. Hiyya bar Abba and R. Assi, both of them speaking in the name of Hezekiah and R. Yohanan.*
D. "One said, 'Interlacing means interlacing warp and woof, and tightening means putting in the warp but not the woof.'
E. "And the other said, 'Interlacing means putting in the warp without the woof, and tightening means he tightens a girth cord if it becomes loose.'"

A talmud to the foregoing now commences:

F. *Is that so? But lo, R. Tahalipa bar Saul taught, "And they concur that they may not insert new cords to begin with." Now that poses no problem to him who maintains that the interlacing that is permitted is,* interlacing warp and woof, and tightening means putting in the warp but not the woof. *In line with that view, R. Tahalipa could say,* "And they concur that they may not insert new cords to begin with." *But from the perspective of him who has said,* Interlacing means putting in the warp without the woof, and tightening means he tightens a girth cord if it becomes loose, *what sense does R. Tahalipa b. Saul's statement make? If you maintain that* interlacing the warp and woof is forbidden, *is there any need to add that* they may not insert new cords to begin with?

G. *That's a problem.*

H. *Said R. Nahman bar Isaac to R. Hiyya bar Abin, "But is there anybody who takes the view that 'interlacing' means inserting a warp without the woof? Have we not learned in the Mishnah:* **R. Meir says, "The bed [becomes susceptible to uncleanness] when one will have knit together on it three rows [of the mesh of the underwebbing]"** [M. Kel. 16:1F]?"

I. *Rather, when Rabin came, he said, "All concur that* interlacing *involves both warp and woof. Where there is a dispute, it concerns tightening. One master takes the view that* the tightening that is permitted means inserting the warp without the woof, *and the other master maintains that what is permitted is* tightening a cord that became loose."

J. *An objection was raised:*

K. "During the intermediate days of a festival they may interlace bed frames, and, it goes without say, they may be tightened," the words of R. Meir.

L. R. Yosé says, "They may be tightened but not interlaced."

M. Some say, "They may not tighten at all."

N.	*Now from the perspective of him who has said, "Tightening means inserting the warp without the woof," then there is a place for "some say" to dissent. But from the perspective of him who says that tightening means tightening the cord that has become slack, then in the view of some, will even this simple improvement not be allowed?*

O.	*Well, yes! For since it is possible to fill up the sag with bedding, we don't have to go to any more trouble than that during the intermediate days of the festival.*

I.1 provides a reason for the Mishnah's rule, and No. 2 then derives from Scripture the consideration that explains the Mishnah's rule. Nos. 3-6+7, 8-10, supplement No. 2, a run-on thematic anthology, each item tied to the foregoing. **II.1** complements the Mishnah with a Tannaite extension, and No. 2 follows suit. **III.1** harmonizes two rulings of the cited authority. No. 2, supplemented by Nos. 3, 4, 5, adds a thematic complement. **IV.1, V.1, VI.1** explain references in the Mishnah.

1:9

A.	They set up an oven or double stove or a hand mill on the intermediate days of a festival.

B.	R. Judah says, "They do not rough the millstones [which are smooth and so not now usable for grinding grain] for the first time."

We begin once more with the analysis of words and phrases, then secondary development of the proposed lexical entry:

I.1	A.	*What is the meaning of* **rough***?*

B.	R. Judah said, "It means chiselling holes into the millstones [so that the grain may be milled]."

C.	R. Yehiel said, "It means fixing an eye hole [on the upper stone, through which the grain is poured in (Lazarus)]."

D.	*An objection was raised:* "**They set up an oven or double stove or a hand mill on the intermediate days of a festival,** on condition that the work is not completely finished," the words of R. Eliezer.

E.	And sages say, "It may even be finished."

F.	R. Judah says in his [Eliezer's] name, "They may set up a new one and roughen an old one."

G.	And some say, "They may not do any roughening at all."

H.	*Now from the perspective of him who says that "rough" means scoring the millstones, that explains why the process pertains also to an old mill [which has been smoothed through use], but from the perspective of him who says that it means fixing an eye hole, how does a used mill require fixing an eye hole [since it already has one]?*

I.	*It would involve, for example, one that requires widening a bit more.*

I.2 A. *R. Huna heard somebody scraping millstones during the intermediate days of a festival. He said, "May the person of him who profanes the intermediate days of the festival be profaned."*

B. *He then takes the position of* "some say [they may not do any roughening at all]."

I.3 A. R. Hama presented this exposition: "On the intermediate days of the festival, people may roughen millstones."

B. In the name of R. Meir one said, "On the intermediate days of the festival one may even trim the hooves of a horse on which he rides or an ass on which he rides, [10B] *but one may not do so to the ass who turns the mill."*

C. *R. Judah permitted trimming the hooves of the ass that turns the mill, setting up a mill, building a mill, constructing a base for the mill, and building a stable for horses.*

D. *Rab permitted currying horses, constructing a bed, or making a mattress box.*

I.4 A. *During the intermediate days of a festival Raba permitted bleeding cattle.*

B. *Said to him Abbayye, "In support of your position it has been taught on Tannaite authority:* During the intermediate days of a festival they may bleed cattle and they do not withhold any means of healing from an animal."

I.5 A. *Raba permitted softening carded sheets of cloth.*

B. *How come?*

C. *It is a process that can be carried out by unskilled labor.*

D. *Said R. Isaac bar Ammi said R. Hisda, "It is forbidden to pleat sleeve ends [Lazarus]. How come? Because that is a process that can be carried out only by skilled labor."*

What follows is a set of rules in the name of a single authority, all of them complementary to the rule of the Mishnah paragraph before us; and all of them are understood in their own terms. The composition has been worked out for its own purpose, then inserted here because it serves the purpose of the framers of the document. In this context, the composition functions as does a Tannaite complement to the Mishnah: it is not analytical, but it also is not paraphrastic. It both stands on its own and also enriches our grasp of the law of the Mishnah. In our catalogue of types of Mishnah commentary, this item finds no place; but in our grasp of how the Bavli overall constitutes a commentary to the Mishnah, this item is of exemplary value and critical importance:

I.6 A. *Said Raba, "One who levels the ground, if it is with the purpose in mind of evening the slope of the threshing floor, that is permitted; if it is with the purpose in mind of leveling the soil, it is forbidden.*

B. *"How so? If he takes up the heaped up soil to heap on soil, or hard soil to lay on hard soil, that indicates that the purpose is to improve the threshing floor. But if he takes heaped up soil and puts it on hard soil, that shows it is to improve the ground."*

I.7 A. *And said Raba, "Someone who collects chips of wood in his field, if it is with gathering firewood in mind, it is permitted; if it is with clearing the ground in mind, it is forbidden.*

    B. *"How so? If he picks up big pieces and leaves little ones, that shows that it is with the purpose of gathering firewood; if he picks up both the big and little pieces, this shows that he has in mind to clear the field."*

I.8 A. *And said Raba, "Someone who opens sluices to let water run off into the field, if it be with the purpose in mind of collecting the fish, it is permitted; if it is to irrigate the field, it is forbidden.*

    B. *"How so? If he opens two flood gates, one above, the other below, that proves it is to collect the fish; but if it is only one gate, that is with the purpose in mind of irrigating the field."*

I.9 A. *And said Raba, "Someone who trims his palm, if it is with the purpose of getting food for his animals, it is permitted. If it is to benefit the palm, it is forbidden.*

    B. *"How so? If he trims only one side, this shows that it is with the need of his cattle that he trims the palm; if he trims both sides, it is to benefit the palm and the act is forbidden on the intermediate dates of the festival."*

I.10 A. *And said Raba, "Unripe tuhalani dates may be picked but not pressed."*

    B. *R. Pappa said, "But if they were getting rotten, then it is like a business deal that would involve a loss if one does not carry it out on the intermediate days of a festival and they may be pressed during the intermediate days of a festival."*

I.11 A. *And said Raba, "Any sort of business deal is forbidden [on the intermediate days of a festival."*

    B. Said R. Yosé bar Abin, "But with regard to a deal that, if not carried out right away, may go sour, it is permitted."

When we come to a set of cases, for example, practical decisions or illustrations of the rule by appeal to actions of a major authority, we know we near the end of the composite assigned to a given clause of the Mishnah. Here is a fine instance:

I.12 A. *Rabina had a deal that would have produced six thousand zuz; he put it off until after the festival and sold the same at twelve thousand.*

I.13 A. *Rabina lent some money to people from Aqra deShanuta. He asked R. Ashi and said, "What about going over there now [during the intermediate days of the festival]?"*

    B. *He said to him, "Since just now they have the ready cash but some other day they may not put their hands on it, it falls into the category of a deal that, if not carried out right away, may go sour, so it is permitted."*

    C. *It has been taught on Tannaite authority along these same lines with regard to dealing with idolators:* [Israelites] may go [11A] to a fair of gentiles and buy from them beasts, slave boys and slave girls, houses, fields, and vineyards, and write deeds and deposit them in their archives, because thereby what one does is rescue [property] from their hands.

I.14   A.   *Rab permitted Hiyya bar Ashi to repair basket traps during the intermediate days of a festival.*

       B.   *How come?*

       C.   This is unskilled work.

       D.   *But mending mesh nets if forbidden.*

       E.   *How come?*

       F.   This is skilled work.

I.15   A.   *R. Judah permitted Ammi the oven maker to build up ovens, and Rabbah bar Ashbi to plait sieves.*

       B.   *Is that so? But did not Rabbah bar Samuel repeat as a Tannaite formulation,* "And they concur that they do not build up an oven to begin with"?

       C.   There is no contradiction, the former ruling applies during the dry season, the latter during the rainy season [Passover, Tabernacles, respectively; in the former period the clay dries quickly and the oven can be used right away, but in the latter festival the rain delays the hardening process, so the oven will not be available right away (Lazarus)].

I.1 defines the principal word of a Mishnah sentence. No. 2 provides a case illustrative of the rule. Nos. 3-15 supplement the foregoing composite.

1:10

       A.   **They make a parapet for a roof or a porch in an unskilled manner,**

       B.   **but not in the manner of a skilled craftsman.**

       C.   **They plaster cracks and smooth them down with a roller, by hand, or by foot, but not with a trowel.**

       D.   **A hinge, socket, roof beam, lock, or key, [any of] which broke**

       E.   **do they repair on the intermediate days of the festival,**

       F.   **so long as one had not [earlier on] had the intention to [postpone the work so as to] do work on it on the intermediate days of the festival.**

       G.   **And all pickled foods which a man can eat during the intermediate days of a festival he also may pickle.**

The starting point, predictably, is explanation of words and phrases:

I.1   A.   **[They make a parapet for a roof or a porch in an unskilled manner, but not in the manner of a skilled craftsman:]** *What is the definition of* **an unskilled manner?**

       B.   *Said R. Joseph,* "With [Lazarus:] *a hurdle made of twigs and daphne stakes.*"

       D.   *In a Tannaite statement it was set forth:* One piles up pebbles but does not hold them down with mortar.

Mishnah criticism moves forward, in the following, with a *reductio ad absurdum,* yielding a clarification of the sense of the Mishnah's language:

II.1   A. **They plaster cracks and smooth them down with a roller, by hand, or by foot, but not with a trowel:**
         B. *Now if it is permitted to use a roller to flatten it down, is there any question that one may do so by hand or by foot?*
         C. *This is the sense of the statement:* They may plaster crevices and flatten down the plaster as with a roller, by hand or by foot, but not with ramming tools.

Words and phrases having been clarified, we proceed to the contradiction between our rule and an intersecting one, and of course the harmonization of the conflict; then the item bears in its wake a talmud of its own.

III.1   A. **A hinge, socket, roof beam, lock, or key, [any of] which broke do they repair on the intermediate days of the festival, so long as one had not [earlier on] had the intention to [postpone the work so as to] do work on it on the intermediate days of the festival:**
         B. *An objection was raised:* Yohanan the High Priest [John Hyrcanus]: until his time, hammers would pound [work was done] in Jerusalem [during the intermediate days of Passover and Sukkot] [M. M.S. 5:15C]. *The meaning then is,* until his time *but not afterward!*
         C. *There is no contradiction. There reference is made to the hammer of a smith, here, it is to the joiner's mallet [which is permitted].*
         D.   *Objected R. Hisda, "Then some will say that a loud noise is forbidden, but a soft one permitted."*
         E.   *Rather, said R. Hisda, "There still is no contradiction: The tool that may be used is a bill hook, the other is an adze"* [Lazarus's translations of the substantives].
         F.   R. Pappa said, "The one speaks of the period prior to the decree, the other, afterward."
         G.   *R. Ashi said, "The one represents the position of R. Judah, the other R. Yosé. For said R. Isaac bar Abdimi, 'Who is the Tannaite authority who takes the view that one has to perform in an extraordinary manner an act that is permitted in a matter in which considerable loss is going to be incurred by postponement? It is not in accord with R. Yosé.'"*
         H.   *Said Rabina, "In accord with whom do we these days deem permitted in the intermediate days of a festival the raising of [Lazarus:] pivot cups of doors? It is in accord with R. Yosé."*

Where, as in the following, we are given a case illustrative of the Mishnah's rule, there will be no prior clarification of the Mishnah, for example, a commentary on its sources, language, or authorities:

IV.1   A. **And all pickled foods which a man can eat during the intermediate days of a festival he also may pickle:**
         B. *At Luba on the Badita Canal everybody went fishing and caught some [at Passover, when fish are abundant], and Raba permitted them to salt them.*

C.   *Said to him Abbayye, "But lo, we have learned in the Mishnah:* **And all pickled foods which a man can eat during the intermediate days of a festival he also may pickle!"**

D.   *He said to him, "Since to begin with they caught them with eating them in mind, and if they leave them, they will rot, it falls into the category of a deal that, if not carried out* right away, may go sour, *so it is permitted."*

E.   *There are those who report the case in this way:*

F.   *Raba permitted them to go trapping. They went and brought in the fish and salted them.*

G.   *Said to him Abbayye, "But lo, we have learned in the Mishnah:* **And all pickled foods which a man can eat during the intermediate days of a festival he also may pickle!"**

H.   *He said to him, "These, too, may be eaten if they are pressed."*

I.   That is in line with the case of Samuel, when they pressed fish in salt sixty times, and he ate it.

IV.2   A.   *Raba visited the household of the exilarch. They made for him fish pressed sixty times, and he ate it.*

IV.3   A.   *Rab visited Bar Shappir, and they set before him a fish that was boiled a third, salted a third, and broiled a third. Said Rab, "Adda the fisherman told me that a fish is best just when it is going to turn putrid."*

B.   *And said Raba, "Said to me Adda the Fisherman, 'Broil the fish with its brother [salt], put it into its father [water], eat it with its son [sauce], and wash it down with its father [water].'"*

C.   *And said Raba, "Said to me Adda the Fisherman, 'After eating fish, fill our belly with cress and milk, don't lie down.'"*

D.   *And said Raba, "Said to me Adda the Fisherman, 'After eating fish, cress and milk, drink water not fermented date juice, or that but not wine.'"*

I.1, II.1 clarifies the sense of the Mishnah's statements, and III.1 then harmonizes the implications of this Mishnah's rule with those of another. IV.1 refines the application of the law, and Nos. 2, 3 then provide an appendix to the foregoing.

III. Rhetorical Paradigms

Our survey of a complete chapter of the Bavli allows us to define the Mishnah's primary discourse as Mishnah commentary. "Primary discourse," it is now clear, refers to the main lines of expression of a coherent document. When the Bavli's authorship, having cited a passage of the Mishnah, begins its statement, it always begins with attention to the cited passage. When further materials, not those of Mishnah commentary follow, these relate to the initial discussion. So while many compositions, and even some very large composites, take shape in their own terms and stand independent of the Mishnah, when they find a place in the Bavli, it is ordinarily in the framework of Mishnah commentary, very often as a secondary expansion of what is set forth to begin with for the exegesis of what is in the Mishnah. The tractate that we have examined leaves no doubt about the coherence, with a cited passage of the Mishnah, of nearly everything in the Bavli. Materials that do not cohere either with Mishnah exegesis, or with secondary amplification of that exegesis, prove sparse indeed. When we recall that sizable components of the Bavli – numerous compositions – stand on their own and not as Mishnah commentary, we realize how much the authorship of the Bavli has done in reframing matters to serve its distinctive purpose: nearly everything that they utilized, they presented in the framework of Mishnah commentary and amplification. Let us now review the types of Mishnah commentary that, over all, forms the Bavli's primary discourse.

1. Scriptural Foundations of the Laws of the Mishnah

The single most commonplace and characteristic inquiry of the Bavli is framed in the question: What is the source of the rule of the Mishnah? Conventionally, this inquiry occurs in simple language, for example, "What is the source of this rule," always with the implication, "in Scripture"? Here is one common way of asking and answering the question:

Bavli Berakhot Chapter One

1:1

A. From what time do they recite the Shema in the evening?

B. From the hour that the priests [who had immersed after uncleanness and awaited sunset to complete the process of purification] enter [a state of cleanness, the sun having set, so as] to eat their heave-offering –

I.1   A. On what basis does the Tannaite authority stand when he begins by teaching the rule, "From what time...," [in the assumption that the religious duty to recite the *Shema* has somewhere been established? In point of fact, it has not been established that people have to recite the *Shema* at all.]

B. Furthermore, on what account does he teach the rule concerning the evening at the beginning? Why not start with the morning?

C. The Tannaite authority stands upon the authority of Scripture, [both in requiring the recitation of the *Shema* and in beginning with the evening], for it is written, "When you lie down and when you rise up" (Deut. 6:7).

D. And this is the sense of the passage: When is the time for the recitation of the *Shema* when one lies down? It is **from the hour that the priests enter [a state of cleanness so as] to eat their heave-offering [M. 1:1B].**

E. And if you prefer, I may propose that the usage derives from the order of the description of creation, for it is said, "And there was evening, and there was morning, one day" (Gen. 1:5).

2. Authorities behind the Laws of the Mishnah

A primary exegetical question concerns whether or not a law stands for an individual's opinion or a consensus of sages. The inquiry takes a variety of forms. The simplest is, "Who is the authority behind the Mishnah's [anonymous] rule?" This allows us to find out whether we have a schismatic (individual) or normative (consensual) opinion; we may further ask whether the cited authority is consistent, testing the principle behind the rule at hand against the evidence of his rulings in other cases in which the same principle determines matters.

1:1-2

I.3

A. *Who is the Tannaite authority who takes the position that work on the intermediate days of a festival is permitted if it is to prevent loss, but if it is to add to gain it is not permitted, and, further, even to prevent loss, really heavy labor is forbidden?*

B. *Said R. Huna,* "It is R. Eliezer b. Jacob, for we have learned in the Mishnah: R. Eliezer b. Jacob says, 'They lead water from one tree to another, on condition that one not water the entire field. Seeds which have not been watered before the festival one should not water on the intermediate days of the festival' [M. 1:3]."

C. *Well, I might concede that there is a representation of R. Eliezer's position that he prohibits work to add to one's gain, but have you heard a tradition that he disallows work in a situation in which otherwise loss will result?*

D. *Rather, said R. Pappa,* "Who is the authority behind this rule? It is R. Judah, for it has been taught on Tannaite authority: 'From a spring that first flows on the intermediate days of a festival they irrigate even a rain-watered field,' the words of R. Meir. And sages say, 'They irrigate from it only a field that depends upon irrigation, which has gone dry.' R. Eleazar b. Azariah says, "Not this nor that, [but they do not irrigate a field from it (namely, a field the spring of which has gone dry) even in the case of an irrigated field]' [T. M.Q. 1:1A-C]. Even further, said R. Judah, 'A person should not clean out a water channel and with the dredging on the intermediate days of a festival water his garden or seed bed.'"

E. *Now what is the meaning of* "that has gone dry"? *If you say that it really has dried up, then what is going to be accomplished by watering it?*

F. *Said Abbayye,* "The point is that this former water source has gone dry and another has just emerged."

G. R. Eleazar b. Azariah says, "Not this nor that": *There is no difference between the case of an old spring that has gone dry or that has not gone dry, in any event a spring that has just flowed may not be utilized on the intermediate days of the festival.*

H. *And how do you know [that it is Judah in particular who takes the position that work on the intermediate days of a festival is permitted if it is to prevent loss, but if it is to add to gain it is not permitted, and, further, even to prevent loss, really heavy labor is forbidden]? Perhaps R. Judah takes the position that he does, that is, that it is permitted to use the water for an irrigated field but not for a field that depends on rain, only in the case of a spring that has just now begun to flow, [2B] since it may cause*

> *erosion, but a spring that has not just now begun to flow and will not cause erosion might be permitted for use even on a field that depends on rain?*

    I.   *If so, then in accord with which authority will you assign our Mishnah paragraph? For in fact, in R. Judah's view, there is no distinction between a spring that has just now flowed and one that has not just now flowed; in either case, an irrigated field may be watered, one that depends on rain may not. And the reason that the passage specifies the spring that has just now flowed is only to show the extent to which R. Meir was prepared to go, even a spring that has just now flowed may be used, and that is, even for a field that depends upon rain.*

The harmonization of conflict will take the form of the comparison of rules of diverse authorities on the same matter. In what follows, the Mishnah's rule is set side by side with a rule in the name of a given authority, and then the conflict is underlined and explained.

3:1-2

II.1   A.   **Who are they who may get a haircut on the intermediate days of a festival? (1) he who comes from overseas or from captivity...:**

        B.   *Our Mishnah paragraph's rule is not in accord with the position of R. Judah. For it has been taught on Tannaite authority:* **R. Judah says, "One who comes home from overseas may not get haircuts during the intermediate days of the festival, because he went abroad at such a season without the permission of sages [who would have told him to go after the festival, so as to avoid this situation]" [T. M.Q. 2:2G].**

        C.   Said Raba, "If he went out merely to sightsee, all parties concur that he is forbidden. If he went out to make a living, all parties concur that he is permitted. They differ only if he made the trip just to make money. *One authority invokes the analogy of going sightseeing, the other, of going to make a living.*"

        D.   An objection was raised: **Said Rabbi, "The opinion of R. Judah makes more sense to me in a case in which one has not gotten permission from sages to go abroad, and that of sages makes more sense in a case in which he has gotten permission from sages to go abroad" [T. M.Q. 2:2I].** *Now what does* **in which one has not gotten permission from sages** *mean? If I should say that it means to go sightseeing, have you not said,* **all parties concur that he is forbidden?** *And could it then mean to make a living? But have you not said,* **all parties concur that he is permitted?** *So it is obvious that it means just to make money.*

        E.   *But then I invoke the concluding clause:* **And that of sages makes more sense in a case in which he has gotten permission from sages to go abroad!** *Now what could "with permission" mean here? If I should say that it means to make a living, have you not said,* **all parties concur that he is permitted?** *And might it be just to make money? But have you not said,* **The opinion of R. Judah makes more sense to me in a case in which one has not gotten permission from sages to go abroad?**

F.   *This is the sense of the statement at hand:* The opinion of R. Judah makes more sense than that of rabbis when he went forth without permission, *and what circumstance might that involve? It is for sightseeing. For sages only differed from R. Judah when it comes to making money. But as to merely sightseeing, they concur with R. Judah.* And the opinion of rabbis seems to make more sense than R. Judah's when he went forth with permission, *and what might that involve? It would be for making a living, for even R. Judah differed with rabbis only when it was to make money. But as to going abroad to make a living, he concurs with them.*

3.   Meanings of Words and Phrases

We come to Mishnah commentary of the most conventional kind: explanation of the meanings of words and phrases of the Mishnah, appealing for scriptural parallels to set forth lexical evidence, on the one side, inquiry into the sense and meaning of sentences of the Mishnah, on the other.

1:1-2
II.2

A.   *And on what basis is it inferred that the meaning of the words "irrigated field" is, a thirsty field [which has to be irrigated]?*

B.   *It is in line with that which is written:* "When you were faint and weary" (Deut. 25:18), *and the Hebrew word for weary is represented in Aramaic by the word that means, "exhausted."*

C.   *And how do we know that the words translated rain-watered field refers to a fucked field?*

D.   "For as a man has sexual relations with a maiden, so shall your sons be as husbands unto you" (Isa. 62:5), *and the word in Aramaic is rendered, "Behold, as a boy fucks a girl, so your sons shall get laid in your midst."*

Another form of explanation of the Mishnah, and the simplest, will be to answer a question left open by the Mishnah and urgent for the explanation of the Mishnah's rule: commentary in its simplest form.

1:4
III.1

A.   **They block up a breach in the intermediate days of a festival. And in the Seventh Year, one builds it in the normal way:**

B.   How is the breach blocked up?

C.   *Said R. Joseph, "With [Lazarus:] a hurdle made of twigs and daphne stakes."*

D.   *In a Tannaite statement it was set forth:* One piles up pebbles but does not hold them down with mortar.

A third form of Mishnah explanation will carry us into the criticism of the language of the Mishnah. In what follows, we ask why the Mishnah paragraph under discussion changes the subject. At stake then is the issue of whether or not the framer of a passage forgets by the end where he started – that is, the issue of the perfection of the verbatim formulation of the document:

4. Text Criticism: The Issue of Repetition

The matter of text criticism covers a variety of distinct inquiries. In the first sort, we want to know why the Mishnah frames matters as it does, with the generative issue being whether or not the document repeats itself. The type of Mishnah commentary is signaled by a single word, "it is necessary," and what will follow is an implicit justification of presenting more than a single rule or case. This form is not limited to Mishnah criticism; on the contrary, it is commonly used for any formulation – Tannaite or other – of a variety of cases that illustrate the same principle, and the form, brief though it is, suitably sets forth the exegetical problem to be solved.

1.1-2

I.1   A.   **[They water an irrigated field on the intermediate days of a festival and in the Seventh Year, whether from a spring that first flows at that time, or from a spring that does not first flow at that time:]** *since it is explicitly stated that they may water from a spring that flows for the first time, which may damage the soil by erosion [making necessary immediate repair of the damage during the intermediate days of the festival], is it necessary to specify that they may water from a spring that does not first flow at that time, which is not going to cause erosion?*

              B.   *One may say that it is necessary to include both the latter and the former, for if the Tannaite framer had given the rule only covering a spring that first flows on the intermediate days of the festival, it is in that case in particular in which it is permitted to work on an irrigated field, but not for a rain-watered field, because the water is going to cause erosion, but in the case of a spring that does not first flow on the intermediate days, which is unlikely to cause erosion, I might have said that even a rain-watered field may be watered. So he tells us that there is no distinction between a spring that flows for the first time and one that does not flow for the first time. The rule is the same for both: an irrigated plot may be watered from it, but a rain-watered plot may not be watered from [either a new or an available spring].*

The key word is simply "necessary," whether introducing a question or a declarative statement. Then the rest follows.

Another kind of text criticism involves the explanation of how a variety of examples hold together; the Mishnah may present three or more examples, and what we want to know is whether a stringency or leniency is conveyed by setting forth examples that do not really cohere. Here is an example of this other sort of analysis of the formulation of the Mishnah:

III.1   A.   **But they do not water [an irrigated field] with (1) collected rain water, or (2) water from a swape well:**

B.   *There is no trouble in understanding why water from a swape well should not be used, since watering in that way involves heavy labor. But what objection can there be to using collected rain water, since what heavy labor can possibly be involved in irrigating with rain water?*

C.   *Said R. Ilaa said R. Yohanan, "It is a precautionary decree, on account of the possibility of the farmer's going on to make use of water from a swape well."*

D.   R. Ashi said, "Rain water itself can be as hard to draw as the water of a swape well."

E.   *At issue between them is what R. Zira said. For said R. Zira said Rabbah bar Jeremiah said Samuel, "From irrigation streams that draw water from ponds it is permitted to irrigate on the intermediate days of the festival." One authority [Ashi] concurs with the position of R. Zira, and the other authority does not concur with the position of R. Zira.*

5. Conflict of Principles Implicit in the Mishnah's Rules

One important issue in the Bavli's Mishnah commentary is whether or not two rules, intersecting in detail or in fundamental principle, cohere. A sustained effort characterizes the Bavli's inquiry into the harmony of the law of the Mishnah, the object of which invariably is to demonstrate that the Mishnah's laws form a single, wholly cogent law, perfect in their harmony. Here is an example of how that interest is expressed:

IX.1   A.   **And go forth [to give warning] against Diverse Kinds:**

B.   *But in fact in the intermediate days of a festival do we go about to inspect whether or not there are mixed seeds in a field? But there is the following contradiction:* **On the first day of Adar they make public announcement concerning [payment of] sheqel dues and concerning the sowing of mixed seeds [Lev. 19:19, Deut. 22:9]. On the fifteenth day of that month they read the Megillah [Scroll of Esther] in walled cities. And they repair the paths, roads, and immersion pools. And they carry out all public needs. And they mark off the graves. And they go forth [to inspect the fields] on account of mixed seeds [M. Sheq. 1:1]***!*

C.   R. Eleazar and R. Yosé bar Hanina –

D.   One said, "The latter refers to the crops that ripen earlier [in mid-Adar], the other, of late ripening crops [and our Mishnah paragraph has a further inspection, now in mid-Nisan, during the intermediate days of the festival of Passover]."

E.   And the other said, "In the one case [in Adar] they go out to inspect the condition of grain fields, in the other, vegetable patches."

F.   Said R. Assi said R. Yohanan, "The rule pertains only in a case in which the sprouts are not yet recognizable [earlier on]; but where it is possible to discern the character of the sprouts early on, they went forth to inspect the situation earlier."

There are various solutions to the problem of conflict between rules, of which the foregoing is one common sort: distinguishing the point of reference of two or more rules, showing that each bears its own distinctive considerations.

We see in what follows that the intersecting rule need not occur in another Mishnah paragraph. The item before us is in the same Hebrew as the Mishnah's rule, but does not bear an explicit indicator of Tannaite origin or formulation; the language forms the taxic indicator.

1:5C-G

I.1   A.   **"Because it is a time of rejoicing for him":**

        B.   *An objection was raised on the basis of the following:*

        C.   He who collects the bones of his mother and father for secondary burial – lo, one observes mourning for them all that day. But in the evening he no longer observes mourning for them. And in that connection said R. Hisda, "Even if he had them tied up in a sheet."

        D.   *Said Abbayye, "Say the rule as follows: 'because the rejoicing of the festival affects him.'"*

6.   Execution of the Law of the Mishnah

Here is an example of how the Bavli will ask about the way in which the law is realized, here meaning, the conditions under which the Mishnah's statement applies:

1:3

I.1   A.   **[On condition that one not water the entire field:]** Said R. Judah, "If the field's soil is clay, he may water it."

        B.   *So, too, it has been taught on Tannaite authority:*

        C.   When they made the rule that it is forbidden to irrigate on the intermediate days of a festival, they made that statement only concerning seed that had not drunk before the festival; but as to seed that had been watered before the festival, they may be watered during the intermediate days of the festival; and if the soil of the field was clay, it is permitted to water it. And a bare field [without a crop at that time] is not watered during the festival week. But sages permit doing so in both cases [where seeds were not watered, watering a bare field].

        D.   *Said Rabina, "That statement leads to the inference that it is permitted to hand-sprinkle a vegetable patch during the intermediate days of a festival. For in the case of a bare field, why is it permitted to do so? It is because that renders the soil fit to be sown or planted, and here, too, that is permitted."*

At stake is where and how the simple rule of the Mishnah pertains; a Tannaite formulation of the same conclusion then reenforces the proposed reading of the Mishnah's rule.

7. The Operative Consideration behind the Law of the Mishnah

One of the exegetically productive initiatives of the Bavli will raise the question of the operative consideration that has led to a given rule in the Mishnah. That inquiry will lead us deep into the principles that are given expression in concrete rules, and we often see how entirely abstract conceptions are conceived to stand behind rather commonplace laws.

V.1   A.   **R. Eleazar b. Azariah says, "They do not make a new water channel on the intermediate days of a festival or in the Seventh Year." And sages say, "They make a new water channel in the Seventh Year, and they repair damaged ones on the intermediate days of a festival":**

        B.   *There is no problem with respect to the prohibition concerning the intermediate days of a festival, since the operative consideration is that this is heavy labor, but why ever not make a channel in the Seventh Year?*

        C.   R. Zira and R. Abba b. Mamel differ on the matter –

        D.   One said, "The reason is that the one who digs appears to be hoeing."

        E.   And the other said, "The reason is that he looks as though he is preparing the banks for sowing."

        F.   *So what's at stake?*

        G.   *At issue is when water comes along immediately. From the perspective of him who has said, "The reason is that he looks as though he is preparing the banks for sowing," it is still objectionable. But from the perspective of him who has said, "The reason is that the one who digs appears to be hoeing," there is no objection.*

        H.   *But should not the one who objects for the reason that it looks as though he is spading also object that he looks as though he is preparing the bank for seed?*

        I.   *Rather, this is what's at stake between the two explanations: it would involve a case in which he takes what is in the trench and tosses it out. From the perspective of him who says, "The reason is that he looks as though he is preparing the banks for sowing," there is no objection; but from the perspective of him who says, "The reason is that the one who digs appears to be hoeing," it is still subject to an objection.*

        J.   *But from the perspective of him who says that he appears to be preparing the sides for seed, would he not also admit that he seems to be hoeing?*

        K.   *Not really, for one who hoes, as soon as he takes up a spadeful, he puts it down again in place.*

What we want to know here is the reason behind the rule, a very familiar inquiry of the Bavli's Mishnah exegetes.

8. The Implications, for the Law in General, of the Mishnah's Particular Formulation

In the following, what generates the sustained discussion of the Talmud is a close reading of the Mishnah's language. This careful analysis produces an inference that has to be investigated in its own terms. Since there is no understanding the sustained discussion apart from the Mishnah's own statement, the entire composition falls into the classification of Mishnah commentary.

VII.1   A. [5A] **They repair damaged waterways in the public domain and dig them out:**

B. *Repairing is all right, but not digging afresh.*

C. Said R. Jacob said R. Yohanan, "They have taught this rule only when the public has no need of the waterways, but if the public needs them, then it is permitted even to dig afresh."

D. *But if the public needs them, is it permitted to do that work? And has it not been taught on Tannaite authority:* Cisterns, pits, and caverns that belong to private property may be cleaned out, and, it goes without saying, those that belong to the public; but cisterns, pits, and caverns belonging to the public may not be dug, and all the more so those of a private person? *Does this not address a case in which the public has need of these facilities?*

E. *No, it addresses a case in which the public has no need of those facilities.*

F. *Along these same lines with respect to a private party, where the private person has no need of the facility, is repairing allowed? And has it not been taught on Tannaite authority:* As to cisterns, pits, and caverns of a private person, they collect water in them but they may not be cleaned out, nor may their cracks be plastered; but as to those belonging to the public, they may be cleaned out and their cracks may be plastered?

G. *Now what is the point here? It is when a private person has need of the facility. And in that case, in regard to what is required for public use, where the public has need of it the same rule pertains? And where the public has need of the facility, is it forbidden to dig? Has it not been taught on Tannaite authority:* As to cisterns, pits, and caverns belonging to a private person, they collect water in them and clean them out, but they may not plaster their cracks nor put scourings into them to fill cracks; as to those serving the public, they may dig them to begin with and plaster them with cement?

H. *So the initial formulation poses a contradiction.*

I. *This is how to iron out the difficulty:* They may clean out wells, ditches, or caverns of a private person, when the private party requires the facility, and, it goes without saying, those that belong to the public *when the public requires use of the facility, in which case even digging them out is permitted.* But they may not dig out wells, ditches, or caverns belonging to the public when the public does not require use of the facility, and, it goes without saying, those belonging to a private party. *When the private party does not require using them, then even cleaning them out is forbidden.*

J. *Said R. Ashi, "A close reading of our Mishnah paragraph yields the same result:* **And they do all public needs.** *Now what is encompassed within the augmentative formulation, all? Is it not to encompass, also, digging?"*

K. *Not at all, it is to encompass what is covered in that which has been taught on Tannaite authority:* On the fifteenth day of Adar agents of the court go forth and dig cisterns, wells, and caves. And they repair immersion pools and water channels. Every immersion pool that contains forty seahs of water is suitable for receiving further drawn water if need be, and to every immersion pool that does not contain forty seahs of water they lead a water course and complete its volume to the measure of forty seahs of water that has not been drawn so that it is suitable to receive further drawn water if need be [T. Sheq. 1:1]. And how on the basis of Scripture do we know that if they did not go forth and carry out all these duties, that any blood that is shed there is credited by Scripture as though they had shed it? Scripture states, "And so blood be upon you" (Deut. 19:10).

L. *Lo, in point of fact the framer of the Mishnah has covered these matters explicitly:* **They repair roads, streets, and water pools. And they do all public needs!** *What is encompassed within the augmentative formulation, all? Is it not to encompass, also, digging?*

M. *Yes, that's the proof!*

Another mode of commentary, in the inquiry into the implications of the Mishnah's rule for law in general, involves presenting a theoretical possibility that is subject to confirmation, or refutation, by a statement of a Mishnah paragraph. That theorizing in response to a rule of the Mishnah then explores the implications of a rule of the Mishnah.

I.1   A. [Writs of betrothal for women:] Said Samuel, "It is permitted for a man to betroth a woman on the intermediate days of the festival, lest someone else get there first."

B. *May we say that the following supports his thesis:* **And these do they write on the intermediate days of a festival: writs of betrothal for women?** *Does this not mean that one quite literally may draw up a writ of betrothal?*

C. *Not at all, it refers, rather, to drawing up preliminary terms, in line with what R. Giddal said Rab said [in defining such an agreement].*

D. For said R. Giddal said Rab, "'How much are you going to give to your son?' 'Thus and so.' 'How much are you going to give to your daughter?' 'Thus and so.' If they then arose and declared the formula of sanctification, they have effected the right of ownership. These statements represent matters in which the right of ownership is transferred verbally."

E. *May one propose, then, that the following supports [Samuel's] thesis:* **They do not take wives on the intermediate days of a festival, whether virgins or widows. Nor do they enter into levirate marriage, for it is an occasion of rejoicing for the groom.** *Lo, it is permitted then to betroth a woman!*

F. *No, the matter is formulated in terms of "it goes without saying," in this manner: Not only may one not betroth a woman, in which case one is not in any event carrying out a religious duty, but even marrying a woman, in which case one is carrying out a religious duty, is forbidden on that occasion. Come and take note of what has been repeated as a Tannaite formulation in the household of Samuel:* **They may betroth, but they may not bring the bride home, and they may not make a feast of betrothal, Nor do they enter into levirate marriage, for it is an occasion of rejoicing for the groom.**

G. *Well, that proves it.*

9. Settling the Point Subject to Dispute in the Mishnah

While not a principal focus of exegetical interest, some attention is given to settling the dispute presented in the Mishnah by a statement of the decided law. Here is an example of that form of Mishnah exegesis:

3:5-6

III.1   A.   **R. Eliezer says, "After the Temple was destroyed, Pentecost is deemed equivalent to the Sabbath." Rabban Gamaliel says, "The New Year and the Day of Atonement are deemed equivalent to festivals." And sages say, "The rule is in accord with the opinion neither of this one nor of that one. But Pentecost is deemed equivalent to a festival, and the New Year and the Day of Atonement are deemed equivalent to the Sabbath":**

        B.   Said R. Giddal bar Menassia said Samuel, "The decided law accords with the position of Rabban Gamaliel."

        C.   *There are those who repeat this statement of R. Giddal bar Menassia in connection with the following:* "Any infant who died within thirty days of birth is carried out for burial in one's arms and is buried by one woman and two men, but not by one man and two women.

        D.   [24B] "Abba Saul says, 'Even by one man and two women.'

        E.   "They do not form a line of mourners on his account, and they do not say on his account the blessing of mourners or the consolation addressed to mourners.

        F.   "As to an infant who died after thirty days of life, he is carried out in a box .

        G.   "R. Judah says, 'Not a box that is carried on the shoulder, but one that is taken in the arms.'

        H.   "They do form a line of mourners on his account, and they do say on his account the blessing of mourners and the consolation addressed to mourners.

        I.   "As to an infant who died after twelve months of life, he is taken out for burial on a bier.

        J.   "R. Aqiba says, 'If he is a year old, but her limbs were like those of a two-year-old, then it is classified as a two-year-old; if it was two years old but the limbs were those of a year old, he is taken out on a bier.'

        K.   "R. Simeon b. Eleazar says, 'In the case of anyone who is carried out on a bier, the community shows public signs of distress, and on account of any that is not carried out on a bier, the community does not show public signs of distress.'

        L.   "R. Eleazar b. Azariah says, 'If he is publicly known, then the public engages in his rites, but if he is not known to the public, the public does not engage with his rites.'

        M.   "And what about a lamentation?

        N.   "R. Meir in the name of R. Ishmael says, 'In the case of the poor, they make a lamentation for a child of three, in the case of the rich, for one of five.'

O. "R. Judah in his name says, 'For a child of the poor [which is all poor people have as pleasure in their lives (Rashi)], they make a lament for a five-year-old, for a child of the rich, six.'

P. "And as for the children of the sages, they are classified as are the children of the poor.

Q. "Said R. Giddal bar Menassia said Rab, 'The decided law accords with the position of R. Judah in the name of R. Ishmael.'"

IV. The Purpose of Commentary

Since a survey of any other tractate will yield the same repertoire, and so far as I know, no tractate will vastly expand the number of issues treated in providing the Mishnah with a sustained talmud, we legitimately ask whether a theological program animates the formation of the Bavli as a Mishnah commentary. A brief statement of the upshot of each of our repeated initiatives in Mishnah exegesis provides the outline of an answer, though a complete answer obviously will emerge only from a survey of not a single tractate but all thirty-seven tractates. What follows, therefore, must be regarded as only a preliminary hypothesis of the theological implications of the Bavli's exegetical program. The sole unproved premise in what follows is that people do not ask questions unless they know in advance they will produce not merely answers, but answers that conform to a larger systemic program.

What purpose is served by the Mishnah commentary set forth in the Talmud of Babylonia? A brief review of our taxonomy shows a highly theological program.

1. Scriptural Foundations of the Laws of the Mishnah

The premise of this question is that every statement of the Mishnah (to which the question is addressed) can indeed be shown to rest on scriptural foundations. Hence, it must follow, the Mishnah overall states what Scripture has already said, spelling out in its details principles or conceptions that the Written Torah has laid forth.

2. Authorities behind the Laws of the Mishnah

The intent of the question, "This passage is/is not in accord with Rabbi X," ordinarily is to demonstrate that the consensus of the sages, not a private individual, stands behind an anonymous statement of the Mishnah. Where an individual is identified, a further issue will be whether his rule here is consistent in its underlying principle with a rule elsewhere that rests on exactly the same principle or its opposite. The intent is to show that sages are consistent in their rulings.

3. Meanings of Words and Phrases

Scripture or common speech ordinarily provides the meaning of otherwise unfamiliar words and phrases.

4. Text Criticism

The purpose of text criticism is to identify flaws in the formulation of the Mishnah and generally to show that the wording of the document is flawless. This will cover proofs that the framers of the document do not repeat themselves and demonstrations that, where the Mishnah seems to say something obvious, it is indeed necessary to make that point, since, if not made explicit, the purpose of the Mishnah's statement will otherwise be lost.

5. Conflict of Principles Implicit in the Mishnah's Rules

The Mishnah's rules give expression, in concrete and exemplary form, to underlying principles. A few weighty principles underlie, and come to realization, in numerous rules. Can we show that the various cases' implicit principles are uniform and harmonious? Always.

6. Execution of the Law of the Mishnah

I see no theological issue inherent in this approach to the explanation of the Mishnah.

7. The Operative Consideration behind the Law of the Mishnah

The Mishnah's rules, when understood in the setting of the considerations at stake in making them up, prove weighty and consequential; the stakes are always high; the operative considerations are always entirely rational and accessible, also, to our reason.

8. The Implications, for the Law in General, of the Mishnah's Particular Formulation

When we understand what is at issue in the Mishnah's exemplary case, we are able to settle a great many more, and larger, questions than those at hand in that case in particular. So the Mishnah addresses weightier questions than its concrete cases apparently suggest, and when we have mastered its law, we may use what we know in a broad exploration of rules not at all set forth in the Mishnah in particular.

9. Settling the Point Subject to Dispute in the Mishnah

Where the Mishnah contains disputes, the sages of the Torah can settle those disputes; the purpose of disputes is not process but proposition, and a decision can always be made upon the conflicted proposition of the Mishnah.

If, therefore, we had to state in a single sentence the exegetical proposition, indeed the hermeneutical principle, that animates the Bavli's reading of the Mishnah, it may be stated very simply: the Mishnah is a supernatural writing, because it can be shown to be flawless in its language and formulation, never repetitious, never slovenly in any detail, always and everywhere the model of perfection in word and thought; the Mishnah is moreover utterly rational in its principles; and of course, the Mishnah is wholly formed upon the solid foundations of the Written Torah of Sinai. No merely human being can have achieved such perfection of language and of thought in conformity with the Torah. That is the point made, over and over again, in the Bavli's primary discourse. In detail, the Bavli proves that, in general, the Mishnah is Torah.

2

Sources and Traditions

The Bavli is made up of sources and traditions, the former, received in an indeterminate process of writing over time, the latter, formulated by the framers of the document itself. "The sources" of the Bavli are those completed, available, and free-standing pieces of writing that the authors of the Bavli used when they wrote their book. "The traditions" of the Bavli are those composites and sustained discussions that the authors of the Bavli set forth in their writing. What I want to know is a simple matter. Upon what kinds of material did the framers of the Bavli draw when, having done their own kind of writing, which was Mishnah commentary, analysis, expansion, and amplification, they filled out their document? For as a matter of simple fact, they augmented their main writing, Mishnah commentary, with a different kind of writing altogether. That other kind of writing is so distinct from the sort that served for their principal purpose that it demands attention in its own terms. When we know what kinds of writing, other than those that formed the stuff of the document and quite different therefrom, were utilized in the framing of the Bavli, we shall know something about the sources, prepared, to be sure, under auspices we cannot identify, for purposes we do not know, and at a time we cannot determine, that ultimately flowed into the foundation document of Judaism.

At stake in the analysis presented here is the answer to a fundamental question about that writing and the Judaic system, the Judaism of the Dual Torah, that that writing set forth. It is this: Is the Talmud of Babylonia a traditional or a systemic writing? By that I mean, does the Bavli merely collect and arrange what it has received, that is, is it merely a medium of tradition? Or do the framers of the Bavli impose their own imprint upon whatever they have received, using whatever they have chosen for the purpose of making what is essentially their own system's statement? To answer the question up front: the Bavli is a highly systemic piece of writing, setting forth its statement of what it conceives to be the tradition. At the same time, the framers of the Bavli did make use of some received sources, in addition to Scripture, the Mishnah, and materials now located in the Tosefta; these it sets forth in evidence, without much indication that its framers have vastly revised these received sources. In this chapter, we shall identify the character of those other sources utilized by the framers of the Bavli. Knowing what they were, meaning, how they are to be classified, will guide us in our ultimate description, analysis, and interpretation of the document that they ultimately helped to constitute.

It is the simple fact that the authorship of the Bavli drew upon a sizable corpus of sources, that is, materials of indeterminate character and substance. Hence the authorship of the Bavli made use of sources, both completed documents, and also sayings and stories, ordinarily of modest proportions. We know about the latter because these received and completed compositions, sayings or sets of sayings and stories alike, were not subjected to ultimate redaction. That fact is shown by a very simple criterion: Does this composition in all its details serve the purpose of the framers who have adduced it in evidence for their purposes? The answer is invariably, rarely in many details, never in all. In fact the received sources are given pretty much in a form quite independent of the purpose for which, in the Bavli, they are adduced in evidence. True, the authorship of the Bavli did whatever it wished with these materials to carry out its own program and to make its own prevailing statement. But although relevant to the purposes of the framers of the Bavli, these received materials were undeniably formulated and transmitted in a process of tradition. They have been so reworked and revised by the penultimate and ultimate authorship that their original character is no longer accessible. Hence we can identify many other such writings that were not only not reformulated but indeed not reshaped in such a way as to win for themselves a clear and cogent position in the passage in which they now appear. These latter kinds of compositions in no way define for the Bavli the syntax of argument and the processes of syllogistic discourse; all they do is supply facts for someone else's case. That is why in the instances of the compositions irrelevant to the thrust and flow of the Bavli's argument, we can still discern traces of received statements or sources.

That fact has now to be set into contrast with the view of many, that the Bavli supposedly draws upon and reshapes available ideas and reworks them into a definitive statement, hence turns sources into a tradition. The kind of material analyzed here contradicts that view, since what we shall see is writing that has not been reworked at all. To test the contrary view I have devised a simple experiment. If the authorship at hand resorts to prior writings and presents us with what is at its foundations a systematic and comprehensive summary and restatement of them, then the Bavli will take up an honorable position at the end of a long process of tradition. But if we find that the authorship of the Bavli follows an essentially independent and fresh program of its own, then the Bavli will prove to have inaugurated a tradition but not to have received and transmitted one. It will follow that, for the Judaism of the Dual Torah, holy Scripture, authoritative sources whether preserved orally or in writing, as such play no categorical role whatsoever. The Bavli will then constitute an independent and fresh statement of its own authorship, not a restatement of what its authorship has received from prior generations, and assuredly not a statement of a cumulative and incremental tradition. The Bavli, rather, will come forth as a statement that in time to come, beyond its redaction, would *become* traditional, but for reasons not related to its own literary let alone theological and legal traits. That set of choices explains the interest and importance of determining the relationship between the Bavli and the extant sources of the Judaism of the Dual Torah that reached closure prior to the Bavli. In fact, the Bavli is mostly the work of its own authorship, acting independently on its singular program of Mishnah exegesis and amplification, alongside its distinctive program of Scripture exegesis and amplification, both programs demonstrably unique to that authorship alone so far as extant sources and documents indicate for our sample. In the Bavli we look in vain for large tractates or even sizable units of discourse that refer to, or depend upon, the plan and program of prior documents. But – and this is what is important for the present monograph – we find something quite to the contrary: sizable units of discourse that do not refer to, or depend upon, the plan and program of the Bavli. These two types of materials – Mishnah commentary and amplification, free-standing compositions out of phase with Mishnah commentary and amplification (or Scripture commentary and amplification) make up the Bavli, in the portion of about 90 percent to 10 percent, depending on the tractate (rarely 80 percent to 20 percent, seldom 95 percent to 5 percent, among the tractates I examined in my *Bavli's One Voice*).

That finding that the Bavli is an essentially free-standing statement, occasionally using other free-standing materials, alas, will contradict familiar and much cherished convictions concerning the character of the Bavli as well as the writings prior to it, in particular, and of Judaism, in general – that is to say, the larger canonical corpus of which it forms a principal representative. That conviction leads us to expect the principal document of Judaism to say pretty much what had been said before, and, many would add, beginning at Sinai. That corpus is held to form a continuous statement, beginning in an earlier writing, standing behind, generating, and therefore continuing in a later one. Consequently, the corpus is called "traditional," in the sense that one document leads to the next, and all of the documents come to their climax and conclusion in the final one of late antiquity. To the documents of the Torah – oral and written – is imputed not only the status of tradition in the sense just now defined but also a relationship of continuity which we may call imputed canonicity, so that, we are told, we may freely cite a passage from one document alongside a counterpart from another, treating them as part of a single – hence, continuous statement, and, in theological terms, one might say, canonical one, though our issue is not to be confused with canonical research. And that claim for the Bavli and the literature prior to it of *traditionality* bears with it not merely theological, but literary implications about the nature of the documents and the correct way of reading them. Because of those implications as to literature we can test the claim at hand and ask whether it indeed so describes the documents as to find substantiation in literary facts.

Let me now specify the kinds of factual information that will permit me to frame a reply to the question before us. If I want to know criteria for authority and sufficiency, I have to ask about the relationship between a document and prior treatments of the topic of said document. For one critical criterion of continuity – of forming a tradition out of available sources – is the capacity to take in, hold together, and rework the entirety of a prior corpus of information, writing, on a given subject. The literary test of traditionality is whether or not the canonical statement has drawn together and reworked in a cogent way whatever lay to hand in prior writings. If the test proves affirmative, then we may propose as one substantial and necessary criterion for traditionality a particular relationship to the entirety of prior writing. If it proves negative, then the entire literary dimension of the problem of traditionality turns out to weigh the wind, measure what has no weight. A different approach to the criteria by which the entirety of the literature of Judaism forms a single canonical statement will require invention and exploration. So to the issue at hand.

That is why my particular concern is the Bavli's relationship to prior treatments of a given subject, with special interest in how the authorship of the Bavli has made use of what it had in hand, and how in its sorting out of available materials it has defined the task of making a full and authoritative statement. In assessing the stance of the Bavli, in making its final statement, vis-à-vis prior writings on a given topic, I can uncover the rules that guide an authorship in its work of summary and systematization: of systemic statement of the whole, all together and all at once, on a given subject. I can conceive of no better way of uncovering how people make a statement we now realize was canonical from the beginning, than situating those people in the setting of what had gone before – and had not attained the canonical status that the Bavli's authorship achieved for their document. So far as traditionality constitutes a literary question concerning rules of how one writes a canonical document, giving the signals to the community that one's writing constitutes a final, authoritative statement, through inductive inquiry into relationships I should be able to answer that question and describe those rules: why this not that. That interest requires me to collect answers to questions deriving from these comparative inquiries:

1. *The topical program* of prior writings on the subject as compared to the topical program of the Bavli on the same subject, with attention to questions such as these: Does the Bavli follow the response to the Mishnah characteristic of the authorship of the Tosefta? The Sifra (or Sifré to Numbers or Sifré to Deuteronomy, where relevant)? Does the Bavli follow the response to relevant passages of Scripture that have caught the attention of compilers of Midrash exegeses in Genesis Rabbah, Leviticus Rabbah, Pesiqta deRab Kahana, and other documents generally thought to have come to closure prior to the Bavli?

2. *The Bavli's use or neglect of the available treatments ("sources") in the prior literature:* If the Bavli does make use of available materials, does it impose its own issues upon those materials or does it reproduce those materials as they occur elsewhere? Has the authorship of the Bavli carried forward issues important in prior writings, or has it simply announced and effected its own program of inquiry into the topic at hand? This is the point at which the present monograph makes its contribution.

3. *The traits of the Bavli's statement, that is, derivative and summary at the end, or essentially fresh and imputed retrospectively?* In consequence of the detailed examination of the Bavli's authorship's use of and response to available sources, how may we characterize the statement of the Bavli as a whole in comparison to prior statements? And, since that statement is canonical by the definition of the entire history of Judaism, we ask about the upshot: the shape and character of a canonical statement on a given subject. Here again we see the Bavli as a document engaged by its own concerns, using what it has received without extensively incorporating all received materials into its own literary framework at all.

Let me now set forth some further facts on the relationship of the Bavli to prior documents:

1.   *The topical program* of prior writings on the subject as compared to the topical program of the Bavli on the same subject, with attention to questions such as these: Does the Bavli follow the response to the Mishnah characteristic of the authorship of the Tosefta? Not systematically, only episodically. As to the Sifra, Sifré to Numbers or Sifré to Deuteronomy, these documents have little in common with ours. Does the Bavli follow the response to relevant passages of Scripture that have caught the attention of compilers of Midrash exegeses in Genesis Rabbah, Leviticus Rabbah, Pesiqta deRab Kahana, and other documents generally thought to have come to closure prior to the Bavli? Quite to the contrary, apart from the Yerushalmi and other authorships within the Bavli itself, our authorship turns out to define unique and uncommon points of interest in verses treated both in the Bavli and in some other document.

2.   *The Bavli's use or neglect of the available treatments ("sources") in the prior literature*: If the Bavli does make use of available materials, does it impose its own issues upon those materials or does it reproduce those materials as they occur elsewhere? The answer to these questions for the present sample is negative. The Bavli does not make extensive use of available materials. Most of what we find in the Bavli, as a matter of fact, turns out to be unique to the Bavli. Where there are materials that occur both here and in other documents, they provide mere facts, not a point of generative discourse. Has the authorship of the Bavli carried forward issues important in prior writings, or has it simply announced and effected its own program of inquiry into the topic at hand? Our authorship has made its own statement in its own way.

3.   *The traits of the Bavli's canonical statement, that is, derivative and summary at the end, or essentially fresh and imputed retrospectively?* In consequence of the detailed examination of the Bavli's authorship's use of and response to available sources, for the sample at hand we may characterize the statement of the Bavli as a whole in comparison to prior statements as original, fresh, and self-defined. And, since that statement is canonical by the definition of the entire history of Judaism, we ask about the upshot: the shape and character of a canonical statement on a given subject. The answer, for the vast sample I have considered in my research, yields a negative finding: the canonical statement does not aim at drawing together available materials and restating a long-term and (assessed in terms of the

extant writings) broadly circulated consensus. Data that constitute evidence for documentary traditionality do not appear to the naked eye – or even to a vision educated to discern literary traits and concerns. Quite to the contrary, the plain truth is that our document does not cite or quote or attempt to summarize and recast available materials, reaching a later authorship out of an earlier and ongoing process of tradition. True, individual sayings may have circulated and may have undergone a process of continuous tradition. But the Bavli as we have it, the work of its penultimate and ultimate authorship, makes its own statement in its own way on its own agenda. It gives us not a tradition out of a remote past but a system of its own, composed, quite obviously, in substantial measure from received materials and in accord with received conventions, but, in all and in essence, a singular, autonomous, and, by its nature, unprecedented statement: a system. I find in the utilization of sources without the extensive revision of those sources for incorporation into the body of the document strong evidence that the Bavli's framers had a clear sense of what mattered to them, and the fact that they kept some writings in pretty much the form that these sources had come down is testimony to that fact. Its authorship does not take over, rework, and repeat what it has received out of prior writings but makes its own statement, on its own program, in its own terms, and for its own purposes – sometimes using, in the received form, what was found interesting out of an indeterminate, antecedent heritage. Now let us turn to the examination of the traits of that heritage of sources as preserved in four tractates of the Bavli.

I. Sources Not *of*, but Merely *in*, the Bavli

I speak here of sources not *of* the Bavli but *in* the Bavli, because I mean to identify and classify the use of materials by the authorship of the Bavli that do not exhibit the traits of writings composed or compiled for the use of that authorship in particular. That is to say, I propose to identify the types of already completed sources that the authorships of tractates of the Bavli utilized in composing the principal composites of which the Talmud of Babylonia is made up. For the present purpose, a simple sample must suffice. I therefore take four tractates and create a classification of the free-standing sources that were utilized in the framing of those tractates. I chose Makkot, Keritot, and Moed Qatan, somewhat shorter tractates in three of the four divisions of the Mishnah that are given talmud commentaries by the Talmud of Babylonia.

In a variety of completed monographs, I have shown that the framers of the traditional system that the Talmud of Babylonia sets forth made use of some received materials, or sources. These monographs are as follows: [1] *The Bavli and Its Sources: The Question of Tradition in the Case of Tractate Sukkah* (Atlanta, 1987: Scholars Press for Brown Judaic Studies); [2] *Making the Classics in Judaism: The Three Stages of Literary Formation* (Atlanta, 1990: Scholars Press for Brown Judaic Studies); [3] *The Rules of Composition of the Talmud of Babylonia. The Cogency of the Bavli's Composite* (Atlanta, 1991: Scholars Press for South Florida Studies in the History of Judaism); [4] *The Bavli's One Voice: Types and Forms of Analytical Discourse and their Fixed Order of Appearance* (Atlanta, 1991: Scholars Press for South Florida Studies in the History of Judaism); and, especially, my most recent study, [5] *The Bavli's Massive Miscellanies. The Problem of Agglutinative Discourse in the Talmud of Babylonia* (Atlanta, 1992: Scholars Press for South Florida Studies in the History of Judaism). In each of these works I have examined pieces of a very large puzzle, and in this chapter, I do the same.

The principal results that set the stage for this work are these: [1] the authorship of the Bavli took charge of the formulation of everything in the Bavli, thus *The Bavli and Its Sources*. But at the same time, a variety of ready-made materials were available. These I identified in two stages. First, in [2] *Making the Classics in Judaism: The Three Stages of Literary Formation*, I simply distinguished between a piece of writing that clearly serves the purpose of the document in which it appears and one that clearly does not. Then, in the next two works, I examined in great detail the writings that clearly are meant to serve the purposes of the authorship of the Talmud of Babylonia, by showing how these writers put together already available material into cogent composites, in [3] *The Rules of Composition of the Talmud of Babylonia*, and then by examining in detail the entire formal repertoire of the Bavli and demonstrating its principal types and their traits, in [4] *The Bavli's One Voice: Types and Forms of Analytical Discourse and Their Fixed Order of Appearance*. From the materials that clearly serve the program of the Bavli's framers, which I had been able to define and demonstrate, I then turned my attention to the writings that, while utilized in the Bavli, do not respond to the program of the framers of the Bavli and clearly were made up with some other documentary purpose in mind, or served no documentary program at all. The results are in [5] *The Bavli's Massive Miscellanies*. Now all of these works have examined the contents of the Bavli from the perspective of the end product itself. But because time and again I have identified materials that are, from that perspective, anomalous, I have now to examine in their own terms compositions in the Bavli that clearly stand on their own and not only or mainly in relationship to the Bavli's authorships' paramount program, which – as my results show beyond any meaningful doubt – was Mishnah commentary and exposition of the principles of the law contained in the Mishnah.

Now let me proceed to give an example of the kind of "sources" I mean to classify in these pages. In *The Bavli's Massive Miscellanies*, I pointed out that the Talmud of Babylonia is made up of large-scale composites of already completed compositions. These already completed compositions supply us with the free-standing sources we are going to examine. To be sure, the document draws upon the already completed writing, the Mishnah, being organized to present the appearance of a commentary to that writing. Second, it cites passages of another already completed piece of writing, the Tosefta. Third, very commonly we are able to identify a single cogent statement, with its own beginning, middle, and end, and furthermore we readily distinguish that statement from a larger framework in which, whole and complete, it is set to serve some larger purpose. None of this is under discussion here; these compositions and composites all serve the single purpose of Mishnah commentary. Most of the Bavli consists of composites of compositions, so that the framers of the whole have made use of (some) already completed pieces of writing, setting them out in such a way as to serve a purpose not contemplated by the author(s) of the original compositions but rather a purpose clearly dictated by the analytical and propositional program of the framers of the Bavli itself. But they also preserved materials that do not serve the Bavli's own analytical and propositional program. These materials were written for some purpose other than the one that, in the Bavli, they are made to serve.

We know them because they appear not as part of a Mishnah-focused composite, or a sustained composition serving a larger purpose, but as essentially free-standing. To understand what I mean, I have to set forth the distinction between composition and composite. Let me explain, to begin with, how the materials that follow are meant to clarify the point at hand: What is a composition and what is a composite? A composition is a fully articulated, cogent statement, which contains everything we need to understand what the author of the writing wishes to say to us. A composite is a collection of such completed pieces of writing, worked out in such a way as to make the point that the framer of the composite, not the authors of the compositions that he uses, wishes to make. As I have explained in *The Rules of Composition of the Talmud of Babylonia. The Cogency of the Bavli's Composite*,[1] the author of a composition sets forth a proposition of his own, while the framer of a composite may make use of a variety of such compositions to make the

---

[1] Atlanta, 1991: Scholars Press for South Florida Studies in the History of Judaism.

quite different point that he has in mind. With this simple distinction in mind, we have, also, carefully to distinguish between glosses, such as – in the example to follow – are found at 2.B, D-E, and free-standing compositions that are utilized for a purpose other than that for which, on the face of it, they were written. What illustrates the classification, composition, in the sample at hand? The statement of Hisda, F, has been set down in its own terms. It is adduced to prove the point of E. So F is a composition, E-F a composite put together to clarify D, itself a gloss of C. Another example of the same is at W, glossed by X. X on its own makes good sense without reference to W or even to the purpose, signaled at X (*But how can they present such an argument, since*), that links Yohanan's statement to the context in which it now occurs. The same is to be said at DD, the gloss of AA-CC, which cites an already completed composition, with its own beginning, middle, and end, of DD, Joseph's statement. Another composition placed into the composite before us is at GG. Still a third is NN-OO. Simeon's statement, OO, is a free-standing one; but the compositor has introduced it as a footnote for the foregoing, NN. Another excellent example of a composition formulated in its own terms and then introduced here for the purposes of the compositor of the whole is at BBB-GGG. HHH contains a fine composition, Judah's citation of Rab, joined by "is this really so" to the larger composite. A still finer instance of the composite is at No. 3, the whole of which is worked out in a framework entirely autonomous of the larger composite in which No. 3 is now positioned. The same may be said of No. 4.

Abodah Zarah

I.2   A.   R. Hanina bar Pappa, and some say, R. Simlai, gave the following exposition [of the verse,"They that fashion a graven image are all of them vanity, and their delectable things shall not profit, and their own witnesses see not nor know" (Isa. 44:9)]: "In the age to come the Holy One, blessed be He, will bring a scroll of the Torah and hold it in his bosom and say, 'Let him who has kept himself busy with it come and take his reward.' Then all the gentiles will crowd together: 'All of the nations are gathered together' (Isa. 43:9). The Holy One, blessed be He, will say to them, 'Do not crowd together before me in a mob. But let each nation enter together with [2B] its scribes, 'and let the peoples be gathered together' (Isa. 43:9), and the word 'people' means 'kingdom': 'and one kingdom shall be stronger than the other' (Gen. 25:23)."

      B.   *But can there be a mob scene before the Holy One, blessed be He? Rather, it is so that from their perspective they not form a mob, so that they will be able to hear what he says to them.*

      C.   [Resuming the narrative of A:] "The kingdom of Rome comes in first."

      D.   *How come? Because they are the most important. How do we know on the basis of Scripture they are the most important?*

Because it is written, "And he shall devour the whole earth and shall tread it down and break it into pieces" (Gen. 25:23), and said R. Yohanan, "This Rome is answerable, for its definition [of matters] has gone forth to the entire world." [Mishcon: "This refers to Rome, whose power is known to the whole world."]

E.   *And how do we know that the one who is most important comes in first? It is in accord with that which R. Hisda said.*

F.   For said R. Hisda, "When the king and the community [await judgment], the king enters in first for judgment: 'That he maintain the case of his servant [Solomon] and [then] the cause of his people Israel' (1 Kgs. 8:59)."...

W.   "They will say to him, 'Lord of the world, in point of fact, did you actually give it to us and we did not accept it?'"

X.   *But how can they present such an argument, since it is written, "The Lord came from Sinai and rose from Seir to them, he shined forth from Mount Paran" (Deut. 33:2), and further, "God comes from Teman" (Hab. 3:3). Now what in the world did he want in Seir, and what was he looking for in Paran? Said R. Yohanan, "This teaches that the Holy One, blessed be He, made the rounds of each and every nation and language and none accepted it, until he came to Israel, and they accepted it."*

Y.   *Rather, this is what they say, "Did we accept it but then not carry it out?"*

Z.   *But to this the rejoinder must be, "Why did you not accept it anyhow!"*

AA.   Rather, "this is what they say before him, 'Lord of the world, Did you hold a mountain over us like a cask and then we refused to accept it as you did to Israel, as it is written, "And they stood beneath the mountain" (Ex. 19:17).'"

BB.   And [in connection with the verse, "And they stood beneath the mountain" (Ex. 19:17),] said R. Dimi bar Hama, "This teaches that the Holy One, blessed be He, held the mountain over Israel like a cask and said to them, 'If you accept the Torah, well and good, and if not, then there is where your grave will be.'"

CC.   "Then the Holy One, blessed be He, will say to them, 'Let us make known what happened first: "Let them announce to us former things" (Isa. 43:9). As to the seven religious duties that you did accept, where have you actually carried them out?'"

DD.   *And how do we know on the basis of Scripture that they did not carry them out? R. Joseph formulated as a Tannaite statement, "'He stands and shakes the earth, he sees and makes the nations tremble' (Hab. 3:6): What did he see? He saw the seven religious duties that the children of Noah accepted upon themselves as obligations but never actually carried them out. Since they did not carry out those obligations, he went and remitted their obligation."*

EE.   *But then they benefited — so it pays to sin!*

FF.   Said Mar b. Rabina, [3A] "What this really proves is that even when they carry out those religious duties, they get no reward on that account."

GG.   *And they don't, don't they? But has it not been taught on Tannaite authority:* R. Meir would say, "How on the basis of Scripture do we know that, even if it is a gentile, if he goes and takes up the study of the Torah as his occupation, he is equivalent to the high priest? Scripture states, 'You shall therefore keep my statutes and my ordinances, which, if a human being does them, one shall gain life through them' (Lev. 18:5). What is written is not 'priests' or 'Levites' or 'Israelites,' but rather, 'a human being.' So you have learned the fact that, even if it is a gentile, if he goes and takes up the study of the Torah as his occupation, he is equivalent to the high priest."

HH.   Rather, what you learn from this [DD] is that they will not receive that reward that is coming to those who are commanded to do them and who carry them out, but rather, the reward that they receive will be like that coming to the one who is not commanded to do them and who carries them out anyhow.

II.   For said R. Hanina, "Greater is the one who is commanded and who carries out the religious obligations than the one who is not commanded but nonetheless carries out religious obligations."...

NN.   "They will say before him, 'Lord of the world, The heaven and earth have a selfish interest in the testimony that they give: 'If not for my covenant with day and with night, I should not have appointed the ordinances of heaven and earth' (Jer. 33:25).'"

OO.   *For said R. Simeon b. Laqish, "What is the meaning of the verse of Scripture,* 'And there was evening, and there was morning, the sixth day' (Gen. 1:31)? This teaches that the Holy One, blessed be He, made a stipulation with all of the works of creation, saying to them, 'If Israel accepts my Torah, well and good, but if not, I shall return you to chaos and void.' *That is in line with what is written:* 'You did cause sentence to be heard from heaven, the earth trembled and was still' (Ps. 76:9). If 'trembling' then where is the stillness, and if stillness, then where is the trembling? Rather, to begin with, trembling, but at the end, stillness."

PP.   [Reverting to MM-NN:] "The Holy One, blessed be He, will say to them, 'Some of them may well come and give testimony concerning Israel that they have observed the entirety of the Torah. Let Nimrod come and give testimony in behalf of Abraham that he never worshiped idols. Let Laban come and give testimony in behalf of Jacob, that he never was suspect of thievery. Let the wife of Potiphar come and give testimony in behalf of Joseph, that he was never suspect of sin. Let Nebuchadnezzar come and give testimony in behalf of Hananiah, Mishael, and Azariah, that they never bowed down to the idol. Let Darius come and give testimony in behalf of Daniel, that he did not neglect even the optional prayers. Let Bildad the Shuhite and Zophar the Naamatite and Eliphaz the Temanite and Elihu son of Barachel the Buzite come and testify in behalf of Israel that they have observed the entirety of the Torah: "Let the nations bring their own witnesses, that they may be justified" (Isa. 43:9).'

QQ.		"They will say before him, 'Lord of the world, give it to us to begin with, and let us carry it out.'

RR.		"The Holy One, blessed be He, will say to them, 'World-class idiots! He who took the trouble to prepare on the eve of the Sabbath [Friday] will eat on the Sabbath, but he who took no trouble on the even of the Sabbath – what in the world is he going to eat on the Sabbath! Still, [I'll give you another chance]. I have a rather simple religious duty, which is called "the tabernacle." Go and do that one.'"

SS.		*But can you say any such thing? Lo, R. Joshua b. Levi has said, "What is the meaning of the verse of Scripture, 'The ordinances that I command you this day to do them' (Deut. 7:11)? Today is the day to do them, but not tomorrow; they are not to be done tomorrow; today is the day to do them, but not the day on which to receive a reward for doing them."*

TT.		*Rather, it is that the Holy One, blessed be He, does not exercise tyranny over his creatures.*

UU.		*And why does he refer to it as a simple religious duty? Because it does not involve enormous expense [to carry out that religious duty].*

VV.		"Forthwith every one of them will take up the task and go and make a tabernacle on his roof. But then the Holy One, blessed be He, will come and make the sun blaze over them as at the summer solstice, and every one of them will knock down his tabernacle and go his way: 'Let us break their bands asunder and cast away their cords from us' (Ps. 23:3)."

WW.	But lo, you have just said, "It is that the Holy One, blessed be He, does not exercise tyranny over his creatures"!

XX.		*It is because the Israelites, too – sometimes [3B] the summer solstice goes on to the Festival of Tabernacles, and therefore they are bothered by the heat!*

YY.		But has not Raba stated, "One who is bothered [by the heat] is exempt from the obligation of dwelling in the tabernacle"?

ZZ.		*Granting that one may be exempt from the duty, is he going to go and tear the thing down?*

AAA.	[Continuing from VV:] "Then the Holy One, blessed be He, goes into session and laughs at them: 'He who sits in heaven laughs' (Ps. 2:4)."

BBB.	Said R. Isaac, "Laughter before the Holy One, blessed be He, takes place only on that day alone."

CCC.	*There are those who repeat as a Tannaite version this statement of R. Isaac in respect to that which has been taught on Tannaite authority:*

DDD. R. Yosé says, "In the coming age gentiles will come and convert."

EEE. *But will they be accepted? Has it not been taught on Tannaite authority:* Converts will not be accepted in the days of the Messiah, just as they did not accept proselytes either in the time of David or in the time of Solomon?

FFF. Rather, "They will make themselves converts, and they will put on phylacteries on their heads and arms and fringes on their garments and a mezuzah on their doors. But when they witness the war of Gog and Magog, he will say to them, 'How come you have come?' They will say, '"Against the Lord and against his Messiah."' For so it is said, 'Why are the nations in an uproar and why do the peoples mutter in vain' (Ps. 2:1). Then each one of them will rid himself of his religious duty and go his way: 'Let us break their bands asunder' (Ps. 2:3). Then the Holy One, blessed be He, goes into session and laughs at them: 'He who sits in heaven laughs' (Ps. 2:4)."

GGG. Said R. Isaac, "Laughter before the Holy One, blessed be He, takes place only on that day alone."

HHH. But is this really so? And has not R. Judah said Rab said, "The day is made up of twelve hours. In the first three the Holy One, blessed be He, goes into session and engages in study of the Torah; in the second he goes into session and judges the entire world. When he realizes that the world is liable to annihilation, he arises from the throne of justice and takes up a seat on the throne of mercy. In the third period he goes into session and nourishes the whole world from the horned buffalo to the brood of vermin. During the fourth quarter he laughs [and plays] with Leviathan: 'There is Leviathan, whom you have formed to play with' (Ps. 104:26)." [This proves that God does laugh more than on that one day alone.]

III. Said R. Nahman bar Isaac, "With his creatures he laughs [every day], but at his creatures he laughs only on that day alone."

I.3 A. Said R. Aha to R. Nahman bar Isaac, "From the day on which the house of the sanctuary, the Holy One, blessed be He, has had no laughter.

B. *"And how on the basis of Scripture do we know that he has had none? If we say that it is because it is written, 'And on that day did the Lord, the God of Hosts, call to weeping and lamentation' (Isa. 22:12), that verse refers to that day in particular. Shall we then say that that fact derives from the verse, 'If I forget you, Jerusalem, let my right hand forget her cunning, let my tongue cleave to the roof of my mouth if I do not remember you' (Ps. 137:5-6)? That refers to forgetfulness, not laughter. Rather, the fact derives from this verse: 'I have long held*

<table>
<tr><td></td><td></td><td>my peace, I have been still, I have kept in, now I will cry' (Isa. 42:14)."</td></tr>
<tr><td>I.4</td><td>A.</td><td>[Referring to the statement that during the fourth quarter he laughs [and plays] with Leviathan,] [*nowadays*] *what does he do in the fourth quarter of the day?*</td></tr>
<tr><td></td><td>B.</td><td>He sits and teaches Torah to kindergarten students: "Whom shall one teach knowledge, and whom shall one make understand the message? Those who are weaned from the milk?" (Isa. 28:19).</td></tr>
<tr><td></td><td>C.</td><td>*And to begin with [prior to the destruction of the Temple, which ended his spending his time playing with Leviathan], who taught them?*</td></tr>
<tr><td></td><td>D.</td><td>*If you wish, I shall say it was Metatron, and if you wish, I shall say that he did both [but now does only one].*</td></tr>
<tr><td></td><td>E.</td><td>And at night what does he do?</td></tr>
<tr><td></td><td>F.</td><td>*If you wish, I shall say that it is the sort of thing he does by day;*</td></tr>
<tr><td></td><td>G.</td><td>*and if you wish, I shall say,* he rides his light cherub and floats through eighteen thousand worlds: "The chariots of God are myriads, even thousands and thousands [shinan]" (Ps. 68:17). Read the letters translated as thousands, shinan, as though they were written, she-enan, meaning, that are not [thus: "the chariots are twice ten thousand less two thousand, eighteen thousand" (Mishcon)].</td></tr>
<tr><td></td><td>H.</td><td>*And if you wish, I shall say,* he sits and listens to the song of the Living Creatures [hayyot]: "By the day the Lord will command his lovingkindness and in the night his song shall be with me" (Ps. 42:9).</td></tr>
</table>

The Bavli at **I.1** begins with a systematic inquiry into the correct reading of the Mishnah's word choices. The dispute is fully articulated in balance, beginning to end. No. 2 then forms a footnote to No. 1. No. 3 then provides a footnote to the leitmotif of No. 2, the conception of God's not laughing. No. 4 returns us to the exposition of No. 2, at III. Nos. 5, 6 are tacked on – a Torah study anthology – because they continue the general theme of Torah study every day, which formed the main motif of No. 2 – the gentiles did not accept the Torah, study it, or carry it out. So that theme accounts for the accumulation of sayings on Torah study in general, a kind of appendix on the theme. Now that the definition of a composition and composite has been amply illustrated, let me proceed to the exposition of the exercise at hand.

A fine instance of a composition that is in, but not of, the Bavli passage where it occurs is No. 3, which is fully articulated, and, while adduced as topically relevant, unaffected by the setting in which it is situated. 3.A sets forth a proposition, B carries forward the same exposition, and the whole is worked out without the slightest acknowledgement of the literary situation in which the little composition is now located. In the foregoing sample, what are other entries that I conceive to be merely in, but not of, the Bavli, meaning, sources that are adduced for purposes quite distinct from those of the framers of the passage that now contains them? To proceed systematically, I point to 2.DD, which can be understood entirely on its own terms and without reference to the passage in which it occurs; 2.GG, which asks and answers its own question; 2.OO, of which the same is to be said; 2.SS. In the pages that follow, I shall identify other such free-standing compositions, entirely out of phase with the exegetical program of the chapters in which they occur. These we shall then classify, and I shall show that a simple and economical taxonomic program encompasses all of the data that our four sizable tractates will present to us.

II. Tractate Makkot

We now survey an entire tractate and identify its sources and traditions. In the case of the composites and compositions that address the Mishnah, I give only the opening line or two. The remainder, following my identification system, will be found in my *The Talmud of Babylonia. An American Translation* (Atlanta, 1984ff: Scholars Press for Brown Judaic Studies).

1:1A-G

A.   **How are witnesses treated [punished] as perjurers?**

I.1   A.   [Instead of the language, **How are witnesses punished as perjurers?**], *what is required is* how are witnesses not punished as perjurers?!

I.2   A.   *What is the source in Scripture for this ruling?*

I.3   A.   Bar Padda says, "It is an argument a fortiori [that we should substitute flogging for a literal sanction]: If the one who by marrying a woman he may not marry desecrates the woman and all her future children [producing an offspring who is disqualified from the priesthood in line with Lev. 21:6-8] is not himself desecrated [but remains a priest], he who proposes to desecrate a priest but has not done so surely should not himself be desecrated!"

II.1   A.   **"We testify concerning Mr. So-and-so, that he is liable to exile," they do not say, "Let this one go into exile in his stead." But he is flogged with forty stripes.**

       B.   *What is the source in Scripture for this ruling?*

II.2   A.   R. Yohanan says, "It is an argument a fortiori: If one who succeeded in committing the murder he intended to commit is not sent into exile [should he escape the death penalty], then surely the conspiracy of perjurers, which did not actually carry out their intention, also should not be sent into exile!"

II.3   A.   Said Ulla, "Whence in the Torah do we find an allusion to the disposition of perjured witnesses?"

II.4   A.   *Our rabbis have taught on Tannaite authority:*

       B.   Four statements have been made with regard to conspiratorial witnesses:

II.5   A.   "They are not punished in retaliation for conspiring to bear false witness in such a matter then punished by being declared the son of a divorcée or the son of a woman who has performed the rite of removing the shoe":

II.6   A.   "They are not sent into exile to the cities of refuge":

II.7   A.   "They are not required to pay ransom":

II.8   A.   *Who is the Tannaite authority behind the view that the payment of the ransom is a form of atonement?*

II.9   A.   "They are not sold as slaves [if they accused someone of having stolen and the accused is to be sold into slavery to pay compensation for the theft]":

II.10   A.   **In the name of R. Aqiba they have said, "They also are not made to pay statutory fines on the basis of their own admission of their guilt":**

       B.   *What is the operative consideration for R. Aqiba?*

II.11   A.   Said Rab, "A conspiring perjurer has to pay in accord with his share."

1:1H-K

       H.   **[If they had said,] "We testify concerning Mr. So-and-so, that he has divorced his wife and not paid off her marriage settlement" –**

I.1   A.   How is this assessment accomplished?

1:1L-N

       L.   **[If they had said,] "We testify concerning Mr. So-and-so, that he owes his fellow a thousand zuz, on condition that he will pay him in thirty days,"**

I.1   A.   Said R. Judah said Samuel, "He who makes a loan to his fellow for ten years – the end of the Sabbatical Year remits the debt, [3B] and that is the case even though one may claim that at the time that the Sabbatical Year came to an end, the commandment 'he shall not exact it of his neighbor' (Deut. 15:2) does not apply, for ultimately that commandment will take effect retroactively."

I.2   A.   And said R. Judah said Samuel, "He who says to his fellow, '...on the stipulation that the advent of the Seventh Year will not abrogate the debts' – the Seventh Year nonetheless abrogates those debts."

I.3   A.   *A Tannaite authority [stated]:*

       B.   **He who lends money to his fellow without further specification has not got the right to dun him for the debt for less than thirty days [T. B.M. 10:1A-B].**

I.4   A.   *Said Samuel to R. Mattenah, "Do not squat down before explaining the following tradition, specifically, the source in Scripture of the following teaching of our rabbis:* **'He who lends money to his fellow without further specification has not got the right to dun him for the debt for less than thirty days [T. B.M. 10:1A-B].** All the same is a loan made on the strength of a bond and one that is made by a merely oral declaration'!"

I.5   A.   And said R. Judah said Rab, "He who on the Sabbath day tears open the neck of a new piece of clothing [unaware that it is the Sabbath] is liable to present a sin-offering."

I.6   A.   And said R. Judah said Rab, "Three logs of water into which fell a qortob of wine, imparting to the whole the color of wine, and the mixture then fell into an immersion pool – the addition of the mixture does not invalidate the pool [as would have been the case if anything other than milk, wine, or fruit juice would have done; these do not disqualify the pool nor bring it up to the volume that is required, being treated as null]."

I.7   A.   *Said R. Joseph, "I never heard this tradition."*

I.8   A.   And said R. Judah said Rab, "A jug filled with water that fell into the Great Sea – one who immerses therein has not gained anything by his immersion, *for we take account of the possibility that the three logs of drawn water [which may not be used for immersion] are collected in one place. And that is the case in particular with the Great Sea, where the water stands still, but in a river in general, that is not the rule."*

1:2-1:3D

A.   [If they had said,] "We testify concerning Mr. So-and-so, that he owes his fellow two hundred zuz,"

I.1   A.   *[4B] There is no problem with the view of rabbis, which, after all, rests on the statement, "...according to his misdeed" (Deut. 25:2), meaning, on the count of a single misdeed do you impose liability upon the person, but you do not impose liability on two counts of misdeed in such a case. But what is the scriptural foundation for the position of R. Meir?*

I.2   A.   *There are those who report that which Ulla has stated in connection with the following, which has been taught on Tannaite authority:*

II.1   A.   [And sages say, "They are flogged only forty stripes":] *and how do rabbis read the verse,* "And you shall not bear false witness against your neighbor" *[for there has been a violation of that commandment as well]?*

1:3E-H

E.   They divide up [among the perjurers] a penalty for making restitution, but they do not divide up the penalty of flogging.

I.1   A.   *How on the basis of Scripture do we know this fact?*

1:4-5

A.   Witnesses are declared to be perjurers only if they [by their own testimony] incriminate themselves.

I.1   A.   *How on the basis of Scripture do we know this fact?*

I.2   A.   Said Raba, "If two witnesses came and said, 'On the east side of the castle Mr. So-and-so killed someone,' and two others came and said, 'Were you two not with us at the west side of the castle,' *we examine the case: If when they are standing at the west side of the castle, they can see the east side of the castle, these are not classified as a conspiracy of perjurers, but if not, lo, they are classified as a conspiracy of perjurers."*

I.3 A. And said Raba, "If two witnesses came and said, 'In Sura, in the morning, on Sunday, So-and-so killed somebody,' and two other witnesses came and said, 'At sunset, on Sunday, you were with us in Nehardea,' *then we examine the case: If it is possible to go from Sura to Nehardea, they are not held to be a conspiracy of perjurers, but if not, they are held to be a conspiracy of perjurers."*

I.4 A. And said Raba, "If two witnesses came and said, 'On Sunday So-and-so killed someone,' and two others came along and said, 'You were with us on Sunday, but on Monday So-and-so killed someone,' and not only so, but even if they say, 'On Friday So-and-so killed someone,' the original witnesses are put to death as a conspiracy of perjurers, *since at the point concerning which they gave testimony, which was Sunday, the accused was not subject to the death penalty at all."*

II.1 A. R. Judah says, "This is a conspiracy, [to confuse the judges], and the only ones to be put to death are those of the first group alone":

B. [5B] *If This is a conspiracy, then even the first set of witnesses also should not be subject to the law!*

II.2 A. *There was a certain woman who produced witnesses in her own behalf, and they were found to be discredited, and who produced more, who also were discredited, and who then produced more, who were not discredited.*

1:6

A. Perjured witnesses [in a capital case] are put to death only at the conclusion of the trial.

I.1 A. *A Tannaite statement in the name of Rabbi:*

B. If they have not killed, they are put to death, if they have killed, they are not put to death [Deut. 17:7 says that the witnesses have to strike the first blow, so, in line with the statement, **they are put to death only at the conclusion of the trial,** if they have not killed the accused, they are put to death, but if they have, they are not.]

1:7-8

A. "At the mouth of two witnesses or three witnesses shall he that is to die be put to death" (Deut. 17:6).

I.1 A. [Just as three witnesses prove two witnesses to be false, two witnesses may prove false even a hundred]:] said Raba, "That rule [on the power of two witnesses to prove a hundred to be perjurers] applies in particular to a case in which all of them testified without significant spells of interruption between one and the next [so that we treat the entire testimony as unified]."

I.2 A. *Said R. Aha of Difti to Rabina, "Since the definition of making a series of statements without significant spells of interruption between one and the next is defined as the interval that it takes a disciple to say, 'Peace to you, my lord and teacher,' it is clear that the evidence of a hundred witnesses is going to take much more time than that!"*

II.1   A.   **R. Aqiba says, "The mention of the third [witness] is only to impose upon him a strict rule and to treat the rule concerning him as the same as that applying to the other two.... Just as, in the case of two [witnesses], if one of them turns out to be a relative or otherwise invalid, the testimony of both of them is null, so in the case of three, [if] one of them turns out to be a relative or otherwise invalid, the testimony of all three of them is null":**

        B.   Said R. Pappa to Abbayye, "Then the murdered party's presence at the murder will itself save the murderer from the death penalty" [Lazarus: since he is an interested party in the case, and a witness of the crime is his own kin, in which case the death penalty could never be applied.]

III.1   A.   **Said R. Yosé, "Under what circumstances? In the case of trials for capital crimes. But in the case of trials in property litigations, the testimony may be confirmed with the remaining [valid witnesses]." Rabbi says, "All the same is the rule governing property cases and capital cases":**

        B.   *What do the judges say to the witnesses?*

IV.1   A.   [But if they had not joined in warning the transgressor, what should two brothers do who saw someone commit homicide?]

        B.   *It has been stated:*

        C.   Said R. Judah said Samuel, "The decided law accords with the position of R. Yosé."

        D.   And R. Nahman says, "The decided law is in accord with Rabbi."

1:9

        A.   **[6B] [If] two saw the incident from one window, and two saw it from another window,**

I.1   A.   Said R. Zutra b. Tobiah said Rab, "How on the basis of Scripture do we know that disjointed testimony is invalid? As it is said, 'At the mouth of one witness he shall not be put to death' (Deut. 17:6). *What is the meaning of the word 'one'? Should we say it actually means one, literally? But that fact we derive from the opening part of the clause:* 'at the mouth of two witnesses or three witnesses shall he that is worthy of death be put to death.' *So what is 'one witness'? It means, 'one and the same testimony.'*"

I.2   A.   *Said R. Pappa to Abbayye, "But if you have maintained that in cases in which* two persons see the criminal, one from one window, one from another, but they cannot see one another; these are not joined together to form a valid testimony, *then what need is there to go on with the case described in the language,* And not only so, but even if the two see the act sequentially from the same window, their testimony is not joined together? *In the former instance, after all, each of the two witnesses saw the entirety of the action. If their testimony is not joined together, then in a case in which the witnesses saw the action only in sequence so one saw only half the act and the other likewise, why specify the rule?* [Testimony is not admissible.]

I.3   A.   Said Raba, "If both witnesses were within sight of the one who gives the admonition, or if the one who gives the admonition saw them both, their testimony does join together."

I.4   A.   And said Raba, "In regard to the admonition of which they spoke, even if it was stated by the victim of the crime himself, or even if it derived from a demon, that suffices."

I.5   A.   Said R. Nahman, "Disjointed testimony in monetary cases is valid, for it is written, 'By the mouth of one witness he shall not be put to death' (Deut. 17:6), meaning, it is in particular in capital cases that such testimony is not valid, but in property cases it is valid."

II.1   A.   **R. Yosé says, "Under no circumstances is one put to death unless both witnesses against him have given warning to him, as it is said, 'At the testimony of two witnesses' (Deut. 17:6)":**

       B.   *Said R. Pappa, "But does R. Yosé really take this position? And have we not learned in the Mishnah: R. Yosé [b. R. Judah] says, 'One who bears enmity [for his victim] is put to death, for he is in the status of one who is an attested danger' [M. Mak. 2:3J]!"*

III.1 A.   **Another matter: At the mouth of two witnesses [directly] – that a sanhedrin should not listen to the testimony through the intervention of a translator:**

       B.   *Some people who spoke a foreign language came before Raba, who appointed an interpreter for them.*

III.2 A.   *[7A] Ilaa and Tubiah were related to one who had given a surety for a loan, but R. Pappa considered validating their evidence, since they were not related to either the debtor or the creditor.*

       B.   *Said R. Huna b. R. Joshua to R. Pappa, "But if the borrower were not in hand, would the creditor not collect from the guarantor of the loan?"*

1:10

       A.   **He whose trial ended and who fled and was brought back before the same court –**

I.1   A.   **He whose trial ended and who fled and was brought back before the same court – they do not reverse the judgment concerning him [and retry him]:**

       B.   Before that court in particular the judgment is not reversed, but it may be reversed before some other court! *But then it is taught further on:* **In any situation in which two get up and say, "We testify concerning Mr. So-and-so that his trial ended in the court of such-and-such, with Mr. So-and-so and Mr. So-and-so as the witnesses against him," lo, this one is put to death!**

II.1   A.   **[Trial before] a sanhedrin applies both in the land and abroad:**
       B.   *What is the source of this rule?*

III.1 A.   **A sanhedrin which imposes the death penalty once in seven years is called murderous. R. Eleazar b. Azariah says, "Once in seventy years":**

       B.   *The question was raised: Does the statement,* **A sanhedrin which imposes the death penalty once in seven years is called murderous** *mean that even one death sentence was enough to mark the sanhedrin as murderous, or is this merely a description of how things are?*

IV.1   A.   **R. Tarfon and R. Aqiba say, "If we were on a sanhedrin, no one would ever be put to death." Rabban Simeon b. Gamaliel says, "So they would multiply the number of murderers in Israel":**

       B.   *So what would they actually do?*

2:1A-L

A.   **These are the ones who go into exile:**

I.1   A.   **[This is the governing principle: Whatever happens en route downward – the person goes into exile:]** *What is the scriptural basis for these distinctions?*

I.2   A.   *Our rabbis have taught on Tannaite authority:*

B.   "That kills any person by error...unaware" (Deut. 19:4) –

I.3   A.   *Our rabbis have taught on Tannaite authority:*

B.   "But if he thrust him suddenly, without enmity, or have cast upon him any thing without lying in wait for him" (Num. 35:22):

I.4   A.   "And as a man goes into the wood with his neighbor" (Deut. 19:5):

B.   Just as the forest is public domain for the entry of the party who was injured and the one who did the injury, so any domain that is equally open to the entry of the injured party and the one who did the injury.

I.5   A.   R. Abbahu raised this question of R. Yohanan: "If someone was climbing up a ladder, and a rung gave way under him so he comes down and kills someone – what is the law? *In such a case do we regard the death as the result of an upward movement or a downward movement?"*

B.   He said to him, "You have reached a case of going down which is required for going up."

I.6   A.   *May we say that the same is taught among a variety of Tannaite statements:*

B.   If he was climbing up a ladder and a rung fell out under him –

2:1M-R

M.   **[If] the iron flew from the heft and killed someone,**

I.1   A.   *It has been taught on Tannaite authority:*

B.   Said Rabbi to sages, "But is it stated, 'and the iron slips from its wood' (Deut. 19:5)? What it says is, 'from the tree.' And 'tree' appears twice, just as in the first instance, the reference is to the tree that is being cut down, so in the second case, it is to the tree that is being cut down."

I.2   A.   Said R. Hiyya bar Ashi said Rab, "And both parties interpret the same verse of Scripture, namely, 'and the iron slips from the tree' (Deut. 19:5).

B.   *"Rabbi maintains that* the unvocalized letters of the text are determinative, *so we may read the word as* 'and was hurled away,' *and rabbis hold that* the vocalization of the letters of the text is determinative, *so we can only read* 'and slipped.'"

I.3   A.   *Said R. Pappa, "Someone who threw a clod at a palm and knocked off some palm fruit, which in falling killed someone – that presents us with a case illustrative of the dispute between Rabbi and rabbis."*

2:2

A.   He who throws a stone into the public domain and so committed manslaughter – lo, this one goes into exile.

I.1 A. **He who throws a stone into the public domain and so committed manslaughter – lo, this one goes into exile:**

B. **[But if that is what he did,] then it is a deliberate action [so why allow the mere penalty of exile]?**

II.1 A. **R. Eliezer b. Jacob says, "If after the stone left the man's hand, the other party stuck out his head and took [the stone on the head], lo, this one is exempt":**

B. *Our rabbis have taught on Tannaite authority:*

C. **"And if it found the neighbor...he shall flee" (Deut. 19:5) – excluding one who made himself available.**

II.2 A. *Does that reading bear the implication that the sense of "find" is that it is finding something there to begin with ["shall have found"]? But the following contradicts that imputation of meaning:*

III.1 A. **Abba Saul says, "Just as cutting wood is optional, so are excluded [from punishment those who do their duty, for example:] the father who hits his son, the master who strikes his disciple, and the court official who committed homicide in the doing of their duty":**

B. *Said one of the rabbis to Raba, "How come the cutting of wood is assumed to be optional? Maybe it was cutting wood for a tabernacle for the Festival of Tabernacles, or the cutting of wood for the wood pile on the altar in the Temple [which are religious duties]? Then it would follow that even under such conditions, the All-Merciful has said that the manslayer should go into exile!"*

III.2 A. *There are those who repeat the foregoing discussion in connection with the following:*

B. **"Six days you shall work but on the seventh day you shall rest, in ploughing time and in harvest you shall rest" (Ex. 34:21) [whatever the need, ploughing and reaping may not be done on the Sabbath or the Sabbatical Year] –**

2:3A-F

A. **The father goes into exile because of [the death of] the son.**

I.1 A. **The father goes into exile because of the death of the son:**

B. *But have you not just said, ...so are excluded [from punishment those who do their duty, for example:] the father who hits his son!*

II.1 A. **And the son goes into exile because of the [the death of] father:**

B. *An objection was raised:*

C. **"He who kills a person" (Num. 35:11) – excluding someone who has killed his father or mother.**

III.1 A. **All go into exile because of [the death of] an Israelite. And an Israelite goes into exile on their account:**

B. *What is encompassed by the language, All go into exile?*

III.2 A. *That is in line with that which our rabbis have taught on Tannaite authority:*

B. **A slave or Samaritan goes into exile or is flogged on account of an action done to an Israelite, and an Israelite goes into exile or is flogged on account of an action done to a slave or a Samaritan [T. Mak. 2:7C-D].**

IV.1 A. **Except on account of [the death of] a resident alien:**

B. *Then it follows that a resident alien is classified as a gentile. But I point to the concluding clause:* **A resident alien goes into exile only on account of [the death of] another resident alien.**

IV.2 A. *There are those who contrast verses of Scripture:*
B. "For the children of Israel and for the stranger and for the sojourner among them shall be these six cities for refuge" (Num. 35:15).

IV.3 A. *They are consistent with views expressed elsewhere, for it has been stated:*
B. If the one who did the killing had thought it was a beast but it turned out to be a man, a Canaanite and it turned out to be a resident alien –

2:3G-N

G. **"A blind person [guilty of manslaughter] does not go into exile," the words of R. Judah.**

I.1 A. **"A blind person [guilty of manslaughter] does not go into exile," the words of R. Judah. R. Meir says, "He goes into exile":**
B. *Our rabbis have taught on Tannaite authority:*

II.1 A. **R. Yosé b. R. Judah says, "One who bears enmity [for his victim] is put to death, for he is in the status of one who is an attested danger."**
B. *But how so? But they have not admonished him in advance!*

III.1 A. **R. Simeon says, "There is one who bears enmity [for the victim] who goes into exile, and there is one who bears enmity who does not go into exile. This is the governing principle : In any case in which one has the power to say, 'He killed knowingly,' he does not go into exile. And if he has the power to say, 'He did not kill knowingly,' lo, this one goes into exile":**
B. *It has been taught on Tannaite authority:*
C. **How is it that there is one who bears enmity [for the victim] who goes into exile, and there is one who bears enmity who does not go into exile? If the rope snapped, lo, this one goes into exile. If it slipped from his hand, lo, he does not go into exile [T. Mak. 2:10F-G].**

2:4-6F

A. **Where do they go into exile?**

I.1 A. *Our rabbis have taught on Tannaite authority:*
B. **Three cities of refuge did Moses set aside in Transjordan, and corresponding to them, Joshua set aside three in the land of Canaan. And they corresponded to the three in Transjordan like two rows of vines in a vineyard. Hebron in Judah corresponded to Boser in the wilderness; Shekhem in the mountains of Ephraim corresponded to Ramot in Gilead; Qadesh in Galilee corresponded to Golan in Bashan.**

What follows is a free-standing composition, wholly worked out in its own terms, a sustained reading of verses of Scripture.

I.2   A.   *[How come] the three cities in Trans]ordan were the same as the three cities for the Land of Israel [since so many more people lived in the Land of Israel]?*

      B.   *Said Abbayye, "In Gilead there were lots of murders, [10A] as it is written,* 'Gilead is a city of those who work iniquity and is covered with footprints of blood' (Hos. 6:8)."

I.3   A.   *What is the meaning of* "covered with footprints"?

      B.   Said R. Eleazar, "They would track down the victims to kill them."

I.4   A.   *How come some are further apart at one side and closer together at the other* [following the reading of Lazarus]?

      B.   *Said Abbayye, "In Shekhem, too, there were lots of murderers, as it is written,* 'And as troops of robbers wait for a man, so does the company of priests murder in the way toward Shekhem' (Hos. 6:9)."

I.5   A.   *What is the meaning of* "the company of priests"?

      B.   Said R. Eleazar, "They formed alliances to commit murder the way priests form alliances to go to the threshing floor at the distribution of the priestly dues."

I.6   A.   *Were there no more than six cities of refuge? Is it not written,* "And to them you shall add forty-two cities...so all the cities shall be forty-eight cities" (Num. 35:6-7, 1 Chr. 6:39-66)?

      B.   Said Abbayye, "These six named cities afforded protection whether explicitly or otherwise [with or without the approval of the municipality], while the others afforded refuge only articulately, but not tacitly."

I.7   A.   And was Hebron classified as a city of refuge? Is it not written, "And they gave Hebron to Caleb, as Moses had said" (Judg. 1:20)?

      B.   Said Abbayye, "He got the suburbs: 'but the fields of the city and the villages thereof they gave to Caleb son of Jephunneh for his possession' (Josh. 21:12)."

I.8   A.   And was Qadesh a city of refuge? And is it not written, "and the fortified cities were Ziddim, Zer, Hammath, Rakkath, and Chinnereth...and Qadesh" (Josh. 19:35-37), and it has been taught on Tannaite authority, **As to these three cities, they do not make them into large cities nor into small towns, but mid-sized cities** [T. Mak. 3:8F].

      B.   *Said R. Joseph, "There were two towns called Qadesh."*

      C.   Said R. Ashi, "For instance, Seleucia and the Fort of Seleucia."

I.9   A.   Reverting to the body of the text partially cited just now: **As to these three cities, they do not make them into large cities nor into small towns, but mid-sized cities. They build them only in a place in which there is adequate water. If they do not have adequate water, they bring water to them [in conduits]. They set them up only in entrepots. And they build them only in populated areas. If the population went down, they bring others and settle them in their place. If their population declined in numbers, they add to them priests, Levites, and Israelites** [T. Mak. 3:8F-J].

I.10 A.   *A Tannaite statement:*

B. A disciple of a sage goes into exile joined by his master, as it is said, 'he may live' (Deut. 4:42), *meaning, do for him whatever is needed for life.*

I.11 A. Said R. Yohanan, "How on the basis of Scripture do we know that if a master goes into exile, the disciples of his session are to go with him?"

What follows is a free-standing composition, devoted to a story about a sage. While the story is used for the larger purpose of the composite at hand, it stands on its own, and does not require any information given in context to be fully understood.

I.12 A. *That is in line with the story involving R. Hisda. He was in session and studying in the household of his master, and the angel of death could not get near him, for his mouth did not close from repeating aloud words of Torah. He went out and took a perch on a cedar of the schoolhouse. When the cedar cracked under his weight, R. Hisda shut up for a moment, and the other overcame him.*

I.13 A. Said R. Tanhum b. Hanilai, "How come the tribe of Judah was awarded the merit of being counted first in the territories assigned to afford refuge? It is because it was he who commenced an argument in favor of affording refuge [to his brother], as it is said, 'And Reuben heard it and he delivered him out of their hand and said, Let us not take his life' (Gen. 37:21)."

I.14 A. Expounded R. Simlai, "*What is the meaning of the verse,* 'Then Moses separated three cities beyond the Jordan, toward sunrise' (Deut. 4:41)? Said the Holy One, blessed be He, to Moses, 'Make the sun rise for those who commit manslaughter.'"

I.15 A. Expounded R. Simlai, "*What is the meaning of the verse,* 'He who loves silver shall not be satisfied with silver, and he who delights in multitude not with increase' (Qoh. 5:9)?

B. "'He who loves silver shall not be satisfied with silver': This refers to our lord, Moses, who knew full well that the three designated cities in TransJordan would not afford protection to manslayers before the three in the Land of Canaan had been selected, but determined, 'A religious duty that comes into my hand shall I most certainly carry out.'"

I.16 A. Said R. Joshua b. Levi, "*What is the meaning of the verse,* 'Our feet stood within your gates, Jerusalem' (Ps. 122:2)? Who made our feet stand in war? The gates of Jerusalem, where students were engaged in the Torah."

B. And said R. Joshua b. Levi, "*What is the meaning of the verse,* 'A song of ascents to David, I rejoiced when they said to me, let us go to the house of the Lord' (Ps. 122:1)?

C. "Said David before the Holy One, blessed be He, 'Lord of the world, I heard people say, "When is this old man going to die, so that his son Solomon will come and build the chosen house, so that we may go up there on a pilgrimage," but I rejoiced to hear it!'

D. "Said to him the Holy One, blessed be He, '"A day in your court is better than a thousand" (Ps. 84:11). Better for me is a single day on which you are engaged in the Torah before me than a thousand burnt-offerings that Solomon, your son, is going to offer before me on the altar.'"

II.1   A.   **And [direct] roads [were prepared] from one to the other, as it is said, "And you shall prepare the way and divide the borders of your land" (Deut. 19:3):**

     B.   *It has been taught on Tannaite authority:*

     C.   **R. Eliezer b. Jacob says, [10B] "They write signs, saying, 'Refuge, refuge,' at the crossroads, so that the manslayer may see and go into exile to the cities of refuge" [T. Mak. 3:5A-B].**

     B.   *Said R. Kahana, "What verse of Scripture makes that point? 'You shall prepare for yourself the way' (Deut. 19:3) – you make preparation for the proper road."*

Now we have a set of unrelated, free-standing compositions, which amplify verses of Scripture. The compositor who put them together thought that because they all refer in some manner or other to "way" or "the way in which a person should go," they belonged together. Each serves to typify a type of composition that came down, in its own terms, to said compositor: a comment on a verse of Scripture, pure and simple.

II.2   A.   *R. Hama bar Hanina opened his course on the subject with this verse of Scripture: "'Good and upright is the Lord, therefore he instructs sinners in the way' (Ps. 25:8). If he instructs sinners, all the more so the righteous!"*

     B.   *R. Simeon b. Laqish opened his course on the subject with this verse of Scripture:* "'And if a man not lie in wait, but God cause it to come to hand, then I will appoint you a place where he may flee' (Ex. 21:13). 'As says the proverb of the ancients, out of the wicked comes forth wickedness, but my hand shall not be upon you' (1 Sam. 24:13-14). Of whom does the former verse of Scripture speak? Of two people who killed someone, one did it inadvertently, the other did it deliberately. Against this one are not witnesses, and against that one are known witnesses. So the Holy One, blessed be He, arranges for them to chance upon the same inn. The one who killed deliberately seats himself under a ladder, and the one who killed inadvertently comes down the ladder and falls on him and kills him. The one who killed deliberately then is killed, and the one who killed inadvertently goes into exile."

II.3   A.   Said Rabbah bar R. Huna said R. Huna, and some say, said R. Huna said R. Eleazar, "From the Torah, the Prophets, and the Holy Writings, it is shown that on the way on which a person wants to go – in that way is he led.

     B.   "From the Torah: 'And God said to Balaam, You shall not go with them' (Num. 22:12), and then: 'If the men came to call you, rise up and go with them' (Num. 22:20);

     C.   "The Prophets: 'I am the Lord your God who teaches you for your profit, who leads you by the way that you should go' (Isa. 48:17);

     D.   "And the Holy Writings: 'If he is of the scorners, he will be allowed to speak scorn, and if he is of the meek, he will show forth grace' (Prov. 3:34)."

II.4   A.   Said R. Huna, "A manslayer who went into exile to a city of refuge, whom the blood-avenger overtook and killed – the latter is exempt from punishment. *He takes the view that* 'and he, not deserving of death' (Deut. 19:6) refers to the blood avenger [in the verse 'he shall flee to one of these cities and live, lest the avenger of blood pursue the manslayer while his heart is hot and overtake him because the way is long and smite him mortally, and he not deserving of death, inasmuch as he hated him not in time past' since it is possible to read, 'the manslayer was not deserving of death' or 'the avenger is not deserving of death']."

II.5   A.   A master has said: **because the incident came to his hand by accident.**

II.6   A.   Said R. Eleazar, "A city the majority of the population of which is made up of murderers does not provide refuge: 'And he shall declare his words in the ears of the elders of the city' (Josh. 20:4) – his cause, not a cause that is equivalent to theirs."

II.7   A.   And said R. Eleazar, "A city that has no elders may not serve as a city of refuge,"
        B.   *for we require 'elders of the city' but there is none!"*

II.8   A.   *It has been stated:*
        B.   A city that has no elders –

II.9   A.   A city that has no elders –
        B.   R. Ammi and R. Assi –

II.10   A.   A city that has no elders –
        B.   R. Ammi and R. Assi –

II.11   A.   Said R. Hama bar Hanina, "How come the passage that deals with murders is stated [11A] in strong language of repeated acts of speech, as it is written, 'And the Lord spoke to Joshua saying, Speak to the children of Israel saying, Appoint for yourselves cities of refuge whereof I spoke to you by the hand of Moses' (Josh. 20:1-2)? It is because it was to carry out what had been stated in the Torah."

II.12   A.   [Explaining how come the passage that deals with murders is stated in strong language of repeated acts of speech, as it is written, 'And the Lord spoke to Joshua saying, Speak to the children of Israel saying, Appoint for yourselves cities of refuge whereof I spoke to you by the hand of Moses' (Josh. 20:1-2),] *There was a difference of opinion between R. Judah and rabbis.*

II.13   A.   On the verse, "And Joshua wrote these words in the book of the Torah of God" (Josh. 24:26), *there was a difference of opinion between R. Judah and R. Nehemiah.*

II.14   A.   As to the suitability of a scroll of the Torah, the parchment skins of which are sewn together with thread of flax, *there was a difference of opinion between R. Judah and R. Meir.*
        B.   One says, "It is valid."
        C.   And the other says, "It is invalid."

2:6G-I

        G.   **All the same are [the deaths of] the high priest who is anointed with anointing oil, the one who is consecrated by being clothed in many garments, and the one who has passed from his anointment**

as high priest – they bring back the murderer [from the city of refuge, his term having ended].

I.1 A. *What is the scriptural basis for these statements?*

B. Said R. Kahana, "Said Scripture, ''And he shall live there until the death of the high priest who was anointed with the holy oil' (Num. 35:25), 'because he should have remained in the city of refuge until the death of the high priest' (Num. 35:28), 'But after the death of the high priest the slayer shall return to the land of his possession' (Num. 35:28)."

II.1 A. **Therefore the mothers of the priests provide food and clothing for those [who are in the cities of refuge,] so that they will not pray that their sons will die:**

B. *So the operative consideration is that they may not say prayers of that kind. Then if they said such prayers, would the sons, the high priests, then die? But has it not been written, "As the flitting bird, as the flying swallow, so the curse that has no cause will not come about" (Prov. 26:2)?*

II.2 A. *There are those who repeat the passage in this language:* **so that they will pray that their sons will not die:**

II.3 A. *That is like the case of the fellow who was eaten by a lion three parasangs from the town where R. Joshua b. Levi lived. On that account, Elijah stayed away from him for three days.*

What follows is an example of a sustained exposition of a proposition, to which Mishnah exposition is tangential or entirely irrelevant.

II.4 A. Said R. Judah said Rab, "The curse of a sage, even for nothing, comes about. How do we know that fact? It is shown by the case of Ahitophel.

B. "When David dug the pits for the Temple's foundations, the waters of the deep welled up and were going to flood the world.

C. *"David said, 'Is there anyone who knows whether or not it is permitted to write the Divine Name on a piece of pottery and to toss it down into the deep so that the water will subside?'*

D. *"No one was around to tell him.*

E. "Said David, 'Whoever knows how to rule but does not state [the rule], will be strangled by the throat.'

F. "Ahitophel reasoned a fortiori on his own [not from tradition] as follows: 'Now if in order to make peace between a man and his wife, the Torah has said, "My name, which is written in a state of sanctification, may be blotted out by water," so as to make peace for the entire world, how much more so [may the Divine Name be written down and blotted out]!'

G. *"[Ahitophel] said to [David], 'It is permitted [to do so].'*

H. *"[David] wrote the Divine Name on a piece of pottery and tossed it into the deep, and the waters subsided by sixteen thousand cubits.*

I. "Nonetheless: 'And when Ahithophel saw that his counsel was not followed, he saddled his ass and arose and went home to his house and to his city, and he put his household in order and hanged himself and died' (2 Sam. 17:23)."

II.5   A.   Said R. Abbahu, "How do we know that a curse of a sage, even if it is subject to a condition, will in any event come about? It is shown by the case of Eli.

        B.   *"For Eli said to Samuel, 'God do this to you and more also if you hide anything from me of all the things he said to you' (1 Sam. 3:17).*

        C.   *"And even though it is written, 'And Samuel told him every whit and hid nothing from him' (1 Sam. 3:18), nonetheless it is written, 'And Samuel's sons did not walk in his ways' (1 Sam. 8:3)."*

II.6   A.   [11B] Said R. Judah said Rab, "How do we know that it is necessary to seek remission from ostracism even though it is conditional [and the condition is not met]?

        B.   "It derives from the case of Judah, for it is written, 'And Judah said to Israel his father, Send the lad with me...if I do not bring him back to you...then let me bear the blame for ever' (Gen. 43:8-9)."

        C.   *And in this connection said R. Samuel bar Nahmani said R. Jonathan, "What is the meaning of the verse of Scripture, 'Let Reuben live and not die, and this for Judah, and let not his men be few; and this is for Judah, and Moses said, Lord, hear the voice of Judah and bring him to his people, let his hands be sufficient for him and be you a help to him from his enemies' (Deut. 33:6-7)?*

        D.   "All those years that the Israelites were in the wilderness, the bones of Judah were rolling around in the coffin, until Moses went and sought mercy for him, saying before him, 'Lord of the ages, who caused Reuben to confess? It was Judah [who set the example].'

        E.   "'And this for Judah.' Forthwith: 'Hear, O Lord, the voice of Judah' (Deut. 33:7).

        F.   *"Each limb then entered its socket [and stopped rolling about].*

        G.   *"But they did not bring him up into the Torah session in the firmament.*

        H.   "[Moses then prayed], 'And bring him in to his people.'

        I.   *"But he could not follow the give and take of the argument [that rabbis were discussing concerning the law].*

        J.   "[Moses prayed]: 'With his hands let him contend for himself' (Deut. 33:7).

        K.   *"He had no tradition in hand pertinent to what was under discussion in the law.*

        L.   "[Moses prayed:] 'Be a help against his adversaries' (Deut. 33:7)."

II.7   A.   *The question was raised: Is it only on the occasion of the death of all of those listed in the Mishnah* [All the same are the deaths of the high priest who is anointed with anointing oil, the one who is consecrated by being clothed in many garments, and the one who has passed from his anointment as high priest – they bring back the murderer from the city of refuge, his term having ended] *that the manslayer comes home, or is it at the death of any one of those listed?*

2:6J-L, 2:7A-N

        J.   [If] after one's trial has ended [with the sentence of exile], a high priest died, lo, this one does not go into exile.

I.1   A.   [[If] after one's trial has ended [with the sentence of exile], a high priest died, lo, this one does not go into exile:]

        B.   *How come?*

II.1 A. **[If] it was before the trial had ended that the high priest died and another was appointed in his stead, and afterward his trial came to an end, he comes back only at the death of the next high priest:**

B. *What is the scriptural source of this rule?*

II.2 A. *Said Abbayye, "We have a tradition:* If the verdict was concluded and the manslayer died, his body is to be carried to one of the cities of refuge: 'that he should come back to dwell in the land until the death of the priest' (Num. 35:32). Now what is 'dwelling in the land'? You have to say, it is burial."

II.3 A. *A Tannaite statement:*

B. If the manslayer died before the high priest died, they bring his bones back to the graves of his ancestors: "And after the death of the high priest the slayer shall return to the land of his possession" (Num. 35:28). Now what is "dwelling in the land of his possession"? You have to say, it is burial.

II.4 A. If his trial had come to an end and the high priest turned out to be the son of a divorcée or of a woman who had performed the rite of removing the shoe –

II.5 A. *May one suppose that at issue between them is what is at issue between R. Eliezer and R. Joshua:*

III.1 A. **If (1) one's trial ended at a time at which there was no high priest, (2) he who kills a high priest, and (3) a high priest who committed involuntary manslaughter – none of these leaves there forever. And one does not leave [the city of refuge] either for giving testimony having to do with a religious duty, or to give testimony having to do with property, or to give testimony having to do with a capital crime. And even if the Israelites need him, and even if he is a general of the Israelite army of the quality of Joab b. Zeruiah:**

B. Said R. Judah said Rab, "Two errors did Joab make at that moment: 'And Joab fled to the tent of the Lord and caught hold of the horns of the altar' (1 Kgs. 2:28). The first was that only the top of the altar affords protection, and he grabbed the horns. Furthermore, only the altar of the eternal house affords protection, and he grabbed the altar of Shilo."

C. *Abbayye says, "In yet another matter did he err:* He erred in that [at the altar] refuge is accorded only to a priest who is engaged in an act of service, and he was a nonpriest."

III.2 A. Said R. Simeon b. Laqish, "Three errors is the angelic prince of Rome destined to make: 'Who is this that comes from Edom with dyed garments from Bozrah' (Isa. 63:1). He will err since only Bezer affords refuge, but he will go instead to Bozrah; he will err in that refuge is accorded only to those who slay inadvertently, but he murders intentionally; he will err in that refuge is accorded only to a human being, and he is an angel."

III.3 A. Said R. Abbahu, "The cities of refuge are not available for places of burial: 'And the cities shall they have to dwell in, and the suburbs of them shall be for their cattle and for their goods and for all their living' (Num. 35:3) – they are assigned for the living, not for burial."

IV.1 A. **Just as the town affords refuge, so the Sabbath limit of the town affords refuge:**

B.   *An objection was raised:* "And he shall abide in it" (Num. 25:25) – in it, not within the area encompassed by its boundary.

V.1   A.   **A manslayer who went beyond the limit, and the avenger of the blood found him – R. Yosé the Galilean said, "It is a religious duty in the hand of the avenger of the blood [to kill the manslaughterer], and it is an option available to anyone else [to do so as well]." R. Aqiba says, "It is an option available to the avenger of the blood, and anyone else bears no liability [if he does so]":**

B.   *Our rabbis have taught on Tannaite authority:*

C.   "'And the avenger of blood shall slay the manslayer, there shall be no bloodguilt for him' (Num. 35:27) – It is a religious duty in the hand of the avenger of the blood [to kill the manslaughterer], and it is an option available to anyone else [to do so as well]," the words of R. Yosé the Galilean.

V.2   A.   Said Mar Zutra bar Tobiah said Rab, "A murderer who went beyond the boundary of the city of refuge and whom the blood avenger found and killed – the latter is put to death on that account."

V.3   A.   *Our rabbis have taught on Tannaite authority:*

B.   "But if the slayer, coming out, should come out beyond the border of his city of refuge...there shall be no blood guilt" (Num. 35:26-27) –

V.4   A.   *One Tannaite statement:* A father who accidentally killed a son – a surviving son serves as the avenger of blood for him.

2:7/O-Q

O.   **A tree standing in the Sabbath limit, with its branches extending outside of the Sabbath limit –**

I.1   A.   *An objection was raised:* **A tree which is standing inside [Jerusalem] and [a bough of which] extends outside [the city],**

B.   **Or [which] is standing outside and [a bough of which] extends inside [Jerusalem] – that which is above [the center of] the wall and inwards is [deemed to be] within [Jerusalem] [and that which is over the center of] the wall and outward is [deemed to be] outside [M. M.S. 3:7A-C].** [The location of the branches is null. In our rule by contrast the status of the root is determined by the branches' location.]

2:7R-S

R.   **[If] one has committed manslaughter in that very town he goes into exile from one neighborhood to another.**

I.1   A.   *Our rabbis have taught on Tannaite authority:*

B.   "Then I will appoint for you a place where he may flee" (Ex. 21:13) –

2:8

A.   **Similarly: a manslayer who went into exile into a city of refuge, whom the townsfolk wanted to honor, must say to them, "I am a manslayer."**

I.1   A.   **["They pay Levites a rental," the words of R. Judah. R. Meir says, "They did not pay them a rental":]** Said R. Kahana, "The dispute concerns the six principal cities of refuge. *For one master maintains, 'and the cities shall be for you for refuge' (Num. 35:6) means, 'for the purpose of refuge and no other purpose,' and the other master takes the view that 'to you' means, 'yours for all your needs.'* But in regard to the other forty-two cities, they concur that the manslayers who settle there do pay rent."...

II.1   A.   **"And he may return to the office which he had held before," the words of R. Meir. R. Judah says, "He did not return to the office which he had held before":**

       B.   *Our rabbis have taught on Tannaite authority:*

       C.   "And he shall return to his family and to the possession of his fathers shall he return" (Lev. 25:41) –

3:1

       A.   **These are the ones who are flogged:**

I.1   A.   *Those that incur a flogging in connection with extirpation are listed, but not those that incur the death penalty by a court decree.*

       B.   *Who is the authority behind this Mishnah paragraph?*

I.2   A.   R. Isaac says, "All those violations of the law that are punishable by extirpation were subject to a single encompassing statement ["For whoever shall do any of these abominations – the persons that do them shall be cut off from among their people" (Lev. 18:29)], and why was the penalty of extirpation made explicit in particular in the case of his sister? It was to impose in that case the penalty of extirpation and not mere flogging."

I.3   A.   *And what is the scriptural basis for R. Aqiba's [excluding from a flogging those who are subject to the death penalty inflicted by the earthly court]?*

I.4   A.   *Raba said, "If the offender was admonished that, if he did the act, the death penalty would follow, all parties concur that, in such a case, the man is not flogged but will be put to death if found guilty. Where there is a dispute, it concerns a case in which there are admonition as to the penalty of flogging [but not death]. R. Ishmael takes the view that* on account of violating a negative commandment that is subject to the admonition that the penalty will be death at the hands of an earthly court may be the occasion of a flogging nonetheless, *and R. Aqiba takes the view that* on account of violating a negative commandment that is subject to the admonition that the penalty will be death at the hands of an earthly court may not be the occasion of a flogging."

I.5   A.   R. Isaac says, "All those violations of the law that are punishable by extirpation were subject to a single encompassing statement ["For whoever shall do any of these abominations – the persons that do them shall be cut off from among their people" (Lev. 18:29)], and why was the penalty of extirpation made explicit in particular in the case of his sister? It was to impose in that case the penalty of extirpation and not mere flogging."

II.1   A.   **[Also subject to flogging are]: (1) an unclean person who ate food in the status of Holy Things: (2) he who enters the Temple unclean [is subject to extirpation and also is flogged]:**

B. *Now there is no problem in understanding why that should be the case for one who enters the Temple unclean, since Scripture explicitly states both the sanction and also the admonition.* The sanction: "He has defiled the tabernacle of the Lord, that soul shall be cut off from Israel" (Num. 19:13). And the admonition: "that the unclean not defile their holy part of the camp" (Num. 5:3).

III.1 A. **[He who enters the Temple unclean:]**

B. Said Rabbah bar bar Hannah said R. Yohanan, "On account of violating any negative commandment that is preceded by a positive commandment people are flogged."

III.2 A. *Said R. Pappa to Raba, "But lo, the prohibition pertaining to it [combining a negative commandment preceded by a positive one] is not comparable to the generative model of a negative commandment, which is the one against muzzling an ox in its threshing (Deut. 25:4)."*

III.3 A. *There we have learned in the Mishnah:* **He who takes the dam with the young – R. Judah says, "He incurs flagellation, but he does not send forth [the dam]." And sages say, "He sends forth [the dam], but does not incur flagellation. This is the general principle: For any negative commandment which encompasses an affirmative one to rise up and do something, one does not incur flagellation" [M. Hul. 12:4].**

IV.1 A. [Also flogged is] **he who eats carrion or terefah meat, forbidden things, or creeping things:**

B. *Said R. Judah, "Someone who ate a worm in a cabbage do we flog, on the count of 'a creeping thing that crawls on the ground' (Lev. 11:43)."*

IV.2 A. Said Abbayye, "If someone ate an eel, he is flogged on four counts [specified at Lev. 11:10-11: a water insect, finless, scaleless, and twice again (Lazarus)]. If someone ate an ant, it is on five counts, the additional one being, 'Any crawling thing that swarms on the earth you shall not eat' (Lev. 11:41-44). If it is a hornet, there are six counts, adding, 'and all winged swarming things are unclean to you, they shall not be eaten (Deut. 14:10)."

V.1 A. **If one ate food liable to tithing from which tithes had not been removed at all, first tithe from which heave-offering had not been removed, second tithe or consecrated food which had not been redeemed, he is liable to flogging:**

B. Said Rab, "If one ate food from which tithes had not been removed, from which poor tithe also had not been removed, he is flogged." [That penalty is not made explicit in Scripture; it would involve forty lashes, that is, two distinct counts (Lazarus).]

VI.1 A. **How much food which had not been tithed at all does one eat so as to be liable? R. Simeon says, "Any amount at all." And sages say, "An olive's bulk":**

B. Said R. Bibi said R. Simeon b. Laqish, "The dispute concerned a grain of wheat, but so far as the required volume of flour, all concur that it is subject to a prohibition and a flogging only if the volume were that of an olive in bulk."

3:3-4

A. **[Also subject to flogging are]: (1) he who eats first fruits over which one has not made the required declaration;**

I.1   A.   **[he who eats first fruits over which one has not made the required declaration:]** Said Rabbah bar bar Hannah said R. Yohanan, "This represents the opinion of R. Aqiba presented without attribution [thus one authority's position is portrayed as the decided law], but sages say, 'As to the presentation of first fruits, the act of placing them before the altar is essential to the rite [and they may not be eaten before that act], but the act of the declaration is not essential to the rite.'"

I.2   A.   *Said Raba, "Any mother who gives birth should give birth to someone like R. Simeon or just not give birth at all! Nonetheless, there are all sorts of challenges that one can raise to his arguments.*

I.3   A.   *In any event, is an admonition [not to do a given deed] going to be constructed merely on the basis of a logical argument [such as Simeon has proposed]? Surely not, for even in the opinion of one who maintains that one may inflict a given punishment solely on the basis of a logical argument resting on Scripture, nonetheless, one may not derive an admonition [not to do a given deed] merely on the basis of a logical argument [such as Simeon has proposed]!*

I.4   A.   *Reverting to the body of the prior composition:* Said Raba, "In R. Simeon's view, a nonpriest who ate meat deriving from a burnt-offering, prior to the tossing of the blood, outside of the wall of Jerusalem, is flogged on five counts":

I.5   A.   Said R. Giddal said Rab, "A priest who ate meat driving from a sin-offering or guilt-offering prior to the sprinkling of the blood is flogged.

I.6   A.   Said R. Eleazar said R. Hoshaia, "As to the presentation of first fruits, the act of placing them before the altar is essential to the rite [and they may not be eaten before that act], but the act of the declaration is not essential to the rite."

I.7   A.   *R. Aha bar Jacob repeated as a statement that R. Assi said R. Yohanan said [presented earlier as follows: Said Rabbah bar bar Hannah said R. Yohanan, "This represents the opinion of R. Aqiba presented without attribution [thus one authority's position portrayed as the decided law], but sages say, 'As to the presentation of first fruits, the act of placing them before the altar is essential to the rite [and they may not be eaten before that act], but the act of the declaration is not essential to the rite'"], and so proposed a contradiction between two statements of R. Yohanan:* "Did R. Yohanan *really say,* 'As to the presentation of first fruits, the act of placing them before the altar is essential to the rite [and they may not be eaten before that act], but the act of the declaration is not essential to the rite'? *Then when R. Assi asked R. Yohanan,* "How soon are first fruits available for the priests to eat," did he not say that those that were presented at the proper time for the declaration were released right after the declaration was made, but those not brought at the proper time for the declaration as soon as they were face to face with the Temple [without declaring what the farmer is required to say]? *Such a statement then would present contradictions on both points, in regard to recital and also in regard to placing the fruit before the altar!*

I.8   A.   Said Raba bar Ada said R. Isaac, "With respect to first fruits, **[19A]** at what point does the obligation to present these particular pieces of fruit take effect [so that one would violate the law if one ate them without proper presentation]? From the moment at which they come face to face with the Temple house."

I.9   A.   Said R. Sheshet, "As to the presentation of first fruits, the act of placing them before the altar is essential to the rite [and they may not be eaten before that act], but the act of the declaration is not essential to the rite."

II.1   A.   **(2) Most Holy Things outside the Temple veils, (3) Lesser Holy Things or second tithe outside the wall [of Jerusalem]:**

       B.   *We have learned this in another Mishnah passage:* **second tithe or consecrated** *food which had not been redeemed* [M. 3:2H]!

II.2   A.   *And what is the source of that rule that one is liable for eating in a state of uncleanness second tithe?*

II.3   A.   Said R. Bibi said R. Assi, "How on the basis of Scripture do we know that second tithe that is uncontaminated may be redeemed even a single step before the wall of Jerusalem? 'When you are not able to bring it up, then you shall turn it into money' (Deut. 15:24)."

II.4   A.   *In session R. Hanina and R. Hoshaia raised this question: "At the very gate to Jerusalem, what is the rule? It is obvious that* if he is outside the gate and his load is inside, the wall of the city has extended its protection over the produce. If he is inside and the burden outside, what is the law?"

II.5   A.   Said R. Assi said R. Yohanan, "How soon are people liable for eating produce in the status of second tithe if they do so [outside of the wall of Jerusalem, that is, at what point is it no longer permitted to redeem the produce for money]? As soon as they were face to face with the interior wall.

3:5

       A.   **(1) He who makes a baldness on his head (Deut. 14:1), (2) he who rounds the corners of his head and (3) mars the corners of his beard (Lev. 19:27), (4) or he who makes a single cutting for the dead (Lev. 19:28) is liable.**

I.1   A.   *Our rabbis have taught on Tannaite authority:*

       B.   **"They shall not make tonsures [upon their heads, nor shave off the edges of their beards, nor make any cuttings in their flesh]":**

I.2   A.   *And just how are the four or five cuts made? If we say that they are made sequentially, one after the other, in the aftermath of five admonitions, then the rule is self-evident!* [20B] *And if it was a single admonition, is he going to be liable on four or five counts? Have we not learned in the Mishnah:* **A Nazirite who was drinking wine all day long is liable on only one count. [If] they said to him, "Don't drink, don't drink!" yet he continued to drink, he is liable on each count** [M. 3:7A-C]?

I.3   A.   And what is the measure of a baldness?

I.4   A.   *A Tannaite statement:*

       B.   One who on the Sabbath removes a scissors' nip of hair is liable [if he did so inadvertently] to a sin-offering." And how much is "a scissors' nip of hair"?

II.1   A.   **he who rounds the corners of his head:**

II.2 A.   B.   *Our rabbis have taught on Tannaite authority: "The corner of the head" is the end of the head, and what constitutes rounding the extreme end of the head?" Leveling the temple growth from the back of the ears to the forehead.*

II.2   A.   *A Tannaite authority repeated before R. Hisda: "All the same are rounding the corners and having someone else round them, both are equally subject to a flogging."*

III.1   A.   **Mars the corners of his beard:**

       B.   *Our rabbis have taught on Tannaite authority:* The corner of the beard means the end of the beard, and what constitutes the end of the beard? The tuft of the beard.

IV.1   A.   **Or he who makes a single cutting for the dead:**

       B.   *Our rabbis have taught on Tannaite authority:* "You shall not make a cutting in your flesh" (Lev. 19:28) –

IV.2   A.   Said Samuel, "He who makes a cut with an instrument is liable [Lazarus: on two counts, as this is prohibited at Lev. 21:5 and Deut. 14:1 respectively]."

       B.   *An objection was raised:* the two distinct terms used for the same action [at Lev. 21:5 and Deut. 14:1 respectively] have the same meaning, but one term refers to doing so by hand, the other with a utensil.

       C.   *Samuel concurs with the position of R. Yosé.*

IV.3   A.   *A Tannaite authority repeated before R. Yohanan: "If one made a cut for the dead, whether by hand or with an instrument, he is liable on one count; if he did so as an act of idolatry, if it was by hand, he is liable, if with an instrument, he is not liable."*

V.1   A.   **For [cutting off the hair of] the head, he is liable on two counts, one for each side of the head.**

       B.   *R. Sheshet pointed out the distinct areas, between the two joints of the head.*

VI.1   A.   **For cutting off the beard, he is liable on two counts for one side, two counts for the other side, and one count for the lower part:**

       B.   *R. Sheshet pointed out the distinct areas, between the junctions of the beard.*

VII.1   A.   **R. Eliezer says, "If he removed all of it at once, he is liable only on one count":**

       B.   *He takes the view that the whole constitutes a single prohibition.*

VIII.1 A.   **And he is liable only if he will remove it with a razor.**

       B.   *Our rabbis have taught on Tannaite authority:*

       C.   "Neither shall the priests shave off the corner of their beard" (Lev. 21:5):

IX.1   A.   **R. Eliezer says, "Even if he removed it with pincers or with an adze, he is liable":**

       B.   *Which way shall we go? If he has in hand an analogy established through verbal intersection [Lev. 14:9 and Num. 8:7, the corner of the beard must be shaved off, shaving involves a razor, in which case the razor is the one forbidden instrument, or the one required one, where a shaving is involved], then he should require use of a razor! And if he does not have in hand an analogy established through verbal intersection, then he should not permit even the use of scissors!*

3:6

A.   **He who tattoos his skin –**

I.1   A.   [**He is liable only if he will write the name of a god:**] *Said R. Aha b. Raba to R. Ashi, "Does that mean, 'he will actually write, "I am the Lord"'?!"*

        B.   *He said to him, "Not at all. It is in accord with that which Bar Qappara repeated as a Tannaite statement:* 'He is liable to a flogging only if he has inscribed the name of some other god, in line with this verse: "Nor put on you any written imprint, I am the Lord," that is, "I am the Lord," there is no other.'"

I.2   A.   Said R. Malkiah said R. Ada bar Ahbah, "It is forbidden for someone to put wood ash on a wound, because it appears to be a tattoo."

I.3   A.   Said R. Nahman [B. A.Z. 29A: Hanina] b. R. Iqa, "Statements about a spear, maidservants, depressions are by R. Malkio; those concerning the forelock, vegetable ashes, and cheese are by R. Malkiah."

        B.   Said R. Pappa, "A statement that pertains to a passage of the Mishnah or to an external Tannaite formulation belong to R. Malkiah. Statements that pertain to what is free-standing belong to R. Malkio."

3:7-9

A.   **A Nazirite who was drinking wine all day long is liable on only one count.**

B.   **[If] they said to him, "Don't drink, don't drink!" yet he continued to drink,**

C.   **he is liable on each count.**

I.1   A.   [Yet he took it off and then put it on, he is liable on each count:] Said R. Bibi said R. Yosé, "It does not have to be actually taking it off and putting it on, taking it off and putting it on, but even if he put his hand in and out of the sleeve [the multiple liabilities are incurred]."

II.1   A.   **There is one who ploughs a single furrow and is liable on eight counts of violating a negative commandment:**

        B.   Said R. Yannai, "In a gathering people voted and decided: he who covers mixed seeds with dirt is liable to a flogging."

II.2   A.   *Which statement of R. Aqiba?*

II.3   A.   *Said Ulla to R. Nahman, "And should he not be flogged also on the count of sowing seed on the festival day?"*

II.4   A.   *Objected R. Hoshaia, "But to the list should also be added him who sows in a 'rough valley,' the associated admonition being:* 'which shall neither be ploughed or sown' (Deut. 21:4)."

II.5   A.   Said R. Hoshaia, "He who breeds with a female an ox that had been sanctified but that was unfit, the farmer is liable on two counts" [Lev. 19:19: "You shall not let your cattle breed with a diverse kind" and Deut. 15:19 (Lazarus)].

3:10-11C

A. How many times do they flog him?

I.1 A. [How many times do they flog him? Forty stripes less one:] What is the scriptural basis for this definition?

I.2 A. *Said Raba, "What jerks! The rest of the people stand up in front of a scroll of the Torah but don't stand up in front of an eminent authority! For in the scroll of the Torah it is written, 'forty,' and it is rabbis who have the wit to cut that number down!"*

II.1 A. R. Judah says, "He is flogged a full forty times." And where does the additional one fall? Between the shoulders:

B. *Said R. Isaac, "What is the scriptural basis behind the position of R. Judah?* It is written, 'And one shall say, what are these wounds between your hands [that is, between the shoulders, explaining the place of the additional one], then he shall answer, I was beaten in the house of my friends' (Zech. 13:6) [who once more make me a friend of God]."

III.1 A. They make an estimate of his capacity to take the flogging [without being irreparably injured or killed] only by a number divisible by three. [If] they estimated him as able to take forty, [if] he then received part of the flogging, and they said that he cannot take all forty, he is exempt:

B. So it follows that, if he has been flogged at all, then that rule applies, but if he has not been flogged at all, that rule does not apply! *But there is the following contradictory statement:* If they estimated that he can take forty stripes, then they estimated that he cannot take forty stripes, he is exempt from a flogging. If they estimated that he can take eighteen and then they estimated that he can take forty, he is exempt. [This statement does not tell us that he has been flogged at all, so the condition of the Mishnah rule is not in play here.]

3:11D-F

D. [If] he committed a transgression on which he is liable on two counts of violating negative commandments, and they make a single estimate [of what he can take, covering both sets],...

I.1 A. *But has it not been taught on Tannaite authority:* An estimate concerning one flogging is not made in connection with the penalty for violating two prohibitions?

3:12-14

A. How do they flog him?

I.1 A. [23A] How do they flog him? One ties his two hands on either side of a pillar, and the minister of the community grabs his clothing – if it is torn, it is torn, and if it is ripped to pieces, it is ripped to pieces – until he bares his chest: *What is the scriptural basis?*

II:1 A. And a strap of cowhide:

B. Said R. Sheshet said R. Eleazar b. Azariah, "How on the basis of Scripture do we know that it is of calf hide? 'Forty lashes shall he strike him' (Deut. 25:4) alongside 'you shall not muzzle the ox in its ploughing' (Deut. 25:4)."

II.2   A.   Said R. Sheshet said R. Eleazar b. Azariah, "How on the basis of Scripture do we know that the deceased childless brother's widow who is obligated to enter into levirate marriage with her late husband's surviving brother, in the case in which the latter is suffering with boils, is not to be muzzled [but may dissent from the marriage]?   It is written, 'you shall not muzzle the ox in its ploughing' (Deut. 25:4), and, alongside, 'if brothers dwell together' (Deut. 25:5)."

II.3   A.   And said R. Sheshet said R. Eleazar b. Azariah, "Whoever treats with contempt the intermediate days of festivals is as though he worshiped an idol.

        B.   "For it is written, 'You shall make no molten gods' (Ex. 34:17), *and, alongside,* 'The feast of unleavened bread you shall keep' (Ex. 34:18-23)."

II.4   A.   And said R. Sheshet said R. Eleazar b. Azariah, "Whoever carries gossip and whoever receives it and whoever bears false witness is worthy of being thrown to the dogs, for it is written, 'you shall throw it to the dogs' (Ex. 22:31), and alongside, 'You shall not carry a false report, do not put your hand with the wicked to be an unrighteous witness' (Ex. 34:1), reading the word as though it were written to yield 'do not beguile someone else.'"

III.1   A.   **...doubled and redoubled, with two straps that rise and fall [fastened] to it:**

        B.   *A Tannaite statement:* It was made of the hide of an ass.

III.2   A.   *That is in line with what a certain Galilean said in this regard before R. Hisda:* "'The ox knows its own, and the ass its master's crib, but Israel does not know, my people does not consider' (Isa. 1:3) –

        B.   "Said the Holy One, blessed be He, 'Let the one come who recognizes its master's crib and exact punishment from one who does not recognize his master's crib.'"

IV.1   A.   **Its handle is a handbreadth long and a handbreadth wide, and its end must reach to his belly button:**

        B.   *Said Abbayye, "That is to say: For each individual we should provide a lash in proportion to his back."*

V.1   A.   **And he hits him with a third of the stripes in front and two-thirds behind:**

        B.   *What is the source in Scripture for this statement?*

VI.1   A.   **And he does not hit [the victim] while he is either standing or sitting, but bending low:**

        B.   [With reference to the detail, **...doubled and redoubled:**] Said R. Hisda said R. Yohanan, "How on the basis of Scripture do we know that the lash is folded? 'And the judge shall have it fall [lie down] and have it strike him [beaten before him] according to the measure of his wicked action, by number' (Deut. 25:2)."

VII.1   A.   **And he who hits him hits with one hand, with all his might:**

        B.   *Our rabbis have taught on Tannaite authority:*

        C.   They appoint in charge of the flogging only those who lack physical power but exhibit abundant knowledge.

VII.2   A.   *A Tannaite statement:*

B.   When he raises up the lash, he raises it up with both hands, but when he smites, he smites with only one hand,

C.   *so that it comes down on its own momentum.*

VIII.1   A.   **And a reader reads: "If you will not observe to do...the Lord will have your stripes pronounced, and the stripes of your seed" (Deut. 28:58ff.) [and he goes back to the beginning of the passage]. "And you will observe the words of this covenant" (Deut. 29:9), and he finishes with, "But he is full of compassion and forgave their iniquity" (Ps. 78:38), and he goes back to the beginning of the passage:**

B.   *Our rabbis have taught on Tannaite authority:*

C.   The most important of the judges makes the recitation, the second does the counting, the third says, "Smite him."

VIII.2   A.   *Our rabbis have taught on Tannaite authority:*

B.   "He shall not exceed an ample flogging" (Deut. 25:3).

IX.1   A.   If the victim dirtied himself, whether with excrement or urine, he is exempt [from further blows]. R. Judah says, "In the case of man, with excrement; and in the case of a woman, with urine":

B.   *Our rabbis have taught on Tannaite authority:*

C.   "All the same are man and woman: the flogging is suspended if the dirtying was with excrement, but not with urine," the words of R. Meir.

IX.2   A.   Said Samuel, "If they tied him to the post and he fled from the court, he is exempt."

IX.3   A.   *Our rabbis have taught on Tannaite authority:*

B.   If they came to an estimate that if he is flogged, he will have loose bowels, they flog him. If they came to an estimate that if he leaves the court, he will have loose bowels, they flog him. If he had loose bowels before he was flogged, they flog him nonetheless, as it is said, "Then if the guilty man deserves to be beaten, the judge shall cause him to lie down and be beaten in his presence with a number of stripes in proportion to his offense; forty stripes may be given him, but no more, lest, if one should go on to beat him with more stripes than these, your brother be degraded in your sight" (Deut. 25:2-3) [T. Mak. 5:14H-J], not if he had already been degraded while in court.

3:15-16

A.   "All those who are liable to extirpation who have been flogged are exempt from their liability to extirpation,..."

I.1   A.   [Said R. Hananiah b. Gamaliel, "Now if one who does a single transgression – Heaven takes his soul on that account, he who performs a single religious duty – how much the more so that his soul will be saved for him on that account!":] Said R. Yohanan, "R. Hananiah b. Gamaliel's colleagues [Aqiba and Ishmael, who insist upon repentance, not punishment, as the condition of avoiding extirpation] differed from him."

I.2   A.   Said R. Adda bar Ahbah said Rab, "The decided law is in accord with R. Hananiah b. Gamaliel."

I.3   A.   *Reverting to the body of the foregoing:* R. Joshua b. Levi said, "Three rulings were made by the earthly court, and the court on high concurred with what they had done."

II.1 A.   **Therefore he gave them abundant Torah and numerous commandments:**

      B.   R. Simelai expounded, "Six hundred and thirteen commandments were given to Moses, three hundred and sixty-five negative ones, corresponding to the number of the days of the solar year, and two hundred forty-eight positive commandments, corresponding to the parts of a man's body."

      C.   *Said R. Hamnuna, "What verse of Scripture indicates that fact?* 'Moses commanded us Torah, an inheritance of the congregation of Jacob' (Deut. 33:4). *The numerical value assigned to the letters of the word Torah is* [24A] *six hundred and eleven, not counting,* 'I am' *and* 'you shall have no other gods,' *since these have come to us from the mouth of the Almighty."*

      D.   [Simelai continues:] "David came and reduced them to eleven: 'A Psalm of David: Lord, who shall sojourn in thy tabernacle, and who shall dwell in thy holy mountain? (i) He who walks uprightly and (ii) works righteousness and (iii) speaks truth in his heart and (iv) has no slander on his tongue and (v) does no evil to his fellow and (vi) does not take up a reproach against his neighbor, (vii) in whose eyes a vile person is despised but (viii) honors those who fear the Lord. (ix) He swears to his own hurt and changes not. (x) He does not lend on interest. (xi) He does not take a bribe against the innocent' (Ps. 15)."

      E.   "He who walks uprightly": This is Abraham: "Walk before me and be wholehearted" (Gen. 17:1).

      F.   "And works righteousness": This is Abba Hilqiahu.

      G.   "Speaks truth in his heart": For instance R. Safra.

      H.   "Has no slander on his tongue": This is our father, Jacob: "My father might feel me and I shall seem to him as a deceiver" (Gen. 27:12).

      I.   "Does no evil to his fellow": He does not go into competition with his fellow craftsman.

      J.   "Does not take up a reproach against his neighbor": This is someone who befriends his relatives.

      K.   "In whose eyes a vile person is despised": This is Hezekiah, king of Judah, who dragged his father's bones on a rope bed.

      L.   "Honors those who fear the Lord": This is Jehoshaphat, king of Judah, who, whenever he would see a disciple of a sage, would rise from his throne and embrace and kiss him and call him, "My father, my father, my lord, my lord, my master, my master."

      M.   "He swears to his own hurt and changes not": This is R. Yohanan.

      N.   For said R. Yohanan, "I shall continue fasting until I get home."

      O.   "He does not lend on interest": Not even interest from a gentile.

      P.   "He does not take a bribe against the innocent": Such as R. Ishmael b. R. Yosé.

      Q.   "He who does these things shall never be moved":

R.	When Rabban Gamaliel *reached this verse of Scripture, he would weep, saying, "If someone did all of these [virtuous deeds], then he will never be moved, but not merely on account of one of them."*

S.	They said to him, "Is it written, 'Who does all of these things;'? What is written is only 'who does these things,' meaning, even one of them."

T.	"For if you do not say this, then there is another verse of Scripture of which we have to take account: 'Do not defile yourselves in all of these things' (Lev. 18:24). Does this mean that one is unclean only if he touches all of these things, but not if he touches only one of them? But does it not mean, only one of them?

U.	"Here, too, it means that only one of these things is sufficient."

V.	[Simelai continues:] "Isaiah came and reduced them to six: '(i) He who walks righteously and (ii) speaks uprightly, (iii) he who despises the gain of oppressions, (iv) shakes his hand from holding bribes, (v) stops his ear from hearing of blood (vi) and shuts his eyes from looking upon evil, he shall dwell on high' (Isa. 33:25-26)."

W.	"He who walks righteously": This is our father, Abraham: "For I have known him so that he may command his children and his household after him" (Gen. 18:19).

X.	"Speaks uprightly": This is one who does not belittle his fellow in public.

Y.	"He who despises the gain of oppressions": For example, R. Ishmael b. Elisha.

Z.	"Shakes his hand from holding bribes": For example, R. Ishmael b. R. Yosé.

AA.	"Stops his ear from hearing of blood": *Who will not listen to demeaning talk about a disciple of rabbis and remain silent.*

BB.	*For instance, R. Eleazar b. R. Simeon.*

CC.	"And shuts his eyes from looking upon evil": That is in line with what R. Hiyya bar Abba said.

DD.	For said R. Hiyya bar Abba, "This is someone who does not stare at women as they are standing and washing clothes.

EE.	Concerning such a man it is written, "He shall dwell on high."

FF.	[Simelai continues:] "Micah came and reduced them to three: 'It has been told you, man, what is good, and what the Lord demands from you, (i) only to do justly and (ii) to love mercy, and (iii) to walk humbly before God' (Mic. 6:8)."

GG.	"Only to do justly": This refers to justice.

HH.	"To love mercy": This refers to doing acts of loving kindness.

II.	"To walk humbly before God": This refers to accompanying a corpse to the grave and welcoming the bread.

JJ.	And does this not yield a conclusion a fortiori: If matters that are not ordinarily done in private are referred to by the Torah as "walking humbly before God," all the more so matters that ordinarily are done in private.

KK.	[Simelai continues:] "Isaiah again came and reduced them to two : 'Thus says the Lord, (i) Keep justice and (ii) do righteousness' (Isa. 56:1).

LL. "Amos came and reduced them to a single one, as it is said, 'For thus says the Lord to the house of Israel: Seek Me and live.'"

MM. *Objected R. Nahman bar Isaac, "Maybe the sense is, 'seek me' through the whole of the Torah?"*

NN. Rather, [Simelai continues:] "Habakkuk further came and based them on one, as it is said, 'But the righteous shall live by his faith' (Hab. 2:4)."

II.2 A. Said R. Yosé bar Hanina, "Four decrees did our lord, Moses, make against Israel. Four prophets came along and anulled them.

B. "Moses said, 'And Israel dwells in safety alone at the fountain of Jacob' (Deut. 33:28). Amos came and annulled it: 'Then I said, O Lord God, stop, I ask you, how shall Jacob stand alone, for he is small,' and it goes on, 'The Lord repented concerning this: This also shall not be, says the Lord God' (Amos 7:5-6).

C. "Moses said, 'And among those nations you shall have no repose' (Deut. 28:65). Jeremiah came and annulled it: 'Thus says the Lord, the people that were left of the sword have found grace in the wilderness, even Israel, when I go to provide him rest' (Jer. 31:1).

D. "Moses said, 'The Lord...visits the sin of the fathers upon the children and upon the children's children to the third and to the fourth generation' (Ex. 34:7), but Ezekiel said, 'the soul that sins it shall die' (Ezek. 18:3-4).

E. "Moses said, 'And you shall perish among the nations' (Lev. 26:38), but Isaiah said, 'And it shall come to pass in that day that a great horn shall sound and they shall come who were lost in the land of Assyria' (Isa. 27:13)."

II.3 A. Said Rab, "I am troubled by this verse: 'And you shall perish among the nations' (Lev. 26:38)."

B. *To this objected R. Pappa,* "Perhaps the meaning is, something that was lost and searched for, in line with this usage: 'I have gone astray like a lost sheep, seek your servant' (Ps. 119:176)?"

C. *At issue for Rab was the end of the same verse:* "And the land of your enemies shall eat you up" (Lev. 26:38).

D. *To this objected Mar Zutra, "But perhaps the meaning is, in the way in which cucumbers and pumpkins are eaten [that is, little by little]."*

Here is another set of stories about sages, worked out for purposes entirely beside the point of Mishnah exegesis.

II.4 A. Once upon a time Rabban Gamaliel, R. Eleazar b. Azariah, R. Joshua, and R. Aqiba were walking along the way and heard the roar of Rome all the way from Puteoli, at a distance of a hundred and twenty miles. They began to cry, but R. Aqiba brightened up.

B. They said to him, "Why so cheerful?"

C. He said to them, "Why so gloomy?"

D. They said to him, "These Cushites worship sticks and stones and burn incense to idolatry but live in safety and comfort, while as to us, the house that was the footstool for our God is burned [24B] with fire! Why shouldn't we cry?!"

E. He said to them, "But that's precisely why I rejoice. If those who violate his will have it so good, those who do his will all the more so!"

II.5 A. Once again, they were going up to Jerusalem. When they got to Mount Scopus, they tore their garments. When they reached the Temple mount, they saw a fox emerge from the house of the Holy of Holies. They began to cry, but R. Aqiba brightened up.

B. They said to him, "Why so cheerful?"

C. He said to them, "Why so gloomy?"

D. They said to him, "The place of which it once was said, 'And the nonpriest who draws near shall be put to death' (Num. 1:51) has become a fox hole, so shouldn't we weep?"

E. He said to them, "But that's precisely why I rejoice. It is written, 'And I will take to me faithful witnesses to record, Uriah the priest and Zechariah son of Jeberechiah' (Isa. 8:2). And what has Uriah the priest to do with Zechariah? Uriah lived during the first Temple, and Zechariah during the second, but Scripture had linked the prophesy of Zechariah to the prophecy of Uriah. In the case of Uriah: 'Therefore shall Zion for your sake be ploughed as a field' (Mic. 3:12). Zechariah: 'Thus says the Lord of hosts, there shall yet old men and old women sit in the broad places of Jerusalem' (Zech. 8:4). Until the prophecy of Uriah was fulfilled, I was afraid that the prophecy of Zechariah might not be fulfilled. Now that the prophecy of Uriah has come about, we may be certain that the prophecy of Zechariah will be fulfilled word for word."

F. They said to him, "Aqiba, you have given us comfort, Aqiba, you have given us comfort."

III. Types of Sources in the Bavli: A Preliminary Taxonomy

Our survey of the above tractate has yielded a small number of "sources," compositions developed in response to a program of writing, and even compilation, entirely out of phase with that of the Bavli, but upon which the framers of the Bavli clearly have drawn. I find these types and no others.

1. A Sustained Reading of Sequential Verses of Scripture

What follows exemplifies the type of composition in which a sequence of verses of Scripture are subjected to a sustained and continuous reading. It is drawn from tractate Makkot, 2:4-6F/I.2.

I.2 A. *[How come] the three cities in TransJordan were the same as the three cities for the Land of Israel [since so many more people lived in the Land of Israel]?*

B. *Said Abbayye, "In Gilead there were lots of murders, [10A] as it is written, 'Gilead is a city of those who work iniquity and is covered with footprints of blood' (Hos. 6:8)."*

I.3 A. *What is the meaning of "covered with footprints"?*

B. Said R. Eleazar, "They would track down the victims to kill them."

I.4   A.   *How come some are further apart at one side and closer together at the other* [following the reading of Lazarus]?

         B.   *Said Abbayye, "In Shekhem, too, there were lots of murderers, as it is written, 'And as troops of robbers wait for a man, so does the company of priests murder in the way toward Shekhem' (Hos. 6:9)."*

I.5   A.   *What is the meaning of* "the company of priests"?

         B.   Said R. Eleazar, "They formed alliances to commit murder the way priests form alliances to go to the threshing floor at the distribution of the priestly dues."

I.6   A.   *Were there no more than six cities of refuge? Is it not written,* "And to them you shall add forty-two cities...so all the cities shall be forty-eight cities" (Num. 35:6-7, 1 Chr. 6:39-66)?

         B.   Said Abbayye, "These six named cities afforded protection whether explicitly or otherwise [with or without the approval of the municipality], while the others afforded refuge only articulately, but not tacitly."

I.7   A.   And was Hebron classified as a city of refuge? Is it not written, "And they gave Hebron to Caleb, as Moses had said" (Judg. 1:20)?

         B.   Said Abbayye, "He got the suburbs: 'but the fields of the city and the villages thereof they gave to Caleb son of Jephunneh for his possession' (Josh. 21:12)."

I.8   A.   And was Qadesh a city of refuge? And is it not written, "and the fortified cities were Ziddim, Zer, Hammath, Rakkath, and Chinnereth...and Qadesh" (Josh. 19:35-37), and it has been taught on Tannaite authority, **As to these three cities, they do not make them into large cities nor into small towns, but mid-sized cities [T. Mak. 3:8F].**

         B.   *Said R. Joseph, "There were two towns called Qadesh."*

         C.   Said R. Ashi, "For instance, Seleucia and the Fort of Seleucia."

2.   Stories about Sages: Singletons and Composites

Here we catalogue the compositions and composites that are devoted to stories about sages, excluding of course those stories that illustrate points of law or decisions of sages in cases. The illustrative case is drawn from the same passage as the exemplum given at No. 1.

I.12   A.   *That is in line with the story involving R. Hisda. He was in session and studying in the household of his master, and the angel of death could not get near him, for his mouth did not close from repeating aloud words of Torah. He went out and took a perch on a cedar of the schoolhouse. When the cedar cracked under his weight, R. Hisda shut up for a moment, and the other overcame him.*

3.   Exposition of Free-Standing, Individual Verses

A composite may be made up of a variety of distinct and free-standing Scripture exegeses, each of them, viewed on its own, a singleton. Thus, for our example:

Makkot 2:4-6

II.1   A.   **And [direct] roads [were prepared] from one to the other, as it is said, "And you shall prepare the way and divide the borders of your land" (Deut. 19:3):**

       B.   *It has been taught on Tannaite authority:*

       C.   R. Eliezer b. Jacob says, [10B] "They write signs, saying, 'Refuge, refuge,' at the crossroads, so that the manslayer may see and go into exile to the cities of refuge" [T. Mak. 3:5A-B].

       B.   *Said R. Kahana, "What verse of Scripture makes that point?* 'You shall prepare for yourself the way' (Deut. 19:3) – you make preparation for the proper road."

II.2   A.   *R. Hama bar Hanina opened his course on the subject with this verse of Scripture:* "'Good and upright is the Lord, therefore he instructs sinners in the way' (Ps. 25:8). If he instructs sinners, all the more so the righteous!"

       B.   *R. Simeon b. Laqish opened his course on the subject with this verse of Scripture:* "'And if a man not lie in wait, but God cause it to come to hand, then I will appoint you a place where he may flee' (Ex. 21:13). 'As says the proverb of the ancients, out of the wicked comes forth wickedness, but my hand shall not be upon you' (1 Sam. 24:13-14). Of whom does the former verse of Scripture speak? Of two people who killed someone, one did it inadvertently, the other did it deliberately. Against this one are not witnesses, and against that one are known witnesses. So the Holy One, blessed be He, arranges for them to chance upon the same inn. The one who killed deliberately seats himself under a ladder, and the one who killed inadvertently comes down the ladder and falls on him and kills him. The one who killed deliberately then is killed, and the one who killed inadvertently goes into exile."

II.3   A.   Said Rabbah bar R. Huna said R. Huna, and some say, said R. Huna said R. Eleazar, "From the Torah, the Prophets, and the Holy Writings, it is shown that on the way on which a person wants to go – in that way is he led.

       B.   "From the Torah: 'And God said to Balaam, You shall not go with them' (Num. 22:12), and then: 'If the men came to call you, rise up and go with them' (Num. 22:20);

       C.   "the Prophets: 'I am the Lord your God who teaches you for your profit, who leads you by the way that you should go' (Isa. 48:17);

       D.   "And the Holy Writings: 'If he is of the scorners, he will be allowed to speak scorn, and if he is of the meek, he will show forth grace' (Prov. 3:34)."

What is important in the foregoing is that each entry makes its own point about a verse that is treated in isolation from any broader composite. What joins the whole, which is to say, what the Bavli's compositors accomplished (if the work was theirs) was linking a variety of statements that have in common reference to "the way." The source that is utilized here, then, is made up of a verse of Scripture and some sort of comment thereon.

4. Proof of a Proposition in No Way Relevant to the Mishnah or Mishnah Exegesis

What follows is an example of a sustained exposition of a proposition, to which Mishnah exposition is tangential or entirely irrelevant. It is from tractate Makkot 2:6G-I/I.4-6, and the proposition is given up front and then provided with a variety of free-standing but entirely coherent proofs.

II.4   A.   Said R. Judah said Rab, "The curse of a sage, even for nothing, comes about. How do we know that fact? It is shown by the case of Ahitophel.

      B.   "When David dug the pits for the Temple's foundations, the waters of the deep welled up and were going to flood the world.

      C.   *"David said, 'Is there anyone who knows whether or not it is permitted to write the Divine Name on a piece of pottery and to toss it down into the deep so that the water will subside?'*

      D.   *"No one was around to tell him.*

      E.   "Said David, 'Whoever knows how to rule but does not state [the rule], will be strangled by the throat.'

      F.   "Ahitophel reasoned a fortiori on his own [not from tradition] as follows: 'Now if in order to make peace between a man and his wife, the Torah has said, "My name, which is written in a state of sanctification, may be blotted out by water," so as to make peace for the entire world, how much more so [may the Divine Name be written down and blotted out]!'

      G.   *"[Ahitophel] said to [David], 'It is permitted [to do so].'*

      H.   *"[David] wrote the Divine Name on a piece of pottery and tossed it into the deep, and the waters subsided by sixteen thousand cubits.*

      I.   "Nonetheless: 'And when Ahithophel saw that his counsel was not followed, he saddled his ass and arose and went home to his house and to his city, and he put his household in order and hanged himself and died' (2 Sam. 17:23)."

II.5   A.   Said R. Abbahu, "How do we know that a curse of a sage, even if it is subject to a condition, will in any event come about? It is shown by the case of Eli.

      B.   *"For Eli said to Samuel, 'God do this to you and more also if you hide anything from me of all the things he said to you' (1 Sam. 3:17).*

      C.   *"And even though it is written,* 'And Samuel told him every whit and hid nothing from him' (1 Sam. 3:18), *nonetheless it is written,* 'And Samuel's sons did not walk in his ways' (1 Sam. 8:3)."

II.6   A.   [11B] Said R. Judah said Rab, "How do we know that it is necessary to seek remission from ostracism even though it is conditional [and the condition is not met]?

      B.   "It derives from the case of Judah, for it is written, 'And Judah said to Israel his father, Send the lad with me...if I do not bring him back to you...then let me bear the blame for ever' (Gen. 43:8-9)."

      C.   *And in this connection said R. Samuel bar Nahmani said R. Jonathan, "What is the meaning of the verse of Scripture,* 'Let Reuben live and not die, and this for Judah, and let not his men be few; and this is for Judah, and Moses said, Lord, hear the voice of Judah and bring him to his people, let his hands be sufficient for him and be you a help to him from his enemies' (Deut. 33:6-7)?

D. "All those years that the Israelites were in the wilderness, the bones of Judah were rolling around in the coffin, until Moses went and sought mercy for him, saying before him, 'Lord of the ages, who caused Reuben to confess? It was Judah [who set the example].'

E. "'And this for Judah.' Forthwith: 'Hear, O Lord, the voice of Judah' (Deut. 33:7).

F. *"Each limb then entered its socket [and stopped rolling about].*

G. *"But they did not bring him up into the Torah session in the firmament.*

H. "[Moses then prayed], 'And bring him in to his people.'

I. *"But he could not follow the give and take of the argument [that rabbis were discussing concerning the law].*

J. "[Moses prayed]: 'With his hands let him contend for himself' (Deut. 33:7).

K. *"He had no tradition in hand pertinent to what was under discussion in the law.*

L. "[Moses prayed:] 'Be a help against his adversaries' (Deut. 33:7)."

5. Sources and Traditions: Types of Compositions in the Talmud of Babylonia

I said at the outset that the sources of the Bavli are those completed, available, and free-standing pieces of writing that the authors of the Bavli used when they wrote their book. The traditions of the Bavli are those composites and sustained discussions that the authors of the Bavli set forth in their writing. We have now seen that, while the Bavli contains a rather negligible proportion of sources that ignore the principal purpose of the document as a whole, it does present us with one type of source that demands considerable attention. The propositional composite on a stated problem, for example, "Is it all right for a person to take the law into his or her own hands?" cannot be dismissed as essentially tangential or even irrelevant to the Bavli's main concerns, as the four types of sources catalogued in the shank of the book can. These four, a sustained reading of sequential verses of Scripture, stories about sages, exposition of free-standing, individual verses, or proof of a proposition in no way relevant to the Mishnah or Mishnah exegesis, tell us that other kinds of documents and types of writing were under way. People wrote compositions that can have been collected, for example, in lives of sages, or in collections of Midrash compilations (in addition to the handful that we have in hand).

Whether the writing took place long before the formation of the Bavli or in the period of the compilation of the document makes little difference in our understanding of the character of the Bavli.[2] The reason

---

[2]I hasten to emphasize that merely because types of sources differ from one another, that does not mean one type must have been written before some other

is very simple. The Bavli contains so slight a proportion of these odds and ends that even if all of them were written prior to the writing of the Bavli, the document as we have it would still form a monument, in the end, principally to the mentality of its ultimate framers or authors or compositors. For whatever they picked or chose beyond their primary foci makes slight impact upon the document as a whole. But the sustained essay on a problem that clearly intersects with the Mishnah, draws upon its laws as cases, investigates principles fundamental to the formation and interpretation of the law of the Mishnah, and yet, abstract, systematic, and not framed by cases and their exegesis but by propositions and their exposition – that is a very different matter.

Here we really do need to work out a method to tell us whether the Bavli's truly important sources were composed within the process of the formulation and closure of the document as a whole or prior to that process. The reason is that the modes of thought represented by these remarkable compositions, their fundamental propositions, and their formidable role in the document as a whole – these marks of great minds engaged in a great enterprise attest to one thing or something else. That is to say, the Bavli is made up of sources that materially affected its formation and composition, or the Bavli's compositors also played the principal role in the formation of the main theoretical expression of the writing itself. How we define those compositors and their work, the way in which we characterize the literary history of the writing, and the role of prior and available sources in the document – these basic issues then will come to the fore as we address the problem of the Bavli's truly important sources.

So I think that the framers of the Bavli drew upon a variety of sources in the formation of their tradition. Most of these appear to have been trivial and to have played no important part in the shaping of the document. But, when, having done their own kind of writing, which was Mishnah commentary, analysis, expansion, and amplification, the framers of the Bavli filled out their document, it was with one kind of writing that vastly expanded the document, turning the exegesis of the Mishnah into something larger and more elegant than a commentary: an essay on the law behind the laws. As I said at the outset, as a matter of simple fact, the authorship of the Bavli augmented their main writing,

---

type. And even though the type of writing I have classified as the sustained inquiry into a legal or moral principle clearly differs from the type of writing I have classified as Mishnah exegesis and amplification, that does not mean that the two types of writings must have been undertaken in different periods. The same writer or writers can write in more than a single way or for more than a single purpose. So difference does not bear implications for the "dating" (or setting into priority, earlier, then later) of types of writing.

Mishnah commentary, with a different kind of writing altogether. That other kind of writing is so distinct from the sort that served for their principal purpose that it demands attention in its own terms. We now know what kinds of writing, other than those that formed the stuff of the document and quite different therefrom, were utilized in the framing of the Bavli, so we realize that there was one type of source that really did make a difference in the character of the document as a whole – therefore also in its consequences.

3

Agglutinative Miscellanies

The pages of the Talmud of Babylonia contain long stretches of apparently disorganized and disconnected writing, on one subject after another. In these miscellaneous entries we have the equivalent of paragraphs but none of those larger compositions of paragraphs setting forth sustained and connected arguments that in general characterize the Bavli. Partly because of these massive miscellanies, the Bavli appears to be disorganized or to adhere to no principle of arrangement that we can discern. If that were so, then the Bavli would radically diverge from the character of the other compilations that make up the canon of the Judaism of the Dual Torah in late antiquity. For prior writings commonly exhibit traits of order and coherence, and none comprises vast conglomerations of free-standing thoughts. None but the Bavli contains sizable sequences that exhibit the appearance of a mere scrapbook – this and that, haphazardly thrown together. Here we analyze these massive miscellanies, and I demonstrate that they adhere to rules of discourse that we can discern, rules that show miscellanies to be anything but miscellaneous and haphazard. In the end, we shall find, to the contrary, the miscellanies, adhering to rules of agglutinative, not propositional and syllogistic, discourse, serve as Mishnah commentaries, as much as do the cogent composites that predominate in the Bavli.

This seems to me to lay to rest the last shreds of the argument, so far as it is based on data, that the Bavli is disorganized or unorganized; that the document adheres to no clear principles of order and that it is really just this, that, and the other thing, all thrown together. Based on a profound misunderstanding of the document and revealing deep ignorance of all but the coherence of words and phrases into sentences and paragraphs, that opinion is broadly held and shows that, until now, the Bavli has really not been properly understood at all. Lest my claim prove implausible, I point to prior writings of mine, where I have extensively cited both received and contemporary statements of the theory that the Bavli is not a well-crafted and carefully edited document. In fact the Bavli is a commentary to the Mishnah, and in this final work of literary analysis, I take up the most intractable type of material – vast stretches of the Bavli that appear to be little more than miscellanies – and I now show that that, too, is little more than Mishnah commentary, of a rather special kind to be sure.

Two conflicting characteristics mark the Bavli, or Talmud of Babylonia. It is, first, a disciplined and well-organized, carefully crafted piece of writing. Most of the document is formulated in accord with a few simple rules, so that it is well organized and easily followed. The Bavli, viewed whole, is carefully set forth as a commentary to the Mishnah, and the vast majority of its composites are put together so as to elucidate the statements of the Mishnah. But in the pages of the Bavli we observe, second, very large composites, not formed into Mishnah commentaries at all. These composites do not follow the rules that govern the formation of the composites that serve as commentaries to the Mishnah. Mishnah commentaries proceed along orderly lines, treating a subject in a way that conforms to our logic, beginning with first things, moving onward, within the limits and logic of the subject, to more complex ones, ending then in subsidiary questions. But the miscellanies go from this to that to the other thing, and it is not easy to explain why one thing is joined to some other, or why one passage is presented before, or after, some other.

Not only so, but the large-scale aggregates to which I refer both have, and also give to the Bavli, when it is viewed by an undiscerning reader, a miscellaneous quality: this, that, the other thing, with no clear pattern or purpose much in evidence. These massive miscellanies – composites that on first glance seem to follow no clear rules of composition at all – are made up of a substantial number of free-standing compositions. They in no way serve the paramount purpose of the Bavli, which demonstrably is to explain the Mishnah. Whoever put the miscellanies together had a different program in mind. And if the framers of the miscellanies had in mind that they ultimately would be collected in a piece of writing of some dimensions, then that writing that they imagined bears no resemblance to the writing in which their miscellanies did end up, that is, the Bavli. In my book, *The Bavli's Massive Miscellanies*,[1] I set forth the rules of conglomeration and agglutination that govern the formation of these massive miscellanies and define the program that, in my view, governed the formation of the Bavli's miscellanies.

---

[1] Atlanta, 1992: Scholars Press for South Florida Studies in the History of Judaism.

Most of the Bavli is made up of extended exercises of Mishnah exegesis and amplification, with, first, exegesis of the Mishnah's language, rules, sources, and authority; and, second, secondary discussions of laws and principles of laws pertinent to a given Mishnah paragraph. These sustained passages, running on for many pages at a time, are remarkably cogent. Even though made up of diverse materials, ready-made and rarely recast or rewritten for the occasion, nearly everything in a given composite will relate in some way or another to the purpose of the composite as a whole; will contribute facts; will provide examples; will address secondary or subsidiary issues; or will otherwise carry forward the analytical, and even propositional, program of Mishnah exegesis that is realized in the entire composite.

But it is the simple fact that the Talmud of Babylonia is made up of large-scale composites of already completed compositions. To begin with, the document draws upon the already completed writing, the Mishnah, being organized to present the appearance of a commentary to that writing. Second, it cites passages of another already completed piece of writing, the Tosefta. Third, very commonly we are able to identify a single cogent statement, with its own beginning, middle, and end, and furthermore we readily distinguish that statement from a larger framework in which, whole and complete, it is set to serve some larger purpose. When I say that the Bavli is made up of composites of compositions, I mean that for the most part, the framers of the whole have made use of (some) already completed pieces of writing, setting them out in such a way as to serve a purpose not contemplated by the author(s) of the original compositions but rather a purpose clearly dictated by the analytical and propositional program of the framers of the Bavli itself. The distinction between composition and composite is fundamental.

To understand what I mean by a an agglutinative miscellany in the context of the Bavli, let me now set forth the traits of the document that, overall, classify the writing as anything but miscellaneous. Then the problem of the literary formations treated in these pages will become entirely clear. For until I have established that most of the Bavli follows easily discerned rules of composition and the formation of composites, and that these rules dictate the character of the document as a whole – a commentary to the Mishnah – my claim to identify and differentiate writing of a quite different character will not be fully understood. Since I propose not only to identify this other kind of writing, but also to define and explain the rules that dictate the making of those composites of the Bavli that serve a different purpose from Mishnah commentary, I had best begin with the norms of the document, and only then to turn to what is different from the normal but also, in its way, governed by reasons we can uncover.

The writers of the Talmud spoke in a single voice. Whatever its writers wished to say, they said in a single way. Viewed as a whole, the Talmud of Babylonia covers thirty-seven of the Mishnah's sixty-three tractates, and, in discussing these thirty-seven Mishnah tractates, the authorship of the Talmud speaks in a single way. A fixed rhetorical pattern and a limited program of logical inquiry governs throughout. Whatever authors wish to say, they say within a severely restricted repertoire of rhetorical choices, and the intellectual initiatives they are free to explore everywhere dictate one set of questions and problems and not any other. The document's "voice," then, comprises that monotonous and repetitious language, which conveys a recurrent and single melody. In the ancient and great centers of learning in which the Talmud of Babylonia is studied today, masters and their disciples – studying out loud and in dialogue with one another and with the text – commonly and correctly say, "the Talmud says...," (Yiddish: *zogt die gemara*; Hebrew: *hattalmud omeret*), meaning, the anonymous, uniform, ubiquitous voice of the document, speaking in the name of no one in particular and within an indeterminate context of space and time, makes a given statement or point. Through years of encounter with the document, within the conventions of centuries of study in continuing circles of learning, by reference to "the Talmud says," the masters express the result of innumerable observations of coherence, uniformity, and cogency. I represent their usage when I speak of "the Talmud's one voice." Why do I claim that the document may be read as a single coherent statement? The reason is that the document as a whole is cogent, doing some few things over and over again; it conforms to a few simple rules of rhetoric, including choice of languages for discrete purposes,[2] and that fact attests to the coherent viewpoint of the authorship at the end – the people who put it all together as we have it – because it speaks, overall, in a single way, in a uniform voice. It is not merely an encyclopaedia of information, but a sustained, remarkably protracted, uniform inquiry into the logical traits of passages of the Mishnah or of Scripture. Most of the Talmud deals with the exegesis and amplification of the Mishnah's rules or of passages of Scripture.

---

[2] I refer to *Language as Taxonomy. The Rules for Using Hebrew and Aramaic in the Babylonian Talmud* (Atlanta, 1990: Scholars Press for South Florida Studies in the History of Judaism). This work is made possible by my translation, which distinguishes between Hebrew and Aramaic by the use of plain and italic type. Then, quite graphically, how each language serves its own distinct, taxonomic purpose, that is, identifying the status and purpose of what is said in that language, is easily portrayed.

Wherever we turn, that labor of exegesis and amplification, without differentiation in topics or tractates, conforms to a few simple rules in inquiry, repeatedly phrased, implicitly or explicitly, in a few simple rhetorical forms or patterns.

The Bavli's one voice governs throughout, about a considerable repertoire of topics speaking within a single restricted rhetorical vocabulary. In the pages of *The Bavli's One Voice: Types and Forms of Analytical Discourse and Their Fixed Order of Appearance*,[3] that vocabulary – the limited repertoire of speech – is set forth through an inductive process, hence "the Bavli's one voice" refers to a remarkably limited set of intellectual initiatives, only this and that, initiatives that moreover always adhere to a single sequence or order: this first, then that – but never the other thing. I can identify the Bavli's authorships' rules of composition. These are not many. Not only so, but the order of types of compositions (written in accord with a determinate set of rules) itself follows a fixed pattern, so that a composition written in obedience to a given rule as to form will always appear in the same point in a sequence of compositions that are written in obedience to two or more rules: type A first, type B next, in fixed sequence. The Talmud's one voice then represents the outcome of the work of the following:

1. An author preparing a composition for inclusion in the Bavli would conform to one of a very few rules of thought and expression; and, more to the point,

2. A framer of a cogent composite, often encompassing a set of compositions, for presentation as the Bavli would follow a fixed order in selecting and arranging the types of consequential forms that authors had made available for his use.[4]

With a clear and specific account of the facts yielding that anticipated result, I shall be well justified in asking about the message of the rhetorical and logical method of the Bavli. The Talmud of Babylonia is made up of large-scale composites – completed units of discourse, with a beginning, middle, and end, which supply all of the data a reader (or

---

[3]Atlanta, 1991: Scholars Press for South Florida Studies in the History of Judaism.
[4]The distinction between composition and composite, which is fundamental to all that follows, is explained in *The Rules of Composition of the Talmud of Babylonia. The Cogency of the Bavli's Composite* (Atlanta, 1991: Scholars Press for South Florida Studies in the History of Judaism). And that distinction begins with my development of an analytical reference system, which makes possible the division of columns of undifferentiated words into much more than sentences, paragraphs, chapters, and the analytical re-presentation of undifferentiated words into their functional components: principal and subordinate. Here again, it would serve no useful purpose to go over familiar results.

listener) requires to understand the point that the framer of that composite wishes to make. A composite commonly draws upon available information, made available in part by prior and completed composites, for example, Scripture, the Mishnah, the Tosefta, and in part by compositions worked out entirely within their own limits, which we might compare with a paragraph of a chapter; or a free-standing composition of a few lines. By "rules of composition" I mean the laws that dictated to the framers of a cogent and coherent composite – such as I allege comprise the whole of the Talmud of Babylonia – precisely how to put together whatever they wished to say, together with the supporting evidence as well as argument, in the composition that they proposed to write. Here, then, "rules of composition" govern how people formed composites that comprise the Bavli: how they are classified, how they are ordered.

Now to set forth the results of the analysis of eleven tractates systematically treated in *The Bavli's One Voice.* It is the simple fact that the Bavli throughout speaks in a single and singular voice. It is single because it is a voice that expresses the same limited set of notes everywhere. It is singular because these notes are arranged in one and the same way throughout. The Bavli's one voice, sounding through all tractates, is the voice of exegetes of the Mishnah. The document is organized around the Mishnah, and that is not a merely formal, but a substantive order. At every point, if the framers have chosen a passage of Mishnah exegesis, that passage will stand at the head of all further discussion. Every turning point brings the editors back to the Mishnah, always read in its own order and sequence. So the Bavli speaks in a single way about some few things, and that is the upshot of my sustained inquiry. It follows that well-crafted and orderly rules governed the character of the sustained discourse that the writing in the Bavli sets forth. All framers of composites and editors of sequences of composites found guidance in the same limited repertoire of rules of analytical rhetoric: some few questions or procedures, directed always toward one and the same prior writing. Not only so, but a fixed order of discourse dictated that a composition of one sort, A, always comes prior to a composite of another type, B. A simple logic instructed framers of composites, who sometimes also were authors of compositions, and who sometimes drew upon available compositions in the making of their cogent composites. So we have now to see the Bavli as entirely of a piece, cogent and coherent, made up of well-composed large-scale constructions. It is coherent not only in its rules of the use of Hebrew and Aramaic, it is even more coherent in its rhetorical laws.

The Bavli's one voice utilizes only a few, well-modulated tones: a scale of not many notes. When we classify more than three thousand composites, spread over eleven tractates, we find that nearly 90 percent of the whole comprises Mishnah commentary of various kinds; not only so, but the variety of the types of Mishnah commentary is limited, as a review of the representation of Temurah in detail, and of the ten tractates of our sample in brief characterization, has shown. Cogent composites are further devoted to Scripture or to topics of a moral or theological character not closely tied to the exegesis of verses of Scripture; these form in the aggregate approximately 10 percent of the whole number of composites, but, of tractates, to begin with, not concerned with scriptural or theological topics (in our sample these are Sanhedrin and Berakhot), they make up scarcely 3 percent of the whole. So the Bavli has one voice, and it is the voice of a person or persons who propose to speak about one document and to do so in some few ways. Let me spell out precisely what I mean. The results of the survey of eleven tractates and classification of all of the composites of each one of them yields firm and one-sided results.

First, we are able to classify all composites in three principal categories: [1] exegesis and amplification of the law of the Mishnah; [2] exegesis and exposition of verses of, or topics in, Scripture; [3] free-standing composites devoted to topics other than those defined by the Mishnah or Scripture. That means that my initial proposal of a taxonomic system left no lacunae.

Second, with the classification in place, much more than four-fifths of all composites of the Bavli address the Mishnah and systematically expound that document. These composites are subject to sub-classification in two ways: Mishnah exegesis and speculation and abstract theorizing about the implications of the Mishnah's statements. The former type of composite, further, is to be classified in a few and simple taxa, for example, composites organized around [1] clarification of the statements of the Mishnah; [2] identification of the authority behind an anonymous statement in the Mishnah; [3] scriptural foundation for the Mishnah's rules; [4] citation and not seldom systematic exposition of the Tosefta's amplification of the Mishnah. That means that most of the Bavli is a systematic exposition of the Mishnah.

Third, the other fifth (or less) of a given tractate will comprise composites that take shape around [1] Scripture or [2] themes or topics of a generally theological or moral character. Distinguishing the latter from the former, of course, is merely formal; very often a scriptural topic will be set forth in a theological or moral framework, and very seldom does a composite on a topic omit all reference to the amplification of a verse or topic of Scripture. The proportion of a given tractate devoted to other-than-Mishnah exegesis and amplification is generally not more than 10 percent. I have demonstrated beyond any reasonable doubt that the

Talmud speaks through one voice, that voice of logic that with vast assurance reaches into our own minds and by asking the logical and urgent next question tells us what we should be thinking. Fixing our attention upon the Mishnah, the Talmud's rhetoric seduces us into joining its analytical inquiry, always raising precisely the question that should trouble us (and that would trouble us if we knew all of the pertinent details as well as the Talmud does). The Bavli speaks about the Mishnah in essentially a single voice, about fundamentally few things. Its mode of speech as much as of thought is uniform throughout. Diverse topics produce slight differentiation in modes of analysis. The same sorts of questions phrased in the same rhetoric – a moving, or dialectical, argument, composed of questions and answers – turn out to pertain equally well to every subject and problem. The Talmud's discourse forms a closed system, in which people say the same thing about everything. The fact that the Talmud speaks in a single voice supplies striking evidence [1] that the Talmud does speak in particular for the age in which its units of discourse took shape, and [2] that that work was done toward the end of that long period of Mishnah reception that began at the end of the second century and came to an end at the conclusion of the sixth century.

When I speak of the Bavli's one voice, as now is clear, I mean to say it everywhere speaks uniformly, consistently, and predictably. The voice is the voice of a book. The message is one deriving from a community, the collectivity of sages for whom and to whom the book speaks. The document seems, in the main, to intend to provide notes, an abbreviated script which anyone may use to reconstruct and reenact formal discussions of problems: about this, one says that. Curt and often arcane, these notes can be translated only with immense bodies of inserted explanation. All of this script of information is public and undifferentiated, not individual and idiosyncratic. We must assume people took for granted that, out of the signs of speech, it would be possible for anyone to reconstruct speech, doing so in accurate and fully conventional ways. So the literary traits of the document presuppose a uniform code of communication: a single voice.

So it is time to ask the purpose of that composition: what the authors, authorships, or framers of the document wished to say through the writing that they have given us. If there is a single governing method, then what can we expect to learn about the single, repeated message? The evidence before us indicates that the purpose of the Talmud is to clarify and amplify selected passages of the Mishnah. We may say very simply that the Mishnah is about life, and the Talmud is about the Mishnah. That is to say, while the Mishnah records rules governing the conduct of the holy life of Israel, the holy people, the Talmud concerns itself with the details of the Mishnah. The one is descriptive and free-standing, the other analytical and contingent. Were there no Mishnah, there would be no Talmud. But what is the message of the method, which is to insist upon the Mishnah's near monopoly over serious discourse? To begin with, the very character of the Talmud tells us the sages' view of the Mishnah. The Mishnah presented itself to them as constitutive, the text of ultimate concern. So, in our instance, the Mishnah speaks of a quarrel over a coat, the Talmud, of the Mishnah's provision of an oath as a means of settling the quarrel in a fair way: substance transformed into process. What the framers of the Bavli wished to say about the Mishnah will guide us toward the definition of the message of their method, but it will not tell us what that message was, or why it was important. A long process of close study of texts is required to guide us toward the center of matters. The upshot is simple. We may speak about "the Talmud," its voice, its purposes, its mode of constructing a view of the Israelite world. The reason is that, when we claim "the Talmud" speaks, we replicate both the main lines of chronology and the literary character of the document. These point toward the formation of the bulk of materials – its units of discourse – in a process lasting (to take a guess) about half a century, prior to the ultimate arrangement of these units of discourse around passages of the Mishnah and the closure and redaction of the whole into the document we now know. What comes next? Well, now that we know that the Bavli is a document of remarkable integrity, repeatedly insisting upon the harmony of the parts within a whole and unitary structure of belief and behavior, we want to know what the Bavli says: the one thing that is repeated in regard to many things. Dismantling ("deconstructing") its components and identifying them, perhaps even describing the kinds of compilations that the authors of those components can have had in mind in writing their compositions – these activities of literary criticism yield no insight into the religious system that guided the document's framers. But the Talmud of Babylonia recapitulates, in grand and acute detail, a religious system, and the generative problematic of that writing directs our attention not to the aesthetics of writing as literature, but to the religion of writing as a document of faith in the formation of the social order.

Our task is to find out [1] just what principles do explain how one thing is joined to the next, [2] why many things are joined all together, and [3] what all this has to do with the Mishnah. At this preliminary stage in my argument, however, I do think I have validated these conclusions:

1. In the miscellany before us, do we identify the first-class, cogent exposition of a proposition? Not at all. Is there the sustained consideration of a given problem? No again.

2. But is it a mere miscellany – disorganized, pointless, a scrapbook of one thing and another? Hardly. And that is the point of this essay.

Well, then, if not exactly a miscellany, but also not a composite of the kind that predominates in the Bavli in its exposition of the Mishnah, then what do we have? This brief account has raised more questions than it has settled. The main point must not be lost. The Bavli contains important composites that differ in their redactional, rhetorical, topical, and logical traits from its paramount composites. Compared to the dominant type of composite, the one that serves as Mishnah commentary and amplification, these other composites exhibit a miscellaneous quality. The real issue is whether before us are anomalies, and for that purpose, we shall have to ask not only whether we deal with miscellanies, viewed in their own terms, but whether or not we confront anomalies, viewed in the context of the chapters that contain them. So let us examine three important composites and see [1] how they hold together, [2] what place they make for themselves in the context of the chapters in which they occur, and [3] how, if at all, the composites or miscellaneous type of composite proposes to expand our understanding of the Mishnah. Three chapters suffice, two that we already have identified in the context of their tractates, Berakhot and Sanhedrin, respectively, and one chosen more or less at random.

Let me now examine one massive miscellany and show how it works. It derives from Bavli Abodah Zarah Chapter One. In the context of this long and important chapter, we have a variety of miscellanies. We shall address the chapter as a whole, first of all asking in context of the individual entries [1] how they hold together, and second, forming a theory, in the setting of the entire chapter, concerning [2] what place the miscellanies make for themselves in the context of the chapters in which they occur. I shall restrict my comments to the issue of how the miscellanies cohere, what principle has guided the compiler of discrete compositions in linking one with another, in the order before us and not in some other. A full exposition of the chapter as a whole is in my *The Talmud of Babylonia. An American Translation.* Atlanta, 1991: Scholars Press for Brown Judaic Studies. XXV.A. *Tractate Abodah Zarah. Chapters One and Two.* To highlight the composites that I regard as miscellanies, I indent those entires at both margins, leaving at the normal margins both the Mishnah and the portion of the Talmud devoted to the exposition of the Mishnah and its principles. I further indent what I regard as footnotes or appendices to principal components of the Bavli's composite. This further clarifies the character of the document before us.

Abodah Zarah 1:1

A. [2A] **Before the festivals of gentiles for three days it is forbidden to do business with them.**

B. **(1) To lend anything to them or to borrow anything from them.**

C. **(2) To lend money to them or to borrow money from them.**

D. **(3) To repay them or to be repaid by them.**

E. **R. Judah says, "They accept repayment from them, because it is distressing to him."**

F. **They said to him, "Even though it is distressing to him now, he will be happy about it later."**

I.1 A. [2A] Rab and Samuel [in dealing with the reading of the key word of the Mishnah, translated festival, the letters of which are 'aleph daled, rather than 'ayin daled, which means, calamity]:

B. *One repeated the formulation of the Mishnah as, "their festivals."*

C. *And the other repeated the formulation of the Mishnah as "their calamities."*

D. *The one who repeated the formulation of the Mishnah as "their festivals" made no mistake, and the one who repeated the formulation of the Mishnah as "their calamities" made no mistake.*

E. *For it is written, "For the day of their calamity is at hand" (Deut. 32:15).*

F. *The one who repeated the formulation of the Mishnah as "their festivals" made no mistake, for it is written, "Let them bring their testimonies that they may be justified" (Isa. 43:9).*

G. *And as to the position of him who repeats the formulation of the Mishnah as "their festivals," on what account does he not repeat the formulation of the Mishnah to yield, "their calamities"?*

H. *He will say to you, "'Calamity' is preferable [as the word choice when speaking of idolatry]."*

I. *And as to the position of him who repeats the formulation of the Mishnah as "their calamities," on what account does he not repeat the formulation of the Mishnah to yield "their festivals"?*

J. *He will say to you, "What causes the calamity that befalls them if not their testimony, so testimony is preferable!"*

K. *And as to the verse, "Let them bring their testimonies that they may be justified" (Isa. 43:9), is this written with reference to gentiles? Lo, it is written in regard to Israel.*

L. For said R. Joshua b. Levi, "All of the religious duties that Israelites carry out in this world come and give testimony in their behalf in the world to come: 'Let them bring their witnesses that they may be justified' (Isa. 43:9), that is, Israel; 'and let them hear and say, It is truth' (Isa. 43:9) – this refers to gentiles."

M. Rather, said R. Huna b. R. Joshua, "He who formulates the Mishnah to refer to their calamities derives the reading from this verse: 'They that fashion a graven image are all of them vanity, and their delectable things shall not profit, and their own witnesses see not nor know' (Isa. 44:9)."

The composite begins with a very long, but coherent exposition of a single theme, which is, God's judgment of the nations. Nos. 2-4 are given on pp. 82-87, and my discussion refers back to those pages. No. 2 holds together rather well, once we realize that it is heavily footnoted. I further indent the footnoted materials of that glossed composition. If we regard the deeply indented materials as footnotes and appendices, attached for thematic reasons, then we can see Nos. 1-4 as an entirely coherent statement, a composite to be sure, but in no way a miscellany. Having examined that set and seen the clear connections between one composition and the next, on the one side, and the coherent character of the whole (with its footnotes and appendix), on the other, we are now ready to look at the miscellany that follows and to ask ourselves how each entry is linked to what is juxtaposed to it, fore and aft. If I had to find a rational explanation for putting No. 5 in at all, it is because it addresses the theme of study of Torah, to which No. 4 has made reference.

I.5   A.   Said R. Levi, "To whoever stops studying the words of the Torah and instead takes up words of mere chatter they feed glowing coals of juniper: 'They pluck salt-wort with wormwood and the roots of juniper are their food' (Job 30:4)."

          B.   Said R. Simeon b. Laqish, "For whoever engages in study of the Torah by night – the Holy One, blessed be He, draws out the thread of grace by day: 'By day the Lord will command his lovingkindness, and in the night his song shall be with me' (Ps. 42:9). Why is it that 'By day the Lord will command his lovingkindness'? Because 'in the night his song shall be with me.'"

          C.   *Some say*, said R. Simeon b. Laqish, "For whoever engages in study of the Torah in this world, which is like the night – the Holy One, blessed be He, draws out the thread of grace in the world to come, which is like the day: 'By day the Lord will command his lovingkindness, and in the night his song shall be with me' (Ps. 42:9). [Supply: Why is it that 'By day the Lord will command his lovingkindness'? Because 'in the night his song shall be with me.']"

The sustaining character of study of the Torah, No. 5, explains the relevance of the composition of No. 6.

I.6   A.   Said R. Judah said Samuel, "*What is the meaning of the verse of Scripture*, 'And you make man as the fish of the sea and as the creeping things, that have no ruler over them' (Hab. 1:14)? Why are human beings compared to fish of the sea? To tell you, just as fish in the sea, when they come up on dry land, forthwith begin to die, so with human beings, when they take their leave of teachings of the Torah and religious deeds, forthwith they begin to die.

          B.   "Another matter: Just as the fish of the sea, as soon as dried by the sun, die, so human beings, when struck by the sun, die."

C. *If you want, this refers to this world, and if you want, this refers to the world to come.*

D. *If you want, this refers to this world, in line with that which R. Hanina [said],* for said R. Hanina, "Everything is in the hands of Heaven except cold and heat: 'cold and heat boils are in the way of the froward, he who keeps his soul holds himself far from them' (Prov. 22:5)."

E. *And if you want, this refers to the world to come, in accord with that which was stated by R. Simeon b. Laqish.* For said R. Simeon b. Laqish, "In the world to come, there is no Gehenna, but rather, the Holy One, blessed be He, brings the sun out of its sheath and he heats the wicked but heals the righteous through it. The wicked are brought to judgment by [4A] it: 'For behold, the days comes, it burns as a furnace, and all the proud and all who do wicked things shall be stubble, and the day that comes shall set them ablaze, says the Lord of hosts, that it shall leave them neither root nor branch' (Mal. 3:19).

F. "'It shall leave them neither root' – in this world; 'nor branch' – in the world to come.

G. "But heals the righteous through it': 'But to you that fear my name shall the sun of righteousness arise with healing in its wings' (Mal. 3:20). They will revel in it: 'And you shall go forth and gambol as calves of the stall' (Mal. 3:20)."

H. [Continuing C, above:] "Another matter: Just as with the fish of the sea, whoever is bigger than his fellow swallows his fellow, so in the case of human beings, were it not for fear of the government, whoever is bigger than his fellow would swallow his fellow."

I. *That is in line with what we have learned in the Mishnah:* R. Hananiah, Prefect of the Priests, says, "Pray for the welfare of the government. For if it were not for fear of it, one man would swallow his fellow alive" [M. Abot 3:2A-B].

The foregoing has mentioned the theme of Gehenna and the world to come, and we shall now pursue that theme, now the contrast between Gehenna and the world to come, the gentiles and Israel, God's anger and God's grace. No. 7 contrasts the time of judgment and the time of God's war against his enemies; No. 8 then deals with the anger of God with the gentiles; Nos. 9, 10 with God's destruction.

I.7 A. *R. Hinena bar Pappa contrasted verses of Scripture:* "It is written, 'As to the Almighty, we do not find him exercising plenteous power' (Job 37:23), but by contrast, 'Great is our Lord and of abundant power' (Ps. 147:5), and further, 'Your right hand, Lord, is glorious in power' (Ex. 15:6).

B. "But there is no contradiction between the first and second and third statements, for the former speaks of the time of judgment [when justice is tempered with mercy, so God does not do what he could] and the latter two statements refer to a time of war [of God against his enemies]."

I.8   A.   *R. Hama bar Hanina contrasted verses of Scripture: "it is written, 'Fury is not in me' (Isa. 27:4) but also 'The Lord revenges and is furious' (Nah. 1:2).*

      B.   *"But there is no contradiction between the first and second statements,* for the former speaks of Israel, the latter of the gentiles."

      C.   R. Hinena bar Pappa said, "'Fury is not in me' (Isa. 27:4), for I have already taken an oath: 'would that I had not so vowed, then as the briars and thorns in flame would I with one step burn it altogether' (Isa. 27:4)."

I.9   A.   *That is in line with what R. Alexandri said, "What is the meaning of the verse,* 'And it shall come to pass on that day that I will seek to destroy all the nations' (Zech. 12:9) –

      B.   "'Seek' – seek permission from whom?

      C.   "Said the Holy One, blessed be He, 'I shall seek in the records that deal with them, to see whether there is a cause of merit, on account of which I shall redeem them, but if not, I shall destroy them.'"

I.10   A.   *That is in line with what Raba said, "What is the meaning of the verse,* 'Howbeit he will not stretch out a hand for a ruinous heap though they cry in his destruction' (Job 30:24)?

      B.   "Said the Holy One, blessed be He, to Israel, 'When I judge Israel, I shall not judge them as I do the gentiles, for it is written, "I will overturn, overturn, overturn it" (Ezek. 21:32), rather, I shall exact punishment from them as a hen pecks.'

      C.   "Another matter: 'Even if the Israelites do not carry out a religious duty before me more than a hen pecking at a rubbish heap, I shall join together [all the little pecks] into a great sum: "although they pick little they are saved" (Job 30:24) [following Mishcon's rendering].'

      D.   "Another matter: 'As a reward for their crying out to me, I shall help them' (Job 30:24) [following Mishcon's rendering]."

The sequence of compositions on the same theme, God's judgment, this world and the world to come, suffering in this world so as to enjoy the world to come, Israel's suffering in this world and its enjoyment of the world to come, goes on through Nos. 11, 12, 13, 14. Then there is a set on God's anger. The movement is imperceptible, since No. 15 simply refers to God's anger in the context of judgment. But forthwith, at No. 16, we move into the theme of divine anger, and that sets us off in a slightly different direction from the one that we have followed up to now.

I.12   A.   *That is in line with what R. Abba said, "What is the meaning of the verse,* 'Though I would redeem them, yet they have spoken lies against me' (Hos. 7:23)? 'I said that I would redeem them through [inflicting a penalty] on their property in this world, so that they might have the merit of enjoying the world to come, "yet they have spoken lies against me" (Hos. 7:23).'"

I.12   A.   *That is in line with what R. Pappi in the name of Raba said, "What is the meaning of the verse,* 'Though I have trained [and] strengthened their arms, yet they imagine mischief against me' (Hos. 7:15)?

B.   Said the Holy One, blessed be He, I thought that I would punish them with suffering in this world, so that their arm might be strengthened in the world to come, "yet they have spoken lies against me" (Hos. 7:23).'"

I.13   A.   *R. Abbahu praised R. Safra to the* minim [in context: Christian authorities of Caesarea], *saying that he was* a highly accomplished authority. *They therefore remitted his taxes for thirteen years.*

B.   *One day they came upon him and said to him,* "It is written, 'You only have I known among all the families of the earth; therefore I will visit upon you all your iniquities' (Amos 3:2). *If one is angry, does he vent it on someone he loves?"*

C.   *He fell silent and said nothing at all. They wrapped a scarf around his neck and tortured him. R. Abbahu came along and found them. He said to them, "Why are you torturing him?"*

D.   *They said to him, "Didn't you tell us that he is* a highly accomplished authority, *but he does not know how to explain this verse!"*

E.   *He said to them, "True enough, I told you that he was a master of Tannaite statements, but did I say anything at all to you about his knowledge of Scripture?"*

F.   *They said to him, "So how come you know?"*

G.   *He said to them, "Since we, for our part, spend a lot of time with you, we have taken the task of studying it thoroughly, while others [in Babylonia, Safra's place of origin] do not study [Scripture] that carefully."*

H.   *They said to him, "So tell us."*

I.   He said to them, "I shall tell you a parable. To what is the matter comparable? To the case of a man who lent money to two people, one a friend, the other an enemy. From the friend he collects the money little by little, from the enemy he collects all at once."

I.14   A.   *Said R. Abba bar Kahana, "What is the meaning of the following verse of Scripture:* 'Far be it from you to do after this manner, to slay the righteous with the wicked' (Gen. 18:25).

B.   "Said Abraham before the Holy One, blessed be He, 'Lord of the world! It is a profanation to act in such a way [a play on the Hebrew letters, shared by the words 'far be it' and 'profanation'], 'to slay the righteous with the wicked' (Gen. 18:25)."

C.   But is it not [so that God might do just that]? And is it not written, "And I will cut off from you the righteous and the wicked" (Ezek. 21:8)?

D.   That speaks of one who is not completely righteous, but not of one who is completely righteous.

E.   And will he not do so to one who is completely righteous? And is it not written, "And begin the slaughter with my sanctuary" (Ezek. 9:6), in which connection R. Joseph repeated as a Tannaite version, "Read not 'with my sanctuary' but rather, 'with those who are holy to me,' namely, the ones who carried out the Torah beginning to end."

F.   *There, too,* since they had the power to protest against the wickedness of the others and did not do so, they were not regarded as completely righteous at all.

I.15   A.   *R. Pappa contrasted verses of Scripture: "It is written, 'God is angry every day' (Ps. 7:12) but also 'who could stand before his anger' (Nah. 1:6).*

        B.   *"But there is no contradiction between the first and second statements,* for the former speaks of the individual, the latter of the community."

The reference to God's anger, No. 16, marks an imperceptible movement to a new theme, namely Balaam, the prophet of the gentiles. Balaam then forms the unifying theme for Nos. 17-19. Because I regard these as footnote entries, I indent them.

I.16   A.   *Our rabbis have taught on Tannaite authority:*

        B.   "God is angry every day" (Ps. 7:12), and how long is his anger? It is for a moment. And how long is a moment? The portion 1/53,848th of an hour is a moment.

        C.   And no creature can determine that moment, except for Balaam that wicked man, of whom it is written, [5A] "who knew the knowledge of the Most High" (Num. 24:16).

        D.   How can it be that a man who did not know the mind of his animal could have known the mind of the Most High?

I.17   A.   *And what is the meaning of the statement that* he did not know the mind of his animal?

        B.   *When they saw him riding on his ass, they said to him, "How come you're not riding on a horse?"*

        C.   *He said to them, "I sent it to the meadow."*

        D.   Forthwith: "The ass said, Am I not your ass" (Num. 22:30).

        E.   *He said to it, "Just as a beast of burden in general."*

        F.   *She said to him, "Upon whom you have ridden" (Num. 22:30).*

        G.   *He said to it, "Only from time to time."*

        H.   *She said to him,* "ever since I was yours {Num. 22:30). And not only so, but I serve you for riding by day and fucking by night."

        I.   For here the word "I was wont" is used, and the same letters bear the meaning of bed mate: "...and she served him as a bed mate" (1 Kgs. 1:2).

I.18   A.   *And what is the meaning of the statement that* he could have known the mind of the Most High?

        B.   For he knew precisely that moment at which the Holy One, blessed be He, was angry.

        C.   *That is in line with what the prophet had said to them,* "O my people, remember now what Balak king of Moab consulted and what Balaam son of Beor answered him from Shittim to Gilgal, that you may know the righteousness of the Lord" (Mic. 6:5).

I.19   A.   ["O my people, remember now what Balak king of Moab consulted and what Balaam son of Beor answered him from Shittim to Gilgal, that you may know the righteousness of the Lord" (Mic. 6:5)]:

        B.   Said R. Eleazar, "Said the Holy One, blessed be He, to Israel, 'My people, see how many acts of righteousness I

> carried out with you, for I did not grow angry with you
> during all those [perilous] days, for if I had grown angry
> with you, there would not have remained from Israel a
> remnant or a survivor.'

C.   "And that is in line with what Balaam says: 'How can I
curse seeing that God does not curse, and how can I be
wrathful, seeing that the Lord has not been wrathful?'
(Num. 23:8)."

We now realize that Nos. 17-19 form a protracted footnote to No. 16, for No. 20 will return us to the theme broken off at No. 16, namely, God's anger. The composite that follows, Nos. 20-23, is held together by that theme.

I.20   A.   And how long is his wrath? It is for a moment. And how long is a
moment? The portion 1/53,848th of an hour is a moment.

B.   And how long is a moment?

C.   Said Amemar – others say, Rabina – "So long as it takes to say the
word 'moment.'"

D.   *And how on the basis of Scripture do we know that his wrath lasts for only
a moment?*

E.   *As it is written,* "For his anger is for a moment, his favor is for a
lifetime" (Ps. 30:6).

F.   *If you prefer:* "Hide yourself for a brief moment, until the wrath be
past" (Isa. 26:20).

I.21   A.   *When is he angry?*

B.   *Said Abbayye, "In the first three hours of the day, when the comb of the
cock is white."*

C.   *Isn't it white all the rest of the day?*

D.   *At other times it has red streaks, but then it has none.*

I.22   A.   *R. Joshua b. Levi – a certain* min *would bother him about verses of
Scripture. Once he took a chicken and put it between the legs of the bed
and watched it. He reasoned, "When that hour comes, I shall curse him."*

B.   *But when that hour came, he was dozing. He said, "What you learn from
this experience is that it is not correct to act in such a way: 'His tender
mercies are over all his works' (Ps. 145:9), 'Neither is it good for the
righteous to inflict punishment' (Prov. 17:26)."*

I.23   A.   *It was taught as a Tannaite version in the name of R. Meir,* "[That time
at which God gets angry comes] when the kings put on their
crowns on their heads and prostrate themselves to the sun.
Forthwith the Holy One, blessed be He, grows angry."

Once again we are at a borderline between one set and another, and once more, the movement is subtle. We have just now referred to times at which God is angry, and times at which he is merciful. God is particularly angry, No. 23, when the kings put their crowns on their heads and worship the sun; No. 24 completes this composite, a different but related distinction between the time to pray and the time not to pray.

I.24   A.   *Said R. Joseph, "A person should not recite the Prayer of the Additional Service for the first day of the New Year [the Day of Judgment] during the first three hours of the day or in private, lest, since that is the time of judgment, his deeds may be examined, and his prayer rejected."*

       B.   *If so, then the prayer of the community also should not be recited at that time?*

       C.   *The merit [accruing to the community as a whole] is greater.*

       D.   *If so, then that of the Morning Service also should not be recited in private?*

       E.   *Since at that time the community also will be engaged in reciting the Morning Prayer, the individual's recitation of the Prayer will not be rejected.*

       F.   *But have you not said,* "In the first three hours the Holy One, blessed be He, goes into session and engages in study of the Torah; in the second he goes into session and judges the entire world"?

       G.   *Reverse the order.*

       H.   *Or, if you prefer, actually do not reverse the order.* For when God is occupied with study of the Torah, called by Scripture "truth" as in "buy the truth and do not sell it" (Prov. 23:23), the Holy One, blessed be He, in any event will not violate the strict rule of justice. But when engaged in judgment, which is not called "truth" by Scripture, the Holy One, blessed be He, may step across the line of strict justice [towards mercy].

No. 25 is going to direct our attention way back to 2.RR. What we have, then, is a massive appendix to that reference, once that was formed in its own terms and is coherent around its own theme. That theme is the religious deeds and duties carried out by Israel, and how these will be rewarded not now but in the world to come. No. 26 introduces David's sin in the context of this discussion, explicitly referring back to No. 25. Then, Nos. 26-27, we pursue a composite devoted to David.

I.25   A.   Reverting to the body of the prior text:

       B.   *R. Joshua b. Levi has said, "What is the meaning of the verse of Scripture, 'The ordinances that I command you this day to do them' (Deut. 7:11)?* Today is the day to do them, but not tomorrow; they are not to be done tomorrow; today is the day to do them, but today is not the day on which to receive a reward for doing them":

       C.   Said R. Joshua b. Levi, "All the religious duties that Israelites do in this world come and give evidence in their behalf in the world to come: 'Let them bring their witnesses that they may be justified, let them hear and say it is truth."

       D.   "Let them bring their witnesses that they may be justified": This is Israel.

       E.   "Let them hear and say it is truth": This refers to the gentiles.

       F.   And said R. Joshua b. Levi, "All the religious duties that Israelites do in this world come and flap about the faces of gentiles in the world to come: 'Keep therefore and do them, for this, your wisdom and understanding, will be in the eyes of the peoples' (Deut. 4:6).

G.   "What is stated here is not 'in the presence of the peoples' but 'in the eyes of the peoples,' which teaches you that they will come and flap about the faces of gentiles in the world to come."

H.   And said R. Joshua b. Levi, "The Israelites made the golden calf only to give an opening to penitents: 'O that they had such a heart as this always, to fear me and keep my commandments' (Deut. 5:26)."

I.26   A.   That is in line with what R. Yohanan said in the name of R. Simeon b. Yohai: "David was really not so unfit as to do such a deed [as he did with Beth Sheva]: 'My heart is slain within me' (Ps. 109:22). [Mishcon: David's inclinations had been completely conquered by himself.] And the Israelites were hardly the kind of people to commit such an act: "O that they had such a heart as this always, to fear me and keep my commandments' (Deut. 5:26). So why did they do it?

B.   [5A] "It was to show you that if an individual has sinned, they say to him, 'Go to the individual [such as David, and follow his example], and if the community as a whole has sinned, they say to them, 'Go to the community [such as Israel].'

C.   *And it was necessary to give both examples. For had we been given the rule governing the individual, that might have been supposed to be because his personal sins were not broadly known, but in the case of the community, the sins of which will be broadly known, I might have said that that is not the case.*

D.   *And if we had been given the rule governing the community, that might have been supposed to be the case because they enjoy greater mercy, but an individual, who has not got such powerful zekhut, might have been thought not subject to the rule.*

E.   *So both cases had to be made explicit.*

I.27   A.   *That is in line with what R. Samuel bar Nahmani said R. Jonathan said, "What is the meaning of the verse of Scripture, 'The saying of David, son of Jesse, and the saying of the man raised on high' (2 Sam. 23:1)?*

B.   "It means, 'The saying of David, son of Jesse, the man who raised up the yoke of repentance.'"

No. 28 brings us back to the general theme of doing a good deed in this world and enjoying the result in the world to come. That theme spills over into No. 29.

I.28   A.   Said R. Samuel bar Nahmani said R. Jonathan, "Whoever does a religious duty in this world – that deed goes before him to the world to come, as it is said, 'And your righteousness shall go before you' (Isa. 58:8).

B.   "And whoever commits a transgression in this world – that act turns aside from him and goes before him on the Day of Judgment, as it is said, 'The paths of their way are turned aside, they go up into the waste and perish' (Job 6:18)."

C.   R. Eliezer says, "It attaches to him like a dog, as it is said, 'He did not listen to her to lie by her or to be with her' (Gen. 39:10).

D.   "'To lie by her' in this world.

E.   "'Or to be with her' in the world to come."

I.29   A.   Said R. Simeon b. Laqish, "Come and let us express our gratitude to our ancestors, for if it were not for their having sinned, we for our part should never have been able to come into the world: 'I said you are gods and all of you sons of the Most High' (Ps. 82:6). Now that you have ruined things by what you have done: 'You shall indeed die like mortals' (Ps. 82:6)."

B.   *Does that statement then bear the implication, therefore, that if they had not sinned, they would not have propagated? But has it not been written,* "And you, be fruitful and multiply" (Gen. 9:7)?

C.   *That applies up to Sinai.*

D.   *But in connection with Sinai it also is written,* "Go say to them, Go back to your tents" (Ex. 19:15), *meaning, to marital relationships. And is it not also written,* "that it might be well with them and with their children" (Deut. 5:26)?

E.   That speaks only to those who were actually present at Mount Sinai.

F.   *But has not R. Simeon b. Laqish stated,* "What is the meaning of that which is written: 'This is the book of the generations of Adam' (Gen. 5:1)? Now did the first Adam have a book? The statement, rather, teaches that the Holy One, blessed be He, showed to the first Adam each generation and its authoritative expositors, each generations and its sages, each generation and those that administered its affairs. When he came to the generation of R. Aqiba, he rejoiced in the master's Torah but he was saddened by the master's death.

G.   "He said, 'How precious are your thoughts to me, O God' (Ps. 139:17)."

H.   And said R. Yosé, "The son of David will come only when all of the souls that are stored up in the body will be used up: 'For I will not contend for ever, neither will I be always angry, for from me proceeds the spirit, and I have made the breath of life' (Isa. 57:16)." [Mishcon: In the face of the foregoing teachings, how could it be stated that had it not been for the sin of the golden calf, we should not have come into the world?]

I.   *Do not, therefore, imagine that the sense of the statement is, we should have not come into the world* [if our ancestors had not sinned], *but rather, it would have been as though we had not come into the world.*

J.   *Does that then bear the implication that, if they had not sinned, they would never have died? But have not the passages been written that deal with the deceased childless brother's widow and the chapters about inheritances* [which take for granted that people die]?

K.   These passages are written conditionally [meaning, if people sin and so die, then the rules take effect, but it is not necessary that they take effect unless that stipulation is fulfilled].

L.   *And are there then any verses of Scripture that are stated conditionally?*

M.   *Indeed so, for said R. Simeon b. Laqish,* "What is the meaning of that which has been written, 'And it was evening and it was morning, the sixth day' (Gen. 1:31)? This teaches that the Holy One, blessed be He, made a stipulation with the works of creation and said, 'If the

            Israelites accept the Torah, well and good, but if not, I shall send you back to the condition of formlessness and void."

N.   *An objection was raised:* "O that they had such a heart as this always, to fear me and keep my commandments, that it may be well with them and their children" (Deut. 5:26): It is not possible to maintain that the meaning here is that he would take away the angel of death from them, for the decree had already been made. It means that the Israelites accepted the Torah only so that no nation or tongue would rule over them: "That it might be well with them and their children after them." [Mishcon: How could R. Simeon b. Laqish hold that but for the golden calf worship Israel would have enjoyed physical deathlessness?]

O.   *[R. Simeon b. Laqish] made his statement in accord with the position of this Tannaite authority, for it has been taught on Tannaite authority:*

P.   R. Yosé says, "The Israelites accepted the Torah only so that the angel of death should not have power over them: 'I said you are gods and all of you sons of the Most High. Now that you have ruined things by what you have done 'you shall indeed die like mortals' (Ps. 82:6)."

Q.   *But to R. Yosé also must be addressed the question, has it not been written,* "O that they had such a heart as this always, to fear me and keep my commandments, that it may be well with them and their children" (Deut. 5:26)? *Goodness is what is promised, but there still will be death!*

R.   *R. Yosé will say to you, "If there is no death, what greater goodness can there ever be?"*

S.   *And the other Tannaite authority – how does he read the phrase, "You shall indeed die"?*

T.   *The sense of "death" here is* "poverty," for a master has said, "Four classifications of persons are equivalent to corpses, and these are they: the poor man, the blind man, the person afflicted with the skin disease [of Lev. 13], and the person who has no children.

U.   "The poor man, as it is written: 'For all the men are dead who sought your life' (Ex. 4:19). *Now who were they? This refers to Dathan and Abiram, and they were certainly not then dead,* they had only lost all their money.

V.   "The blind man, as it is written: 'He has made me dwell in darkness as those that have been long dead' (Lam. 3:6).

W.   "The person afflicted with the skin disease, as it is written: 'Let her, I pray you, not be as one who is dead' (Num. 12:12).

X.   "And the person who has no children, as it is written: 'Give me children or else I die' (Gen. 30:1)."

A new composite of compositions now commences. No. 30 begins with reference to Israel's sin. The connection to No. 29, so far as I can see, is simple. We have dealt with Israel's good deeds in this world, which yield the world to come. No. 29 also has referred to the penalties for sin, and how these are appropriate. Now we turn to Israel's bad deeds. The composite on Israel's sins will continue through Nos. 30-33.

I.30   A.   *Our rabbis have taught on Tannaite authority:*
       B.   "If you walk in my statutes" (Lev. 26:3) – the word "if" is used in the sense of supplication, as in the verse, O that my people would hearken to me, that Israel would walk in my ways....I should soon subdue their enemies" (Ps. 81:14-15); "O that you had listened to my commandments, then my peace would have been as a river, your seed also would have been as the sand" (Isa. 48:18).
I.31   A.   *Our rabbis have taught on Tannaite authority:*
       B.   "O that they had such a heart as this always, to fear me and keep my commandments, that it may be well with them and their children" (Deut. 5:26).
       C.   Said Moses to the Israelites, "You are a bunch of ingrates, children of ingrates. When the Holy One, blessed be He, said to you, 'O that they had such a heart as this always, to fear me and keep my commandments, that it may be well with them and their children' (Deut. 5:26), they should have said, 'You give it.'
       D.   "They were ingrates, since it is written, 'Our soul loathes [5B] this light bread' (Num. 21:5).
       E.   "The children of ingrates: 'The woman whom you gave to be with me, she gave me of the fruit of the tree and I ate it' (Gen. 3:12).
       F.   "So our rabbi, Moses, gave an indication of that fact to the Israelites only after forty years: 'And I have led you forty years in the wilderness...but the Lord has not given you a heart to know and eyes to see and ears to hear to this day' (Deut. 29:3, 4)."
I.32   A.   ["And I have led you forty years in the wilderness...but the Lord has not given you a heart to know and eyes to see and ears to hear to this day" (Deut. 29:3, 4):]
       B.   Said Raba, "This proves that a person will fully grasp the mind of his master only after forty years have passed."
I.33   A.   *Said R. Yohanan in the name of R. Benaah, "What is the meaning of the verse of Scripture, 'Happy are you who sow beside all waters, that send forth the feet of the ox and the ass' (Isa. 32:20)? 'Happy are you, O Israel, when you are devoted to the Torah and to doing deeds of grace, then their inclination to do evil is handed over to them, and they are not handed over into the power of their inclination to do evil.*
       B.   "For it is said, 'Happy are you who sow beside all waters.' For what does the word 'sowing' mean, if not 'doing deeds of grace,' in line with the use of the word in this verse: 'Sow for yourselves in righteousness, reap according to mercy' (Hos. 10:12), and what is the meaning of 'water' if not Torah: 'Oh you who are thirsty, come to the water' (Isa. 55:1)."
       C.   As to the phrase, "That send forth the feet of the ox and the ass":
       D.   It has been taught by the Tannaite authority of the household of Elijah:
       E.   "A person should always place upon himself the work of studying the Torah as an ox accepts the yoke, and as an ass, its burden."

That completes the miscellany. It certainly plays no role in Mishnah exegesis. It also sets forth no proposition, in a way in which compositions of Mishnah exegesis, and even composites thereof, commonly do. Rather, we have a set of compositions of a rather diverse quality, which are grouped by common themes; the points that they make jointly are at best commonplaces. The grouping of the compositions into subcomposites is fairly easy to explain, and their further agglutination into the large-scale composite before us lies within the range of reasonable explanation. We have something more than a random scrapbook of this-and-that. The survey just now concluded leaves us with an impression somewhat different from what we expected at the outset. First of all, identifying the supplementary entries – footnotes, appendices – shows us that a fair amount of the miscellany in fact is made up of secondary expansions of a quite coherent text. Within the technical limitations of our authorship, who, after all, had no way of signifying footnotes and appendices, the framers of the whole had no choice but to gloss. Second, the rather sizable sequence of free-standing compositions in the aggregate is made up of conglomerates, the cogency of which we are able to explain. Third, the order of the conglomerates is not entirely beyond reason, since if we were to state the propositions not proved but illustrated by what is before us, we would have these simple statements:

1.   Study of the Torah on the part of a human being elicits in God a counterpart response, one of grace.

2.   Israel lives through study of the Torah.

3.   God favors Israel, by reason of Israel's study of the Torah, and is angry with the gentiles.

4.   Israel's good deeds in this world will be rewarded not now but in the world to come.

We then end with what is labelled as an appendix to materials introduced earlier. Now while we can hardly claim that the enormous composite made up of Nos. 2 through 33 is a sustained and well-crafted whole, we also cannot settle for the characterization of the set as a mere miscellany. It is made up of clearly identifiable composites, each of them comprising already made-up compositions. Where there is a movement from one to the next, there is ordinarily a clear connection, for example, a reference to a subtheme now given principal place as a main theme; an allusion to a person, now formed into the focus of a set of compositions. What holds the parts together, one to the next, is a connection of a formal, generally thematic character. What holds the whole together is a sequence of unfolding themes. It would claim far too much to allege that we have a demonstration of a single proposition, for example, God hates and is angry with idolators and loves and rewards Israel. But it would be obtuse not to observe that that theme, remarkably coherent with the

Mishnah tractate overall and with the opening paragraph of the Mishnah in particular, is present and is treated.

Let me now summarize the whole. **I.1** begins with a systematic inquiry into the correct reading of the Mishnah's word choices. The dispute is fully articulated in balance, beginning to end. No. 2 then forms a footnote to No. 1. No. 3 then provides a footnote to the leitmotif of No. 2, the conception of God's not laughing, and No. 4 returns us to the exposition of No. 2, at HHH. Nos. 5, 6 are tacked on – a Torah study anthology – because they continue the general theme of Torah study every day, which formed the main motif of No. 2 – the gentiles did not accept the Torah, study it, or carry it out. So that theme accounts for the accumulation of sayings on Torah study in general, a kind of appendix on the theme. Then – so far as I can see, because of the reference to God's power – No. 7 begins with a complement to 6.I. The compositions, Nos. 7, 8, then are strung together because of a point that is deemed to link each to its predecessor. No. 7 is linked to the foregoing because of the theme of God's power; but it also intersects with 2.HHH and complements that reference; the entire sequence beyond No. 2 then in one way or another relates to either No. 2, theme or proposition, or to an item that is tacked on to No. 2 as a complement. Thus No. 8 is joined to No. 7 because of the shared method of contrasting verses. Then No. 9 is tacked on because it continues the proposition of No. 8. No. 10 continues the foregoing. No. 11 is tacked on to No. 10 for the reason made explicit: it continues what has gone before. The same is so for No. 12. No. 13 continues the theme, but not the form or the proposition, of the prior compositions, namely, punishment little by little, for example, in this world, in exchange for a great reward later on. The established theme then is divine punishment and how it is inflicted: gently to Israel, harshly to the gentiles; the preferred form is the contrast among two verses. That overall principle of conglomeration – form and theme – explains the inclusion of Nos. 14, 15+16, which is tacked on to 15. But then the introduction of Balaam, taken as the prototype for the min, accounts for the inclusion of a variety of further sayings on the same theme, specifically, No. 17, a gloss on the foregoing; No. 18, a continuation of the foregoing process of glossing; No. 19, an amplification on the now dominant theme; No. 20, a reversion to No. 16; No. 21, a story on the theme of how difficult it is to define precisely the matter dealt with in the foregoing. Nos. 21, 22, 23 complete the discussion of that particular time at which God is angry, a brief moment but one that is marked by a just cause. No. 23 then introduces the theme of choosing the right time – that is not the moment of divine wrath – for prayer. This seems to me a rather miscellaneous item, and it marks the conclusion of the systematic expansion begun much earlier. That that is the fact is shown by the character of No. 24, which cites 2.HHH, and by No. 25, which explicitly reverts to 2.SS, which justifies my insistence that the entire corpus of materials that follows No. 2 simply amplifies and augments No. 2, and that is done in a very systematic way. Some of the sets, as we have seen, were formed into conglomerates prior to insertion here, but once we recognize that all of the sets serve the single task at hand, we see the coherence of what on the surface appears to be run-on and miscellaneous. In my *Rules of Composition*, Chapter Two, I show in a graphic way how these materials serve No. 2, some as footnotes, some as appendices, and some as footnotes or appendices to footnotes or appendices. No. 26 is a fine case in point. It complements 25.H, and is tacked on for that reason. Then No. 27 complements No. 26's statements concerning David. Bearing a formal tie to No. 27, with the same authority, No. 28 fits in also because it reverts to the theme of No. 25, the power of the religious duties that one carries out. No. 29 continues the theme of No. 28, that is, death and the day of judgment. Simeon's statement defines the center of gravity of the passage, which obviously was complete prior to its inclusion here. The reason it has been added is its general congruence to the discussions of sin, penitence, death, and forgiveness. No. 30 is attached to No. 31, and No. 31 is tacked on because it refers to the prooftext in the prior composition. No. 32 takes up the prooftext of No. 31. No. 33 writes a solid conclusion to the whole, addressing as it does the basic theme that Israel's actions define their fate, and that study of the Torah is what determines everything else. That is a thematic conclusion to a composite largely devoted, one way or another, to that one theme.

What then leads us to see Nos. 2 through 33 as a miscellany? It is the contrast between that composite and the amazingly coherent character of the Talmud's Mishnah commentary. And since the Talmud is made up mostly of Mishnah commentary, what holds together its thematic sets, and what accounts for their relationship to the Mishnah, are considerations that are easy to miss. But in the case of what is before us, we can readily see both what holds the several composites together, what links one composite to the next, and what defines the relationshp of the entire group of composites to the Mishnah paragraph that stands at the head. The upshot may be easily stated. The miscellanies really are not at all miscellaneous. They form an integral part of the Talmud's program of Mishnah commentary. But they are made up of materials that, on their own, do not address the language or propositions of the Mishnah, only its (implicit) themes. As a result, they do not exhibit the literary cogency that makes the bulk of the Talmud so remarkably coherent. Viewed in their own terms, however, the materials we have examined answer the question the Mishnah paragraph raises and respond to its topical program: gentiles observe holy days in the service of idols. Israel should have nothing to do with such things. God loves Israel, who study the Torah, forgives their sins, and in the world to come will give them their lasting and just reward. In light of the propositions of the Mishnah, we can hardly have asked for a more appropriate set of compositions than those selected and arranged in the massive "miscellany" at hand.

Traits of Agglutinative Discourse in the Talmud of Babylonia

It is now very simple to define agglutinative discourse in the context of the Bavli. The Talmud of Babylonia makes use of two distinct principles for the formation of large-scale composites of distinct compositions, and the framers of the document very rarely set forth a composition on its own, standing without clear ties to a larger context. Ordinarily, they brought together distinct and free-standing compositions in the service of Mishnah exegesis and amplification of law originating in the Mishnah paragraph under analysis. For that purpose they would then draw upon already written compositions, which would be adduced as cases, statements of principles, fully exposed analyses, inclusive of debate and argument, in the service of that analysis. So all of the compositions in a given composite would serve the governing analytical or propositional purpose of the framer of the composite. Where a composition appears to shade over into a direction of its own, that very quickly is seen to serve as a footnote or even an appendix to the composite at hand.

In addition to propositional and even analytical composites, the framers of the Bavli also formed compositions into thematic composites, and on the face of it, this second type of composite presents the appearance of a miscellany. But far from forming a mere rubbish heap of this and that, this other type of composite proves not at all miscellaneous. Clear, governing, and entirely predictable principles allow us to explain how one composition is joined to another. Ordinarily, a sizable miscellany will tell us more about a subject that the Mishnah addresses or richly illustrate a principle that the Mishnah means to set forth through its cases and examples. In that sense, the miscellaneous kind of composite is set forth as Mishnah commentary of a particular kind. As we have seen, an agglutinative composite may be formed by appeal to a common theme, ordinarily stated by the Mishnah or at least suggested by its contents, and several closely related themes will then come under exposition in a massive miscellany. One common theme will be a passage of Scripture, systematically examined. A subordinate principle of agglutination will join composites attributed to the same authority or tradent, though it would be unusual for the compositions so joined to deal with entirely unrelated topics. So the principal point of differentiation between propositional composites and agglutinative ones is that the former analyze a problem, the latter illustrate a theme or even a proposition.

It follows that two modes of forming composites serve the framers of the Bavli, the paramount, propositional and analytical mode, and the subordinate, agglutinative sort. The one joins together a variety of distinct compositions into a propositional statement, commonly enriched with analytical initiatives, and frequently bearing a burden of footnotes and appendices. The other combines distinct compositions into a thematic composite, the proposition of which is ordinarily rather general and commonplace. A second principle of agglutinative composite making appeals to common attributions, though when two or more compositions are joined into a composite because they are assigned to the same authority or tradental chain, they very likely will also bear in common an interest in a single theme, if not in a uniform proposition in connection with that theme.

Since all of the miscellanies we have examined concern theological or exegetical subjects, none focusing upon a problem of law, we should be tempted to propose that agglutinative discourse governs the treatment of one type of subject matter, theology or exegesis, but not another, the more prominent, and generally held, normative one, of law. To demonstrate that the distinction between lore and law (*aggadah* and *halakhah*) makes no difference in whether compositions will be linked into composites by appeal to propositional analytical or merely agglutinative principles of formation, let me give a fine example of an agglutinative legal ("halakhic") passage, which shows beyond any doubt that there is no important point of distinction, so far as agglutinative discourse is concerned, between compositions and subcomposites of one kind and of the other. We find in both types of subject matter precisely the same literary traits of composite making.

Here the compositions are joined agglutinatively, by reference to a common subject matter; but the composite that results does not make a point, for example of proposition, analysis, or argument. Rather, it serves to illustrate a theme. We deal with Bavli Baba Batra, Chapter Five.

Baba Batra 5:11

A.   Said Rabban Simeon b. Gamaliel, "Under what circumstances?

B.   "In the case of liquid measures.

C.   "But in the case of dry measures, it is not necessary."

D.   [88B] And [a shopkeeper] is liable to let the scales go down by a handbreadth [to the buyer's advantage].

	E.	[If] he was measuring out for him exactly, he has to give him an overweight –
	F.	one part in ten for liquid measure,
	G.	one part in twenty for dry measure.
	H.	In a place in which they are accustomed to measure with small measures, one must not measure with large measures;
	I.	with large ones, one must not measure with small;
	J.	[in a place in which it is customary] to smooth down [what is in the measure], one should not heap it up;
	K.	to heap it up, one should not smooth it down.

III.1 A. In a place in which they are accustomed to measure with small measures, one must not measure with large measures; with large ones, one must not measure with small; in a place in which it is customary to smooth down what is in the measure, one should not heap it up; to heap it up, one should not smooth it down:

B. *Our rabbis have taught on Tannaite authority:*

C. How on the basis of Scripture do we know that **in a place in which it is customary to smooth down what is in the measure, one should not heap it up; to heap it up, one should not smooth it down?** Scripture says, "A perfect measure" (Deut. 25:15). [Slotki: Deviating from the usual practice the buyer or the seller may defraud or mislead others.]

D. And how do we know that if one said, "Lo, where it is customary to heap up, I will level it off, and reduce the price,' or, in a place where they level, I will heap it up, and raise the price," they do not listen to him [he may not do so]?

E. Scripture says, "A perfect and just measure you shall have" (Deut. 25:15).

III.2 A. *Our rabbis have taught on Tannaite authority:*

B. How on the basis of Scripture do we know that in a place where the practice is to allow an overweight, they do not give the exact weight, and in a place in which they give an exact weight, they do not give an overweight?

C. Scripture says, "A perfect weight" (Deut. 25:15).

D. And how on the basis of Scripture do we know that if one said in a place in which they give an overweight, "Lo, I shall give an exact weight and charge him less," or in a place in which they give an exact weight, "Lo, I shall give him an overweight and add to the price," they do not listen to him?

E. Scripture says, "A perfect weight and a just one" (Deut. 25:15).

F. Said R. Judah of Sura, "'You shall not have anything in your house' (Deut. 25:14). Why? Because of your 'diverse weights' (Deut. 25:13). But if you keep 'a perfect and just weight, you shall have' (Deut. 25:15) things, 'if a perfect and just measure, you shall have....'"

There is no problem in explaining why No. 2 is tacked on to No. 1. The proposition is the same, so is the form. But what follows is another matter, since we are now going to entertain a different proposition altogether.

III.3 A.   *Our rabbis have taught on Tannaite authority:*
     B.   "You shall have...": this teaches that they appoint market supervisors to oversee measures, but they do not appoint market supervisors to control prices.

No. 4 will now illustrate the foregoing.

III.4 A.   *The household of the patriarch appointed market supervisors to oversee measures and to control prices. Said Samuel to Qarna, "Go, repeat the Tannaite rule to them:* They appoint market supervisors to oversee measures, but they do not appoint market supervisors to control prices.
     B.   *He went out and instructed them:* "They appoint market supervisors to oversee measures and to control prices."
     C.   *He said to him, "What do they call you? Qarna [horn]? Let a horn grow out of your eye." A horn grew out of his eye.*
     D.   *And as for Qarna, in accord with what authority did he reach this conclusion?*
     E.   *It was in accord with what Rammi bar Hama said R. Isaac said,* "They appoint market supervisors to oversee measures and to control prices, on account of crooks."

Now we have a miscellany, meaning, a set of compositions, each standing on its own foundation, all making clearly articulated points, none related except in a shared theme to what stands fore or aft. What we shall also observe is subsets, clearly joined to one another, but connected to the larger context only by the general theme. These subsets do not require explicit specification, being obvious on the face of it.

III.5 A.   *Our rabbis have taught on Tannaite authority:*
     B.   If somebody ordered a litra, he should measure out a litra; if he ordered a half-litra, he should measure out for him a half-litra; a quarter-litra, he should measure out a quarter.
     C.   *So what does that passage tell us?*
     D.   *It is that we provide weights in these denominations.*
III.6 A.   *Our rabbis have taught on Tannaite authority:*
     B.   If someone ordered three-quarters of a litra, he should not say to him, "Weigh out for me three-quarters of a litra one by one," but he should say to him, "Weigh out a litra for me but leave out a quarter-litra with the meat" [Slotki: on the other scale].
III.7 A.   *Our rabbis have taught on Tannaite authority:*
     B.   If someone wanted to order ten litras, he should not say to him, "Weigh them out for me one by one and allow an overweight for each," but all of them are weighed together, with one overweight covering the whole order [cf. T. B.B. 5:9B-I].
III.8 A.   *Our rabbis have taught on Tannaite authority:*
     B.   [Slotki:] The hollow handle in which the tongue of the balance rests must be suspended in the air three handbreadths [removed from the roof from which the balance hangs], and it must be three handbreadths above the ground.

C. The beam and the rope that goes with it should be twelve handbreadths, and the balances of wool dealers and glassware dealers must be suspended two handbreadths in the air from the ceiling and two above the ground. The beams and ropes that go with them must be nine handbreadths in length. The balance of a shopkeeper and a householder must be suspended a handbreadth in the air from above and a handbreadth above the ground. The beam and ropes that go with them must be six handbreadths. A gold balance must be suspended three fingerbreadths in the air from above and three above the ground. I don't know the length of the beam and the cords.

D. *What kind of balance is the one mentioned first [before the specific rulings for those of the wool dealers, glassware dealers, and so on]?*

E. **[89B]** *Said R. Pappa, "The one used for heavy pieces of metal."*

III.9 A. Said R. Mani bar Patish, "Just as they have specified certain restrictions with regard to disqualifying balances for commercial purposes, so they have laid down disqualifications with regard to their constituting utensils for the purpose of receiving cultic uncleanness."

B. *What does he tell us that we do not learn from the following:* **The cord of the scales of the storekeepers and [or] of householders – [to be susceptible to uncleanness must be in length at least] a handbreadth. A handle of the ax at its front – a handbreadth. The projection of the shaft of a pair of compasses – a handbreadth. The shaft of a stonemason's chisel – a handbreadth. A cord of the balances of wool dealers and of glass weighers – two handbreadths. The shaft of a millstone chisel – two handbreadths. The battle ax of the legions – two handbreadths. The goldsmith's hammer – two handbreadths. And of the carpenter's – three handbreadths] [M. Kel. 29:5-6]***!* [Slotki: Since this restriction has been applied to one kind of balance, are not the other kinds of balance to be implied?]

C. The statement that he made is necessary to deal with the sizes of the beam and cords [that are not dealt with at the parallel].

A subset now follows, Nos. 10-13, glossed by No. 14.

III.10 A. *Our rabbis have taught on Tannaite authority:*
       B. They make weights out of neither tin or led or alloy but of stone or glass.

III.11 A. *Our rabbis have taught on Tannaite authority:*
       B. They make the strike not out of a board, because it is light, nor out of metal, because it is heavy, but out of olive, nut, sycamore, or box wood.

III.12 A. *Our rabbis have taught on Tannaite authority:*
       B. They do not make the strike thick on one side and thin on the other.
       C. They do not make the strike with a single quick movement, because striking in that way brings loss to the seller and advantage to the buyer, nor very slowly, since this is a loss to the buyer but a benefit to the seller.

D. In regard to all of these shady practices, said Rabban Yohanan b. Zakkai, "Woe is me if I speak, woe is me if I do not speak. If I speak, then sharpers will learn from me, and if I don't speak, then the sharpers will say, 'The disciples of sages haven't got the slightest idea what we are doing.'"

III.13 A. *The question was raised: "So did he speak of them or didn't he?"*

B. Said R. Samuel bar R. Isaac, "He did speak of them: 'For the ways of the Lord are right, and the just walk in them; but transgressors stumble therein' (Hos. 14:10)."

III.14 A. *Our rabbis have taught on Tannaite authority:*

B. "You shall do no unrighteousness in judgment, in surveying, weight, or in measure" (Lev. 19:35):

C. "In surveying": This refers to surveying the real estate, meaning, one should not measure for one party in the dry season and another in the rainy season.

D. "Weight": One should not keep one's weights in salt.

E. "In measure" (Lev. 19:35): One should not make the liquid form a head.

F. And that yields an argument a fortiori: If with reference to a mere "measure" (Lev. 19:35), which is merely one-sixth of a log, the Torah demanded meticulous attention, how much the more so must one give meticulous care in measuring out a hin, half a hin, a third of a hin, a quarter of a hin, a log, a half a log, a quarter of a log, a toman, half a toman, and an uqla.

III.15 A. Said R. Judah said Rab, "It is forbidden for someone to keep in his house a measure that is either smaller or larger than the norm, even for the purpose of a piss pot."

B. *Said R. Pappa, "But we have stated that rule only in a place where measures are not properly marked with a seal, but where they are properly sealed, they are permitted, since, if the purchaser sees no mark, he is not going to accept their use. And even in a place where measures are not properly marked with a seal, we have stated that rule only in a case in which they are not supervised [by administrative officers of the market], but if they are ordinarily supervised, we should have no objection."*

C. *But that is not the case, for sometimes the buyer may come by at twilight and may happen to take a faulty measure. And so, too, that has been taught on Tannaite authority:* It is forbidden for someone to keep in his house a measure that is either smaller or larger than the norm, even for the purpose of a piss pot. But he may make a seah measure, a tarqab, a half-tarqab, a qab, a half-qab, a quarter-qab, a toman, [90B] and an uqla measure. How much is an uqla measure? It is a fifth of a quarter of a qab. In the case of liquid measures, one may make a hin, a half-hin, third-hin, quarter-hin, log, half-log, quarter-log, eighth-log, and eighth of an eighth, which is a qortob.

D. *So why shouldn't someone also make a double-qab measure?*

E. *It might be confused with a tarqab.*

F. *Therefore people may err by as much as a third.*

G. *If so, then a qab also people should not make, since they might confuse it with a half-tarqab. Rather, as to a double-qab, this is the reason that one is not to make it, specifically, that one will confuse it with a half-tarqab.*

H. *And this proves that one may err by a quarter.*

    I.   *If so, a half-toman and an uqla measure are things people should not make.* [Slotki: The difference between a half-toman, a sixteenth-qab, and an uqla, a twentieth-qab, is only one eightieth of a qab, which is a fifth of the half-toman, less than a quarter, so that these two measures could certainly be mistaken for one another.]

    J.   *Said R. Pappa, "With small measures people are quite expert."*

    K.   *What about a third of a hin and a fourth of a hin — shouldn't people be forbidden to make these?*

    L.   *Since these were utilized in the sanctuary, rabbis made no decree in their regard.*

    M.   *Well, shouldn't there be a precautionary decree with respect to the sanctuary?*

    N.   *The priests are meticulous in their work.*

III.16 A.   Said Samuel, "They may not increase the size of the measures [whether or not people concur] by more than a sixth, nor the coins by more than a sixth, and he who makes a profit must not profit by more than a sixth."

    B.   What is the operative consideration for the first of these three rulings?

    C.   *If we say that it is because the market prices will rise, then for that same consideration, it should not be permitted to increase the size of the measures even by a sixth. And if the operative consideration is overreaching, so that the transaction should not have to be annulled, did not* Raba say, "One can retract from an agreement that involves fraud in measure, weight, or number, even though it is less than the standard, a sixth, of overreaching." *And if the operative consideration is that the dealer may not incur any loss, then is the whole purpose of the law to guard him from loss? Is he not entitled to make a profit? But "buy and sell at no profit, merely to be called a merchant!"*

    D.   *Rather, said R. Hisda, "Samuel identified a verse of Scripture and interpreted it,* 'And the sheqel shall be twenty gerahs, twenty sheqels, twenty-five sheqels, ten and five sheqels shall be your maneh' (Ezek. 45:12). [90B] *Now was the maneh to be two hundred forty denars?* [But it is supposed to be twenty-five sheqels or a hundred denars (Cashdan).] *But three facts are to be inferred from this statement:* [1] The maneh used in the sanctuary is worth double what the maneh is usually worth; [2] they may not increase the size of the measures [whether or not people concur] by more than a sixth, and [3] the sixth is added over and above the original [so to add a sixth, the original is divided into five parts and another part of equal value, making a sixth one, then is added to it, so the maneh consisted of two hundred forty denars (Cashdan, *Menahot*)]."

III.17 A.   *R. Pappa bar Samuel ordained a measure of three qepizi. They said to him,* "Lo, said Samuel, 'They may not increase the size of the measures [whether or not people concur] by more than a sixth'!"

    B.   *He said to them, "What I am ordaining is an entirely new measure." He sent it to Pumbedita, and they did not adopt it. He sent it to Papunia and they adopted it, naming it the Pappa-measure.*

Any doubt that we are dealing with a miscellany is removed by what follows, which in no way pertains to the foregoing in any detail. And yet it is introduced for a very clear purpose, which is to make a point about a common theme and proposition: fair dealing in the market, giving and getting true value.

III.18 A. *Our rabbis have taught on Tannaite authority:*
        B. Concerning those who store up produce, lend money on usury, falsify measures, and price gouge, Scripture says, "Saying, when will the new moon be gone, that we may sell grain, and the Sabbath, that we may set forth grain? Making the ephah small and the sheqel great and falsifying the balances of deceit" (Amos 8:5). And in their regard, Scripture states, "The Lord has sworn by the pride of Jacob, surely I will never forget any of their works" (Amos 8:7).
        C. *What would be an example of those who store up produce?*
        D. *Said R. Yohanan, "Like Shabbetai the produce hoarder."*
III.19 A. *The father of Samuel would sell produce at the early market price when the early market price prevailed [that is, cheap, so keeping prices down through the year (Slotki)]. Samuel his son held the produce back and sold it when the late market prices prevailed, but at the early market price.*
        B. *They sent word from there, "The father is better than the son. How come? Prices that have been held down remain down."*
III.20 A. Said Rab, "Someone may store up his own produce" [but may not hoard for trading purposes (Slotki)].
        B. *So, too, it has been taught on Tannaite authority:*
        C. [Following Tosefta's version:] They do not hoard in the Land of Israel things upon which life depends, for example, wine, oil, fine flour, and produce. But things upon which life does not depend, for instance, cummin and spice, lo, this is permitted. And they put things in storage for three years, the eve of the Seventh Year, the Seventh Year itself, and the year after the Seventh Year.
        D. Under what circumstances.
        E. In the case of that which one purchases in the market.
        F. But in the case of what one puts aside from what he himself has grown, even for a period of ten years it is permitted.
        G. But in a year of famine even a qab of carobs one should not put into storage, because he brings a curse on the prices [by forcing them upward through artificial demand] [T. A.Z. 4:1A-G].
III.21 A. *Said R. Yosé b. R. Hanina to Puga his servant, "Go, store up fruit for me for the next three years: the eve of the Sabbatical Year, the Sabbatical Year, and the year after the Sabbatical Year."*
III.22 A. *Our rabbis have taught on Tannaite authority:*
        B. They do not export from the Land of Israel to Syria things upon which life depends, for example, wine, oil, and fine flour.
        C. R. Judah b. Betera says, "I say that they export wine to Syria, because in doing so, one diminishes silliness [in the Land of Israel]."
        D. Just as they do not export to Syria, so they do not export from one hyparchy to another.
        E. And R. Judah permits doing so [91A] from one hyparchy to another [T. A.Z. 4:2].
III.23 A. *Our rabbis have taught on Tannaite authority:*

B.   **They are not to make a profit in the Land of Israel from the necessities of life, for instance, wine, oil, and flour.**

C.   **They said concerning R. Eleazar b. Azariah that he would make a profit from wine and oil all his life [T. A.Z. 4:1H-J].**

D.   *In the matter of wine, he concurred with the view of R. Judah [b. Batera], and in the matter of oil, as it happens, in the place where R. Eleazar b. Azariah lived, oil was abundant.*

III.24 A.   *Our rabbis have taught on Tannaite authority:*

B.   People are not to profit from eggs twice.

C.   *Said Mari bar Mari, "There was a dispute between Rab and Samuel. One says, 'Two for one' [selling for two what was bought for one], and the other said, 'Selling by a dealer to a dealer' [making two profits on the same object]."*

III.25 A.   *Our rabbis have taught on Tannaite authority:*

B.   They sound the alarm on account of a collapse in the market in trading goods even on the Sabbath.

C.   Said R. Yohanan, "For instance, linen clothing in Babylonia and wine and oil in the Land of Israel."

D.   *Said R. Joseph, "But that is the case when these are so cheap that ten go for the price of six."*

III.26 A.   *Our rabbis have taught on Tannaite authority:*

B.   **A person is not allowed to emigrate from the Land of Israel unless wheat goes at the price of two seahs for a sela.**

C.   **Said R. Simeon, "Under what circumstances? Only in a case in which he does not find any to buy even at that price. But if he finds some to buy at that price, even if a seah of grain goes for a sela, he should not emigrate."**

D.   **And so did R. Simeon bar Yohai say, "Elimelech, Machlon, and Kilion were the great men of his time, and one of those who sustained the generation. But because he went abroad, he and his sons died in famine. But all the Israelites were able to survive on their own land, as it is said, 'and when they came to Bethlehem, the whole town was stirred because of them' (Ruth 1:19). This teaches that all of the town had survived, but he and his sons had died in the famine" [T. A.Z. 4:4A-H].**

III.27 A.   "And when they came to Bethlehem, the whole town was stirred because of them, and the women said, 'Is this Naomi?'" (Ruth 1:19):

B.   *What is the meaning of the phrase, "Is this Naomi"?*

C.   Said R. Isaac, "They said, 'Did you see what happened to Naomi, who emigrated from the Land to a foreign country?'"

III.28 A.   And said R. Isaac, "The day that Ruth the Moabite emigrated from the Land to a foreign land, the wife of Boaz died. *That is in line with what people say: 'Before a person dies, his successor as master of the house is appointed.'"*

III.29 A.   Said Rabbah bar R. Huna said Rab, "Isban is the same as Boaz."

B.   *So what in the world does that mean?*

C.   *It is in line with what Rabbah b. R. Huna further said, for* said Rabbah bar R. Huna said Rab, "Boaz made for his sons a hundred and twenty wedding banquets: 'And Isban had thirty sons and thirty daughters he sent abroad, and thirty daughters he brought from abroad for his sons, and he judged Israel seven years' (Judg. 12:9).

For each one of them he made two wedding feasts, one in the household of the father, the other in the household of the father-in-law. But to none of them did he invite Manoah, for he said, '*How will that barren mule ever repay my hospitality?*' And all of them died in his lifetime. That is in line with what people say, '*In your lifetime you begot sixty? What good are the sixty? Marry again and get another one, brighter than all sixty.*'"

III.30 A. Said R. Hanan bar Raba said Rab, "Elimelech and Salmon and 'such a one' (Ruth 4:1) and the father of Naomi were all sons of Nahshon b. Amminadab (Ex. 6:23, Num. 10:14)."

B. *So what in the world does that mean?*

C. It is that even if one has a substantial store of unearned merit gained from his answers, it will serve him no good when he emigrates from the Land to a foreign land."

III.31 A. And said R. Hanan bar Raba said Rab, "*The mother of Abraham was named Amathelai, daughter of Karnebo; the name of the mother of Haman was Amatehilai, daughter of Orabti; and the mnemonic will be, 'unclean to the unclean, clean to the clean.' The mother of David was Nizbeth daughter of Adael, the mother of Samson was Zlelponit, and his sister was Nasyan.*"

B. *So what?*

C. For answering heretics.

III.32 A. And said R. Hanan bar Raba said Rab, "For ten years our father, Abraham, was kept in prison, three in Kuta, seven in Kardu."

B. *And R. Dimi of Nehardea repeats the matter in reverse order.*

C. *Said R. Hisda, "The lesser Kuta is the same as Ur of the Chaldees [Gen. 11:31]."*

III.33 A. And said R. Hanan bar Raba said Rab, "The day on which our father, Abraham, died, all of the principal authorities of the nations of the world formed a line and said, 'Woe is the world that has lost [91B] its leader, woe to the ship that has lost its helmsman.'"

III.34 A. "And you are exalted as head above all" (1 Chr. 29:11):

B. *Said R. Hanan bar Raba said Rab, "Even the superintendent of the water supply is appointed by Heaven."*

III.35 A. Said R. Hiyya bar Abin said R. Joshua b. Qorhah, "God forbid! Even if [Elimelech and his family] had found bran, they would never have emigrated. So why were they punished? Because they should have besought mercy for their generation but failed to do so: 'When you cry, let them that you have gathered deliver you' (Isa. 57:13)."

III.36 A. Said Rabbah bar bar Hannah said R. Yohanan, "This [prohibition against emigration] has been taught only when money is cheap [and abundant] and produce expensive, but when money is expensive [and not to be found, there being no capital], even if four seahs cost only a sela, it is permitted to emigrate."

B. *Said R. Yohanan, "I remember when four seahs of grain cost a sela and many died of starvation in Tiberias, not having an issar for bread."*

C. *And said R. Yohanan, "I remember when workmen wouldn't agree to work on the east side of town, where workers were dying because of the scent of bread [which they could not afford to buy]."*

III.37 A.   *And said R. Yohanan, "I remember when a child would break open a carob pod and a line of honey would run over both his arms."*

       B.   *And said R. Eleazar, "I remember when a raven would grab a piece of meat and a line of oil would run down from the top of the wall to the ground."*

       C.   *And said R. Yohanan, "I remember when boys and girls would promenade in the market at the age of sixteen or seventeen and not sin."*

       D.   *And said R. Yohanan, "I remember when they would say in the house of study, 'Who agrees with them falls into their power, who trusts in them — what is his becomes theirs."*

III.38 A.   It is written, "Mahlon and Chilion" (Ruth 1:2) and it is written "Joash and Saraph" (1 Chr. 4:22)!

       B.   Rab and Samuel —

       C.   One said, "Their names really were Mahlon and Chilion, and why were they called Joash? Because they despaired of redemption [the words for Joash and despair using the same letters]. And Saraph? Because they become liable by the decree of the Omnipresent to be burned."

       D.   And the other said, "Their names really were Joash and Saraph, but they were called Mahlon and Chilion: Mahlon, because they profaned their bodies [the words for Mahlon and profane using the same letters], and Chilion, because they were condemned by the Omnipresent to destruction [the words for destruction and Chilion using the same letters]."

       E.   *It has been taught on Tannaite authority in accord with the view of him who said that their names really were Mahlon and Chilion. For it has been taught on Tannaite authority:* What is the meaning of the verse, "And Jokim and the men of Cozeba and Joash and Saraph, who had dominion in Moab, and Jashubilehem, and the things are ancient"? (1 Chr. 4:22)?

       F.   "Jokim": This refers to Joshua, who kept his oath to the men of Gibeon (Josh. 9:15, 26).

       G.   "And the men of Cozeba": These are the men of Gibeon who lied to Joshua [the words for lie and Cozeba using the same letters] (Josh. 9:4).

       H.   "And Joash and Saraph": Their names really were Mahlon and Chilion, and why were they called Joash? Because they despaired of redemption [the words for Joash and despair using the same letters]. And Saraph? Because they become liable by the decree of the Omnipresent to be burned.

       I.   "Who had dominion in Moab": They married wives of the women of Moab.

       J.   "And Jashubilehem": This refers to Ruth of Moab, who had returned [using letters that are shared with Jashub] and remained in Bethlehem of Judah.

       K.   "And the things are ancient": These things were stated by the Ancient of Days.

III.39 A.   "These were the potters and those that dwelt among plantations and hedges; there they dwelt occupied in the kings work" (1 Chr. 4:23):

       B.   "These were the potters": This refers to the sons of Jonadab, son of Rahab, who kept the oath of their father (Jer. 35:6).

C. "And those that dwelt among plantations": This speaks of Solomon, who in his rule was like a fecund plant.

D. "And hedges": This refers to the Sanhedrin, who hedged in the breaches in Israel.

E. "There they dwelt occupied in the kings work": This speaks of Ruth of Moab, who lived to see the rule of Solomon, her grandson's grandson: "And Solomon caused a throne to be set up for the king's mother" (1 Kgs. 2:19), in which connection R. Eleazar said, "For the mother of the dynasty."

III.40 A. *Our rabbis have taught on Tannaite authority:*

B. "And you shall eat of the produce, the old store" (Lev. 25:22) – without requiring preservatives.

C. *What is the meaning of* without requiring preservatives?

D. R. Nahman said, "Without grain worms."

E. And R. Sheshet said, "Without blast."

F. *It has been taught on Tannaite authority in accord with the view of R. Sheshet, and it has been taught on Tannaite authority in accord with the view of R. Nahman.*

G. *It has been taught on Tannaite authority in accord with the view of R. Nahman:*

H. "And you shall eat the old store" (Lev. 25:22) – might one suppose that the sense is that the Israelites will be eager for the new produce because last year's has been destroyed [by the grain worm]? Scripture says, "until her produce came in," that is, until the produce will come on its own [without an early, forced harvest (Slotki)].

I. *It has been taught on Tannaite authority in accord with the view of R. Sheshet:*

J. "And you shall eat of the produce, the old store" (Lev. 25:22) – might one suppose that the sense is that the Israelites will be eager for the new produce because last year's has been spoiled [Slotki: by the blast]? Scripture states, "until her produce came in," that is, until the new crop will come in the natural way.

III.41 A. *Our rabbis have taught on Tannaite authority:*

B. "And you shall eat old store long kept" (Lev. 26:10) – whatever is of an older vintage than its fellow is better in quality than its fellow.

C. I know that that is so only of things that are ordinarily aged. What about things that are not ordinarily aged?

D. Scripture is explicit: "Old store long kept" (Lev. 26:10) – in all cases.

III.42 A. "And you shall bring forth the old from before the new" (Lev. 26:10) –

B. This teaches that the storehouses will be full of last year's crop, and the threshing floors, this year's crop, and the Israelites will say, "How are we going to remove the one before the other?"

C. *Said R. Pappa, "Everything is better when aged, except for dates, beer, and fish hash."*

III.1, 2 provide a scriptural basis for the rule and principle of the Mishnah. The key verse of No. 2 accounts for the inclusion of No. 3, which carries in its wake No. 4. Further Tannaite thematic supplements are at Nos. 5-8. No. 8 is glossed by No. 9, and then Nos. 10-12+13, 14 continue the Tannaite supplement. Carrying forward the general theme at hand, Nos. 15-42 form a miscellany built around the general theme before us. I see no formal differences between the miscellany at hand and those we have already examined. The only difference is subject matter – but not *classification of subject matter.* Is it possible, then, to state the propositions of the subsets of the miscellany? These seem to me to state the paramount proposals:

1. People are to employ honest measures and when selling, to give accurate and honest measures: Nos. 5-17.

2. People are not to take advantage of shortages nor create shortages: Nos. 18-25.

3. If there are shortages, people are to try to remain in the Land of Israel if they possibly can: Nos. 26-28+29-36, 37-40.

One might argue that the combination of the set yields the syllogism that honesty in buying and selling the necessities of life is what makes possible Israel's possession of the Holy Land, but that does not seem to me a plausible proposal. I see here only a thematic composite, all the numbered items addressed to that single theme, perhaps, furthermore, with a number of cogent propositions joining some compositions as well.

The Media of Agglutination:
Topic, Attribution, or Verses of Scripture

The conclusion may be stated very simply. We have now formed a hypothesis that quite random compositions, each with its own focus, will be formed into a composite on the basis of one of three theories of linkage: [1] topic, [2] attribution, or [3] sequence of verses of a passage of Scripture. The agglutination of topically coherent compositions predominates. And this leads to a further theory on the miscellany. The conglomerates of random compositions formed into topical composites ordinarily serve as an amplification of a topic treated in the Mishnah, or are joined to a composite that serves in that way, so that, overall, the miscellanies are made to extend and amplify the statements of the Mishnah, as much as, though in a different way from, the commonplace propositional, analytical, and syllogistic composite.

What appears to be a random hodgepodge of this and that and the other thing in fact forms a considered and even crafted composite, the agglutinative principles of which we may readily discern. In fact what we have in the miscellany is nothing more than a Mishnah commentary of a peculiar sort, itself extended and spun out, as the more conventional Mishnah commentaries of the Bavli tend to be extended and spun out. The miscellany may be defined, therefore, in a very simple way: it is, specifically, a composite that has been compiled so as to present for the Mishnah a commentary intending to provide information on topics introduced by the Mishnah – that, and not much more than that. True, the miscellany is not propositional, and it is certainly not analytical. But it is very much a composite in the sense in which I have defined that literary structure in the present context: purposeful, coherent, and I think, elegant. I do not claim that the pages of tractates Berakhot and Sanhedrin may compete in power and intellect with the pages of tractate Baba Qamma. I do claim that what appears by contrast to those pages to be odd, incoherent, pointless, rambling, to the contrary attests in its own way to the single and definitive program of the Bavli's framers. Whatever those framers wished to say on their own account they insisted on setting forth within the framework of that received document upon the structure of which they made everything to depend. All the more reason to admire the remarkable originality and genuinely fresh perspective – and statement – that, in the guise of a commentary, the Bavli was to make.

4

How the Bavli Shaped Rabbinic Discourse

Sometime between the closure of the Talmud of the Land of Israel, ca. 400, and the conclusion of the Talmud of Babylonia, ca. 600, *talmud*, a common noun that can connote the rigorous and systematic, critical analysis of a received document of Tannaite standing in the canon of the Judaism of the Dual Torah, became a proper noun, The Talmud. The Talmud was a composite of critical analysis organized around, and focused solely upon, the Mishnah. There would be two Talmuds, the Talmud of the Land of Israel, the Talmud of Babylonia, both of them limited, for purposes of structure and organization, in focus to the Mishnah. Other writings accorded Tannaite standing could have had talmuds and did enjoy that critical dialectical reading that the Mishnah did. But only the Mishnah was privileged to receive the Talmud, and all other Tannaite writings were denied the talmuds that had accumulated around them during the centuries from ca. 200 through ca. 600. That is the hypothesis set forth in this chapter. Viewed from the perspective of the redactional program of the Bavli, these other analytical critical readings of documents other than the Mishnah served no purpose that the Bavli's ultimate redactors defined for themselves in their sustained reading of the Bavli and their episodic and rather sparse reading of all other writings. But those readings did serve those other documents, and in the sherds and remnants in our hands, we can see how a rigorous and systematic reading of those other writings was being written even while the Bavli's materials came forth. On redactional grounds, then, I maintain that the Bavli contains compositions and even composites that reached closure under auspices separate from the Bavli's. I further insist that it was the framers of the Bavli that dictated the shape of rabbinic discourse – not only for the future, but, more to the point, retrospectively as well: this but not that.

I. The Proposition

The framers of the Bavli not only defined rabbinic discourse for the future, but they also redefined the discourse of the prior centuries. They were the ones who decided that only the Mishnah would receive a *talmud*, that is, a sustained exercise in applied reason and practical logic, set forth in a moving or dialectical argument aimed at holding together in a single, coherent structure a variety of facts and principles. The Mishnah would have a *talmud*, which then was *The Talmud* (whether of Babylonia or of the Land of Israel) – but not the Sifra, the Tosefta, or other received compositions and composites assigned Tannaite standing along with the Mishnah. Other *talmuds*, for those other Tannaite materials, can have been and were composed. But only one document, the Mishnah, would in the end have a *talmud*, and the other *talmuds* that were under way prior to the closure of the talmud were either never brought to conclusion and closure or were simply suppressed, I think the former the more likely of the possibilities. So the Talmud, meaning both Talmuds, the Talmud of the Land of Israel and the Talmud of Babylonia, decisively shaped rabbinic discourse not only by what was done but also what was not done but left half done. That the framers of the Bavli decided to do, and that they did.

I begin with the simple observation that the Mishnah is not the sole document of the initial writings of the canon of the Judaism of the Dual Torah – those classified as Tannaite in authority or standing – that was subjected to the sustained application of practical reason and critical analysis that, for the Mishnah, yielded the Talmud of Babylonia. Three other classifications of materials enjoyed that same remarkable reading: the Tosefta, the Sifra, and statements marked as Tannaite (for example, with such sigla as TNY', TN', and the like). Each of these classifications of received statements were read exactly as was the Mishnah, and the results of that reading were expressed in the rhetorical and logical program that characterizes the Talmud to the Mishnah. Not only so, but at a determinate age in the unfolding of the rabbinic writings, defined solely by the point of redaction of various writings, people working on the Mishnah and on these other compilations contemplated a *talmud* not only for the Mishnah, but also for the Tosefta, the Sifra, and some other compositions and even composites bearing Tannaite standing. So – from the perspective of the treatment of those other documents, besides the Mishnah – there can have been a *talmud* to the Tosefta, the Sifra, and other Tannaite formations or conglomerations of sayings. I shall show precisely what those other *talmuds* would have looked like by citing passages, sustained and well executed, of Sifra, Tosefta, and baraita criticism and amplification that are indistinguishable in every detail from passages of Mishnah criticism.

When the reading of the Mishnah that yielded our Talmud was under way, these other documents, or materials of the same status – Tannaite – as the Mishnah, also were being read along the same lines. But those other *talmuds* never reached us, and although the Bavli contains ample indication that such *talmuds* could have come into being, it also contains no evidence that, in any sustained way, they did. Once we realize that ours is not the only Talmud that was under way from the closure of the Mishnah to the conclusion of the Bavli, 200-600, we then grasp how profoundly the framers of the Talmud of Babylonia reshaped all prior discourse, since they made certain that there would be only one *talmud*, the Talmud, and only one privileged document entitled to such a *talmud*, namely, the Mishnah.

Accordingly, what I show here is that the compositors of the Bavli, or the Talmud of Babylonia, preserve evidence that, just as the Talmud of Babylonia was worked out as an analysis and critique of the Mishnah, so other documents were subjected to the same kind of critical analysis. These compositors provide us with important samples of the written result of that analysis. When we examine those samples, we see beyond doubt that, just as the Mishnah was studied in a systematic and orderly way so as to yield the Bavli as we have it, so the Sifra and the Tosefta (among numerous documents closed prior to the Bavli) were studied in the same way. Not only so, but certain types of statements, accorded the status of Tannaite, were systematically analyzed in their own terms as well. The bearing of these facts upon the problem of how to find out what passages of the Bavli attest to opinion held prior to the closure of the Bavli is simple. What we are going to see is the simple fact that the Mishnah was not the only book produced in the earlier centuries of the Common Era to have been subjected to that sustained analytical criticism that yielded the Bavli (and the Yerushalmi). Other books, and other classifications of statements, also were subjected to that same critical exegetical process. But while the Mishnah's exegesis led to the Bavli, the Sifra's and the Tosefta's did not. A kind of writing that addressed several documents then can have yielded not only the Bavli but an equivalent exegesis, a *talmud* so to speak, for the Sifra and the Tosefta and other materials as well – but we do not have the *talmud* for any other book but the Mishnah. The conclusion I draw from that fact, which I mean to demonstrate in these pages, is that, where we find writing in the Bavli but not pertinent to the requirements of the Bavli's framers, that writing was carried out separate from the work on the Mishnah that led to the Bavli.

In an earlier work, *Making the Classics in Judaism. The Three Stages of Literary Formation,* I have set forth a fresh approach to the issue of how we may identify passages in a document that can have reached closure prior to the redaction of that document. My approach simply disregards attributions altogether and addresses the character of the document at hand, hence it may be called a documentary approach to identifying earlier writings in the composite formed of a later compilation. I move a step beyond *Three Stages.* The distinctions that that work set forth, in the framework of Midrash compilations, are here utilized in a quite fresh way. There I argued that we can identify in a given compilation materials that served the purpose of the redactors of that document; these may or may not have been written prior to the undertaking of the redaction of that document. On the basis of that same criterion, which requires no very subjective opinion, we may furthermore identify materials that clearly do not serve the purpose of the redactors of that document. For example, they may simply talk about things that, otherwise, the redactors do not discuss. The contrast between compositions that clearly serve the purposes of a composite and those that do not permits us then to conclude that these compositions that fall outside of the redactional framework of a document cannot have been made up by the ultimate redactors of the document in which they occur for the purposes of said document. They stand as likely candidates for classification as writings made up prior to the redaction of that document.

The upshot is that the framers of the Bavli imposed upon the entirety of rabbinic discourse their own definition of not only what would be said, but also what would not be said: how matters would be organized and categorized, and how they would not be so set forth. The Mishnah would be the only received document that would be accorded a *talmud,* not the Sifra or the Tosefta or the compositions or composites of sayings marked as Tannaite. Not only so, but, still more important, the *talmud* that the Mishnah would receive would be framed by the framers of the Bavli acting on their own, and not as mere heirs and glossators of prior exegesis of the Mishnah. So the Mishnah would have as its *talmud* the only *talmud, The Talmud,* the Bavli (in succession after the Yerushalmi). That is precisely how the Talmud shaped rabbinic discourse – not only for time to come, but also for time past. The Bavli reshaped what its authors had received and defined what its heirs would discuss: the Mishnah as they read it, that alone. But that sufficed.

The polemical context in which these rather humble results are set forth requires only brief explanation, since the epilogue and appendix explain in the context of the ideas and methods of other scholars what is at stake in these pages. Documents of the canon of the Judaism of the Dual Torah attribute statements to authorities who flourished at various periods. Most historians of Judaism until now have treated those attributions as fact and so maintained that attributed statements in documents represent opinion held long prior to the closure of those documents. They propose histories of Judaism based upon the premise that the classical writings attest not only to opinion held at the time of their redaction but to views maintained over many centuries before that time. But once the critical issue of how we know what is attributed to a given authority really was said by him, the entire question of whether a document tells us anything about the age prior to its redaction once more takes center stage. Three positions encompass regnant opinion. The first, held in circles of the faithful, is that since the canonical writings are holy, whatever they say is so. The second, broadly espoused among scholars who regard themselves as critical, is that while we do not take at face value the attribution of a statement to a named authority, nonetheless, what is attributed to named authorities can guide us to opinions characteristic of ages prior to that of the final closure of the document itself. The third, which is mine, is that while documents may contain materials that reached closure prior to the formation of those documents themselves, compositions written earlier have to be identified on grounds other than the claim that a given authority really said what is assigned to him.

II. Literary History and the Perspective of Ultimate Redaction –
A Reprise of the Argument of *Making the Classics in Judaism:*
The Three Stages of Literary Formation

Each of the score of documents that make up the canon of Judaism in late antiquity exhibits distinctive traits in logic, rhetoric, and topic, so that we may identify the purposes and traits of form and intellect of the authorship of that document. It follows that documents possess integrity and are not merely scrapbooks, compilations made with no clear purpose or aesthetic plan. But, as is well known, some completed units of thought – propositional arguments, sayings, and stories for instance – travel from one document to another. It follows that the several documents intersect through shared materials. Furthermore, writings that peregrinate by definition do not carry out the rhetorical, logical, and topical program of a particular document. In framing a theory to accommodate the facts that documents are autonomous but also connected through such shared materials, therefore, we must account for the history of not only the documents in hand but also the completed pieces of writing that move from here to there. We have at present no theory of the formation of the various documents of the rabbinic literature that derives from an inductive sifting of the evidence. Nor do we have even a theory as to the correct method for the framing of a hypothesis for testing against the evidence.

My theory on the literary history of the rabbinic canon posits three stages in the formation of writing. I began with the discovery that an objective corpus of indicative evidence, permitting us to differentiate among compositions in a document and even to identify compositions that can have taken shape prior to the redaction of the document in which they appear, may derive from a simple observation. It is that some compositions and even whole composites in a document conform to the paramount traits of that document and clearly serve the purposes of the framers of the document, those who gave the document that distinctive character that it now has. Other compositions and even composites, by contrast, respond to the requirements of not the document in which they occur but some other document now in our hands (or none at all). These types of compositions and composites do not serve the framers of the document in which they occur, they do not conform to the indicative logic and rhetoric of that document, and they therefore were formulated outside of the circle of the framers of the document that now preserves them. It is this simple theory that I review here, before venturing the refinements of the present monograph.

Moving from the latest to the earliest, one stage is marked by the definition of a document, its topical program, its rhetorical medium, its logical message. The document as we know it in its basic structure and main lines therefore comes at the end. It follows that writings that clearly serve the program of that document and carry the purposes of its authorship were made up in connection with the formation of *that* document. Another, and I think, prior stage is marked by the preparation of writings that do not serve the needs of a particular document now in our hands, but can have carried out the purposes of an authorship working on a document of a *type* we now have. The existing documents then form a model for defining other kinds of writings worked out to meet the program of a documentary authorship.

But different from, and possibly prior to, the formulation of materials that suit the documents that contain them, there are other types of writings that in no way serve the needs or plans of any document we now have, and that, furthermore, also cannot find a place in any document of a type that we now have. These writings, as a matter of fact, very commonly prove peripatetic, traveling from one writing to another, equally at home in, or alien to, the program of the documents in which they end up. These writings therefore were carried out without regard to a documentary program of any kind exemplified by the canonical books of the Judaism of the Dual Torah. They form what I conceive to be the earliest in the three stages of the writing of the units of completed thought that in the aggregate form the canonical literature of the Judaism of the Dual Torah of late antiquity.

As a matter of fact, therefore, a given canonical document of the Judaism of the Dual Torah draws upon three classes of materials, and these were framed in temporal order. Last comes the final class, the one that the redactors themselves defined and wrote; prior is the penultimate class that can have served other redactors but did not serve these in particular; and earliest of all in the order of composition (at least, from the perspective of the ultimate redaction of the documents we now have) is the writing that circulated autonomously and served no redactional purpose we can now identify within the canonical documents.

III. The Correct Starting Point

In beginning the inquiry with the traits of documents seen whole, I reject the assumption that the building block of documents is the smallest whole unit of thought, the lemma, nor can we proceed in the premise that a lemma traverses the boundaries of various documents and is unaffected by the journey. The opposite premise is that we start our work with the traits of documents as a whole, rather than with the traits of the lemmas of which documents are (supposedly) composed. I have set forth the documentary hypothesis for the analysis of the rabbinic literature of late antiquity. But how shall we proceed, if we take as our point of entry the character and conditions of the document, seen whole? And what are the results of doing so?

Having demonstrated beyond any doubt that a rabbinic text is a document, that is to say, a well-crafted text and not merely a compilation of this and that, and further specified in acute detail precisely the aesthetic, formal, and logical program followed by each of those texts, accordingly, I am able to move to the logical next step. That is to show that in the background of the documents that we have is writing that is *not* shaped by documentary requirements, writing that is not shaped by the documentary requirements of the compilations we now have, and also writing that is entirely formed within the rules of the documents that now present that writing. These then are the three kinds of writing that form, also, the three stages in the formation of the classics of Judaism.

IV. Redaction and Writing: The Extreme Case of the Mishnah

My example of a document that is written down essentially in its penultimate and ultimate stages, that is, a document that takes shape within the redactional process and principally there, is, of course, the Mishnah. In that writing, the patterns of language, for example, syntactic structures, of the apodosis and protasis of the Mishnah's smallest whole units of discourse are framed in formal, mnemonic patterns. They follow a few simple rules. These rules, once known, apply nearly everywhere and form stunning evidence for the document's cogency. They permit anyone to reconstruct, out of a few key phrases, an entire cognitive unit, and even complete intermediate units of discourse. Working downward from the surface, therefore, anyone can penetrate into the deeper layers of meaning of the Mishnah. Then and at the same time, while discovering the principle behind the cases, one can easily memorize the whole by mastering the recurrent rhetorical pattern dictating the expression of the cogent set of cases. For it is easy to note the shift from one rhetorical pattern to another and to follow the repeated cases, articulated in the new pattern downward to its logical substrate. So syllogistic propositions, in the Mishnah's authors' hands, come to full expression not only in *what* people wish to state but also in *how* they choose to say it. The limits of rhetoric define the arena of topical articulation.

Now to state my main point in heavy emphasis: *the Mishnah's formal traits of rhetoric indicate that the document has been formulated all at once, and not in an incremental, linear process extending into a remote (mythic) past, (for example, to Sinai).* These traits, common to a series of distinct cognitive units, are redactional, because they are imposed at that point at which someone intended to join together discrete (finished) units on a given theme. The varieties of traits particular to the discrete units and the diversity of authorities cited therein, including masters of two or three or even four strata from the turn of the first century to the end of the second, make it highly improbable that the several units were formulated in a common pattern and then preserved, until, later on, still further units, on the same theme and in the same pattern, were worked out and added. The entire indifference, moreover, to historical order of authorities and concentration on the logical unfolding of a given theme or problem without reference to the sequence of authorities, confirm the supposition that the work of formulation and that of redaction go forward together.

The principal framework of formulation and formalization in the Mishnah is the intermediate division rather than the cognitive unit. The least formalized formulary pattern, the simple declarative sentence, turns out to yield many examples of acute formalization, in which a single distinctive pattern is imposed upon two or more (very commonly, groups of three or groups of five) cognitive units. While an intermediate division of a tractate may be composed of several such conglomerates of cognitive units, it is rare indeed for cognitive units formally to stand wholly by themselves. Normally, cognitive units share formal or formulary traits with others to which they are juxtaposed and the theme of which they share. It follows that the principal unit of formulary formalization is the intermediate division and not the cognitive unit. And what that means for our inquiry, is simple: we can tell when it is that the ultimate or penultimate redactors of a document do the writing. Now let us see that vast collection of writings that exhibit precisely the opposite trait: a literature in which, while doing some writing of their own, the redactors collected and arranged available materials.

V. When the Document Does Not Define the Literary Protocol: Stories Told But Not Compiled

Now to the other extreme. Can I point to a kind of writing that in no way defines a document now in our hands or even a type of document we can now imagine, that is, one that in its particulars we do not have but that conforms in its definitive traits to those that we do have? Indeed I can, and it is the writing of stories about sages and other exemplary figures. To show what might have been, I point to the simple fact that the final organizers of the Bavli, the Talmud of Babylonia had in hand a tripartite corpus of inherited materials awaiting composition into a final, closed document. First, the first type of material, in various states and stages of completion, addressed the Mishnah or took up the principles of laws that the Mishnah had originally brought to articulation. These the framers of the Bavli organized in accord with the order of those Mishnah tractates that they selected for sustained attention. Second, they had in hand received materials, again in various conditions, pertinent to Scripture, both as Scripture related to the Mishnah and also as Scripture laid forth its own narratives. These they set forth as Scripture commentary. In this way, the penultimate and ultimate redactors of the Bavli laid out a systematic presentation of the two Torahs, the oral, represented by the Mishnah, and the written, represented by Scripture.

And, third, the framers of the Bavli also had in hand materials focused on sages. These in the received form, attested in the Bavli's pages, were framed around twin biographical principles, either as strings of stories about great sages of the past or as collections of sayings and comments drawn together solely because the same name stands behind all the collected sayings. These can easily have been composed into biographies. In the context of Christianity and of Judaism, it is appropriate to call the biography of a holy man or woman, meant to convey the divine message, a gospel. This is writing that is utterly outside the documentary framework in which it is now preserved; nearly all narratives in the rabbinic literature, not only the biographical ones, indeed prove remote from any documentary program exhibited by the canonical documents in which they now occur.

The Bavli as a whole lays itself out as a commentary to the Mishnah. So the framers wished us to think that whatever they wanted to tell us would take the form of Mishnah commentary. But a second glance indicates that the Bavli is made up of enormous composites, themselves closed prior to inclusion in the Bavli. Some of these composites – around 35 percent to 40 percent of Bavli's, if my sample is indicative[1] – were selected and arranged along lines dictated by a logic other than that deriving from the requirements of Mishnah commentary. The components of the canon of the Judaism of the Dual Torah prior to the Bavli had encompassed amplifications of the Mishnah, in the Tosefta and in the Yerushalmi, as well as the same for Scripture, in such documents as Sifra to Leviticus, Sifré to Numbers, another Sifré, to Deuteronomy, Genesis Rabbah, Leviticus Rabbah, and the like. But there was no entire document, now extant, organized around the life and teachings of a particular sage. Even The Fathers According to Rabbi Nathan, which contains a good sample of stories about sages, is not so organized as to yield a life of a sage, or even a systematic biography of any kind. Where events in the lives of sages do occur, they are thematic and not biographical in organization, for example, stories about the origins, as to Torah study, of diverse sages; death scenes of various sages. The sage as such, whether Aqiba or Yohanan ben Zakkai or Eliezer b. Hyrcanus, never in that document defines the appropriate organizing principle for sequences of stories or sayings. And there is no other in which the sage forms an organizing category for any material purpose.

Accordingly, the decision that the framers of the Bavli reached was to adopt the two redactional principles inherited from the antecedent century or so and to reject the one already rejected by their predecessors, even while honoring it. [1] They organized the Bavli around the Mishnah. But [2] they adapted and included vast tracts of antecedent materials organized as scriptural commentary. These they inserted whole and complete, not at all in response to the Mishnah's program.

---

[1] I compared Bavli and Yerushalmi tractates Sukkah, Sanhedrin, and Sotah, showing the proportion of what I call Scripture units of thought to Mishnah units of thought. See my *Judaism. The Classic Statement. The Evidence of the Bavli* (Chicago, 1986: University of Chicago Press).

But, finally, [3] while making provision for small-scale compositions built upon biographical principles, preserving both strings of sayings from a given master (and often a given tradent of a given master) as well as tales about authorities of the preceding half-millennium, they *never* created redactional compositions, of a sizable order, that focused upon given authorities. But sufficient materials certainly lay at hand to allow doing so.

We have now seen that some writings carry out a redactional purpose. The Mishnah was our prime example. Some writings ignore all redactional considerations we can identify. The stories about sages in the Fathers According to Rabbi Nathan for instance show us kinds of writing that are wholly out of phase with the program of the document that collects and compiles them. We may therefore turn to Midrash compilations and find the traits of writing that clearly are imposed by the requirements of compilation. We further identify writings that clearly respond to a redactional program, but not the program of any compilation we now have in hand. There is little speculation about the identification of such writings. They will conform to the redactional patterns we discern in the known compilations, but presuppose a collection other than one now known to us. Finally, we turn to pieces of writing that respond to no redactional program known to us or susceptible to invention in accord with the principles of defining compilation known to us.

VI. Pericopes Framed for the Purposes of the Particular Document in Which They Occur

My analytical taxonomy of the writings now collected in various Midrash compilations point to not only three stages in the formation of the classics of Judaism. It also suggests that writing went on outside of the framework of the editing of documents, and also within the limits of the formation and framing of documents. Writing of the former kind then constituted a kind of literary work to which redactional planning proved irrelevant. But the second and the third kinds of writing respond to redactional considerations. So in the end we shall wish to distinguish between writing intended for the making of books – compositions of the first three kinds listed just now – and writing not in response to the requirements of the making of compilations.

The distinctions upon which these analytical taxonomies rest are objective and in no way subjective, since they depend upon the fixed and factual relationship between a piece of writing and a larger redactional context.

[1]   We know the requirements of redactors of the several documents of the rabbinic canon, because I have already shown what they are in the case of a large variety of documents. When, therefore, we judge a piece of writing to serve the program of the document in which that writing occurs, it is not because of a personal impulse or a private and incommunicable insight, but because the traits of that writing self-evidently respond to the documentary program of the book in which the writing is located.

[2]   When, further, we conclude that a piece of writing belongs in some other document than the one in which it is found, that, too, forms a factual judgment.

My example is a very simple one: writing that can serve only as a component of a commentary on a given scriptural book has been made up for the book in which it appears (or one very like it, if one wants to quibble). My example may derive from any of the ten Midrash compilations of late antiquity. Here is one among innumerable possibilities.

Sifré to Numbers I

VII.1 A.   "[The Lord said to Moses, 'Command the people of Israel that they put out of the camp every leper and every one having a discharge, and every one that is unclean through contact with the dead.] You shall put out both male and female, putting them outside the camp, that they may not defile their camp, in the midst of which I dwell'" (Gen. 5:1-4).

B.   I know, on the basis of the stated verse, that the law applies only to male and female [persons who are suffering from the specified forms of cultic uncleanness]. How do I know that the law pertains also to one lacking clearly defined sexual traits or to one possessed of the sexual traits of both genders?

C.   Scripture states, "...putting *them* outside the camp." [This is taken to constitute an encompassing formulation, extending beyond the male and female of the prior clause.]

D.   I know, on the basis of the stated verse, that the law applies only to those who can be sent forth. How do I know that the law pertains also to those who cannot be sent forth?

E.   Scripture states, "...putting them outside the camp." [This is taken to constitute an encompassing formulation, as before.]

F.   I know on the basis of the stated verse that the law applies only to persons. How do I know that the law pertains also to utensils?

G.   Scripture states, "...putting *them* outside the camp." [This is taken to constitute an encompassing formulation.]

VII.2 A.   [Dealing with the same question as at 1.F,] R. Aqiba says, "'You shall put out both male and female, putting them outside the camp.' Both persons and utensils are implied."

B.   R. Ishmael says, "You may construct a logical argument, as follows:

  C. "Since man is subject to uncleanness on account of *negaim* ["plagues"], and clothing [thus: utensils] is subject to uncleanness on the same count, just as man is subject to being sent forth [ostracism], likewise utensils are subject to being sent forth."

  D. No, such an argument is not valid [and hence exegesis of the actual language of Scripture, as at A, is the sole correct route]. If you have stated the rule in the case of man, who imparts uncleanness when he exerts pressure on an object used for either sitting or lying, and, on which account, he is subject to ostracism, will you say the same rule of utensils, which do not impart uncleanness when they exert pressure on an object used for sitting and lying? [Clearly there is a difference between the uncleanness brought about by a human being from that brought about by an inanimate object, and therefore the rule that applies to the one will not necessarily apply to the other. Logic by itself will not suffice, and, it must follow, the proof of a verse of Scripture alone will suffice to prove the point.]

  E. [No, that objection is not valid, because we can show that the same rule does apply to both an inanimate object and to man, namely] lo, there is the case of the stone affected with a *nega*, which will prove the point. For it does not impart uncleanness when it exerts pressure on an object used for sitting or lying, but it does require ostracism [being sent forth from the camp, a rule that Scripture itself makes explicit].

  F. Therefore do not find it surprising that utensils, even though they in general do not impart uncleanness when they exert pressure on an object used for sitting or lying, are to be sent forth from the camp." [Ishmael's logical proof stands.]

VII.3 A. R. Yosé the Galilean says, "'You shall put out both male and female, putting them outside the camp, that they may not defile their camp, in the midst of which I dwell.'

  B. "What marks as singular male and female is that they can be turned into a generative source of uncleanness [when they die and are corpses], and, it follows, they are to be sent forth from the camp when they become unclean [even while alive], so anything which can become a generative source of uncleanness will be subject to being sent forth from the camp.

  C. "What is excluded is a piece of cloth less than three by three fingerbreadths, which in the entire Torah is never subject to becoming a generative source of uncleanness."

VII.4 A. R. Isaac says, "Lo, Scripture states, '[And every person that eats what dies of itself or what is torn by beasts, whether he is a native or a sojourner, shall wash his clothes and bathe himself in water and be unclean until the evening; then he shall be clean.] But if he does not wash them or bathe his flesh, he shall bear his iniquity' (Lev. 17:15-16).

  B. "It is on account of failure to wash one's body that Scripture has imposed the penalty of extirpation.

  C. "You maintain that it is on account of failure to wash one's body that Scripture has imposed the penalty of extirpation. But perhaps Scripture has imposed a penalty of extirpation only on account of the failure to launder one's garments.

D.   "Thus you may construct the argument to the contrary [*sui eipas*]: If in the case of one who has become unclean on account of corpse uncleanness, which is a severe source of uncleanness, Scripture has not imposed a penalty merely because of failure to launder one's garments, as to one who eats meat of a beast that has died of itself, which is a minor source of uncleanness, it is a matter of reason that Scripture should not impose a penalty on the account of having failed to launder the garments."

Why do I maintain that the composition can serve only the document in which it occurs? The reason is that we read the verse in a narrow framework: What rule do we derive from the *actual* language at hand? No. 1 answers the question on the basis of an exegesis of the verse. No. 2 then provides an alternative proof. Aqiba provides yet another reading of the language at hand. Ishmael goes over the possibility of a logical demonstration. I find it difficult to see how Yosé's pericope fits in. It does not seem to me to address the problem at hand. He wants to deal with a separate issue entirely, as specified at C. No. 4 pursues yet another independent question. So Nos. 3, 4 look to be parachuted down. On what basis? No. 3 deals with our base verse. But No. 4 does not. Then what guided the compositors to introduce Nos. 1, 2, 3, and 4? Nos. 1, 2 deal with the exegesis of the limited rule at hand: How do I know to what classifications of persons and objects ostracism applies? No. 1 answers two questions, first, the classifications, then the basis for the rule. No. 2 introduces the second question: On what basis do we make our rule? The answer, as is clear, is Scripture, not unaided reason. Now at that point the issue of utensils emerges. So Yosé the Galilean's interest in the rule governing a utensil – a piece of cloth – leads to the intrusion of his item. And the same theme – the rule governing utensils, garments – accounts for the introduction of I:VII.4 as well. In sum, the redactional principle is clear: treat the verse, then the theme generated by the verse. Then this piece of writing can have been formed only for the purpose of a commentary to the book of Numbers: Sifré to Numbers is the only one we have. Q.E.D.

VII. Pericopes Framed for the Purposes of a Particular Document But Not of a Type We Now Possess

A piece of writing that serves no document we now know may nonetheless conform to the rules of writing that we can readily imagine and describe in theory. For instance, a propositional composition, that runs through a wide variety of texts to make a point autonomous of all of the texts that are invoked, clearly is intended for a propositional document, one that (like the Mishnah) makes points autonomous of a given prior writing, for example, a biblical book, but that makes points that for one reason or another cohere quite nicely on their own. Authors of propositional compilations self-evidently can imagine that kind of redaction. We have their writings, but not the books that they intended to be made up of those writings. A single example suffices. It derives from Sifra.

If the canon of Judaism included a major treatise or compilation on applied logic and practical reason, then a principal tractate, or set of tractates, would be devoted to proving that reason by itself cannot produce reliable results. And in that treatise would be a vast and various collection of sustained discussions, which spread themselves across Sifra and Sifré to Numbers and Sifré to Deuteronomy, the Yerushalmi and the Bavli, as well as other collections. Here is a sample of how that polemic has imposed itself on the amplification of Lev. 1:2 and transformed treatment of that verse from an exegesis to an example of an overriding proposition. It goes without saying that where we have this type of proof of the priority of Scripture over logic, or of the necessity of Scripture in the defining of generative taxa, the discussion serves a purpose that transcends the case, and on that basis I maintain the proposition proposed here. It is that there were types of collections that we can readily imagine but that were not made up. In this case, it is, as is clear, a treatise on applied logic, and the general proposition of that treatise is that reliable taxonomy derives only from Scripture.

Sifra Parashat Vayyiqra Dibura Denedabah Parashah 2 III

I.1 A. "Speak to the Israelite people [and say to them, 'When any [Hebrew: Adam] of you presents an offering of cattle to the Lord, he shall choose his offering from the herd or from the flock. If his offering is a burnt-offering from the herd, he shall offer a male without blemish; he shall offer it at the door of the tent of meeting, that he may be accepted before the Lord;] he shall lay [his hand upon the head of the burnt-offering, and it shall be accepted for him to make atonement for him]'" (Lev. 1:2):

B. "He shall lay his hand": Israelites lay on hands, gentiles do not lay on hands.

C. [But is it necessary to prove that proposition on the basis of the cited verse? Is it not to be proven merely by an argument of a logical order, which is now presented?] Now which measure [covering the applicability of a rite] is more abundant, the measure of waving or the measure of laying on of hands?

D. The measure of waving [the beast] is greater than the measure of laying on of hands.

E. For waving [the sacrifice] is done to both something that is animate and something that is not animate, while the laying on of hands applies only to something that is animate.

F. If gentiles are excluded from the rite of waving the sacrifice, which applies to a variety of sacrifices, should they not be excluded from the rite of laying on of hands, which pertains to fewer sacrifices? [Accordingly, I prove on the basis of reason the rule that is derived at A-B from the verse of Scripture.]

G.   [I shall now show that the premise of the foregoing argument is false:] [You have constructed your argument] from the angle that yields waving as more common and laying on of hands as less common.

H.   But take the other angle, which yields laying on of hands as the more common and waving as the less common.

I.   For the laying on of hands applies to all partners in the ownership of a beast [each one of whom is required to lay hands on the beast before it is slaughtered in behalf of the partnership in ownership of the beast as a whole],

J.   but the waving of a sacrifice is not a requirement that applies to all partners in the ownership of a beast.

K.   Now if I eliminate [gentiles' laying on of hands] in the case of the waving of a beast, which is a requirement applying to fewer cases, should I eliminate them from the requirement of laying on of hands, which applies to a larger number of cases?

L.   Lo, since a rule pertains to the waving of the sacrifice that does not apply to the laying on of hands, and a rule pertains to the laying on of hands that does not apply to the waving of the sacrifice, it is necessary for Scripture to make the statement that it does, specifically:

M.   "He shall lay his hand": Israelites lay on hands, gentiles do not lay on hands.

The basic premise is that when two comparable actions differ, then the more commonly performed one imposes its rule upon further actions, the rule governing which is unknown. If then we show that action A is more commonly performed than action B, other actions of the same classification will follow the rule governing A, not the rule governing B. Then the correct route to overturn such an argument is to show that each of the actions, the rule governing which is known, differs from the other in such a way that neither the one nor the other can be shown to be the more commonly performed. Then the rule governing the further actions is not to be derived from the one governing the two known actions. The powerful instrument of analytical and comparative reasoning proves that diverse traits pertain to the two stages of the rite of sacrifice – the waving, the laying on of hands – which means that a rule pertaining to the one does not necessarily apply to the other. On account of that difference we must evoke the specific ruling of Scripture. The polemic in favor of Scripture, uniting all of the components into a single coherent argument, then insists that there really is no such thing as a genus at all, and Scripture's rules and regulations serve a long list of items, each of them *sui generis*, for discovering rules by the logic of analogy and contrast is simply not possible.

VIII. Pericopes Framed for the Purposes Not Particular to a Type of Document Now in Our Hands

Some writings stand autonomous of any redactional program we have in an existing compilation or of any we can even imagine on the foundations of said writings. Compositions of this kind, as a matter of hypothesis, are to be assigned to a stage in the formation of classics prior to the framing of all available documents. For, as a matter of fact, all of our now extant writings adhere to a single program of conglomeration and agglutination, and all are served by composites of one sort, rather than some other. Hence we may suppose that at some point prior to the decision to make writings in the model that we now have but in some other model people also made up completed units of thought to serve these other kinds of writings. These persist, now, in documents that they do not serve at all well. And we can fairly easily identify the kinds of documents that they can and should have served quite nicely indeed. These then are the three stages of literary formation in the making of the classics of Judaism.

Of the relative temporal or ordinal position of writings that stand autonomous of any redactional program we have in an existing compilation or of any we can even imagine on the foundations of said writings we can say nothing. These writings prove episodic; they are commonly singletons. They serve equally well everywhere, because they demand no traits of form and redaction in order to endow them with sense and meaning. Why not? Because they are essentially free-standing and episodic, not referential and allusive. They are stories that contain their own point and do not invoke, in the making of that point, a given verse of Scripture. They are sayings that are utterly ad hoc. A variety of materials falls into this – from a redactional perspective – unassigned, and unassignable, type of writing. They do not belong in books at all. By that I mean, whoever made up these pieces of writing did not imagine that what he was forming required a setting beyond the limits of his own piece of writing; the story is not only complete in itself but could stand entirely on its own; the saying spoke for itself and required no nurturing context; the proposition and its associated proofs in no way was meant to draw nourishment from roots penetrating nutriments outside of its own literary limits.

Where we have utterly hermetic writing, able to define its own limits and sustain its point without regard to anything outside itself, we know that here we are in the presence of authorships that had no larger redactional plan in mind, no intent on the making of books out of their little pieces of writing. We may note that, among the "unimaginable" compilations is not a collection of parables, since parables rarely[2] stand free and never are inserted for their own sake. Whenever in the rabbinic canon we find a parable, it is meant to serve the purpose of an authorship engaged in making its own point; and the point of a parable is rarely, if ever, left unarticulated. Normally it is put into words, but occasionally the point is made simply by redactional setting. It must follow that, in this canon, the parable cannot have constituted the generative or agglutinative principle of a large-scale compilation. It further follows, so it seems to me, that the parable always takes shape within the framework of a work of composition for the purpose of either a large-scale exposition or, more commonly still, of compilation of a set of expositions into what we should now call the chapter of a book; that is to say, parables link to purposes that transcend the tale that they tell (or even the point that the tale makes). Let me now give one example of what I classify as a free-standing piece of writing, one with no place for itself in accord with the purposes of compilers either of documents we now have in hand or of documents we can readily envisage or imagine. My example again derives from Sifra, although, as a matter of fact, every document of the canon yields illustrative materials for all three types of writing.

The issue of the relationship between the Mishnah and Scripture deeply engaged a variety of writers and compilers of documents. Time and again we have evidence of an interest in the scriptural sources of laws, or of greater consequence in the priority of Scripture in taxonomic inquiry. We can show large-scale compositions that will readily have served treatises on these matters. But if I had to point to a single type of writing that is quite commonplace in the compilations we do have, but *wholly* outside of the repertoire of redactional possibilities we have or can imagine, it must be a sustained piece of writing on the relationship of the Mishnah to Scripture. Such a treatise can have been enormous, not only because, in theory, every line of the Mishnah required attention. It is also because, in practice, a variety of documents, particularly Sifra, the two Sifrés, and the Talmuds, contain writing of a single kind, meant to amplify the Mishnah by appeal to Scripture (but never to amplify Scripture by appeal to the Mishnah!). It is perfectly clear that no one imagined compiling a commentary to the Mishnah that would consist principally of proofs, of a sustained and well-crafted sort, that the Mishnah in general depends upon Scripture (even though specific and sustained proofs that the principles of taxonomy derive from Scripture are, as I said, susceptible of compilation in such treatises). How do we

---

[2]I should prefer to say "never," but it is easier to say what is in the rabbinic literature than what is never there.

know that fact? It is because, when people did compile writings in the form of sustained commentaries to the Mishnah, that is to say, the two Talmuds, they did not focus principally upon the scriptural exegesis of the Mishnah; that formed only one interest, and, while an important one, it did not predominate; it certainly did not define the plan and program of the whole; and it certainly did not form a center of redactional labor. It was simply one item on a list of items that would be brought into relationship, where appropriate, with sentences of the Mishnah. And even then, it always was the intersection at the level of sentences, not sustained discourses, let alone with the Mishnah viewed whole and complete.

And yet – and yet if we look into compilations we do have, we find sizable sets of materials that can have been joined together with the Mishnah, paragraph by paragraph, in such a way that Scripture might have been shaped into a commentary to the Mishnah. Let me now give a sustained example of what might have emerged, but never did emerge, in the canonical compilations of Judaism. I draw my case from Sifra, but equivalent materials in other Midrash compilations as well as in the two Talmuds in fact are abundant. In boldface type are direct citations of Mishnah passages. I skip Nos. 2-12, because these are not germane to this part of my argument.

Sifra Parashat Behuqotai Parashah 3 CCLXX

I.1   A.   ["The Lord said to Moses, Say to the people of Israel, When a man makes a special vow of persons to the Lord at your Valuation, then your Valuation of a male from twenty years old up to sixty years old shall be fifty sheqels of silver according to the sheqel of the sanctuary. If the person is a female, your Valuation shall be thirty sheqels. If the person is from five years old up to twenty years old, your Valuation shall be for a male twenty sheqels and for a female ten sheqels. If the person is from a month old up to five years old, your Valuation shall be for a male five sheqels of silver and for a female your Valuation shall be three sheqels of silver. And if the person is sixty years old and upward, then your Valuation for a male shall be fifteen sheqels and for a female ten sheqels. And if a man is too poor to pay your Valuation, then he shall bring the person before the priest, and the priest shall value him; according to the ability of him who vowed the priest shall value him" (Lev. 27:1-8).]

    B.   **"Israelites take vows of Valuation, but gentiles do not take vows of Valuation [M. Ar. 1:2B].**

    C.   "Might one suppose they are not subject to vows of Valuation?

    D.   "Scripture says, 'a man,'" the words of R. Meir.

    E.   Said R. Meir, "After one verse of Scripture makes an inclusionary statement, another makes an exclusionary statement.

    F.   "On what account do I say that gentiles are subject to vows of Valuation but may not take vows of Valuation?

G. "It is because greater is the applicability of the rule of subject to the pledge of Valuation by others than the applicability of making the pledge of Valuation of others [T. Ar. 1:1A].

H. "For lo, a deaf-mute, idiot, and minor may be subjected to vows of Valuation, but they are not able to take vows of Valuation [M. Ar. 1:1F]."

I. R. Judah says, "Israelites are subject to vows of Valuation, but gentiles are not subject to vows of Valuation [M. Ar. 1:2C].

J. "Might one suppose that they may not take vows of Valuation of third parties?

K. "Scripture says, 'a man.'"

L. Said R. Judah, "After one verse of Scripture makes an inclusionary statement, another makes an exclusionary statement.

M. "On what account do I say that gentiles are not subject to vows of Valuation but may take vows of Valuation?

N. "It is because greater is the applicability of the rule of pledging the Valuation of others than the applicability of being subject to the pledge of Valuation by others [T. Ar. 1:1C].

O. "For a person of doubtful sexual traits and a person who exhibits traits of both sexes pledge the Valuation of others but is not subjected to the pledge of Valuation to be paid by others" [M. Ar. 1:1D].

I.13 A. And how do we know that the sixtieth year is treated as part of the period prior to that year?

B. Scripture says, "from twenty years old up to sixty years old" –

C. This teaches that the sixtieth year is treated as part of the period prior to that year.

D. I know only that that is the rule governing the status of the sixtieth year. How do I know the rule as to assigning the fifth year, the twentieth year?

E. It is a matter of logic:

F. Liability is incurred when one is in the sixtieth year, the fifth year, and the twentieth year.

G. Just as the sixtieth year is treated as part of the period prior to that year,

H. so the fifth and the twentieth years are treated as part of the period prior to that year.

I. But if you treat the sixtieth year as part of the prior period, imposing a more stringent law [the Valuation requiring a higher fee before than after sixty],

J. shall we treat the fifth year and the twentieth year as part of the period prior to that year, so imposing a more lenient law in such cases [the Valuation being less expensive]?

K. Accordingly, Scripture is required to settle the question when it refers repeatedly to "year,"

L. thus establishing a single classification for all such cases:

M. Just as the sixtieth year is treated as part of the prior period, so the fifth and the twentieth years are treated as part of the prior period.

N.   And that is the rule, whether it produces a more lenient or a more stringent ruling [M. Ar. 4:4M-Q, with somewhat different wording].

I.14   A.   R. Eliezer says, "How do we know that a month and a day after a month are treated as part of the sixtieth year?

       B.   "Scripture says, 'up...':

       C.   "Here we find reference to 'up...,' and elsewhere we find the same. Just as 'up' used elsewhere means that a month and a day after the month [are included in the prior span of time], so the meaning is the same when used here. [M. Ar. 4:4R: R. Eleazar says, "The foregoing applies so long as they are a month and a day more than the years which are prescribed."]

I.15   A.   I know only that this rule applies after sixty. How do I know that the same rule applies after five or twenty?

       B.   It is a matter of logic:

       C.   One is liability to pay a pledge of Valuation if the person to be evalued is older than sixty, and one is liable if such a one is older than five or older than twenty.

       D.   Just as, if one is older than sixty by a month and a day, the person is as though he were sixty years of age, so if the one is over five years or twenty years by a month and a day, lo, these are deemed to be the equivalent of five or twenty years of age.

I.16   A.   "And if a man is too poor to pay your Valuation":

       B.   this means, if he is too impoverished to come up with your Valuation.

I.17   A.   "Then he shall bring the person before the priest":

       B.   This then excludes a dead person.

       C.   I shall then exclude a corpse but not a dying person?

       D.   Scripture says, "Scripture says, 'Then he shall bring the person before the priest, and the priest shall value him" –

       E.   One who is subject to being brought is subject to being valuated, and one who is not subject to being brought before the priest [such as a dying man] also is not subject to the pledge of Valuation.

I.18   A.   Might one suppose that even if someone said, "The Valuation of Mr. So-and-so is incumbent on me," and he died, the man should be exempt?

       B.   Scripture says, "And the priest shall value him."

       C.   That is so even if he is dead.

I.19   A.   "And the priest shall value him":

       B.   This means that one pays only in accord with the conditions prevailing at the time of the Valuation.

I.20   A.   "According to the ability of him who vowed the priest shall value him":

       B.   It is in accord with the means of the one who takes the vow, not the one concerning whom the vow is taken,

       C.   whether that is a man, woman, or child.

       D.   In this connection sages have said:

       E.   The estimate of ability to pay is made in accord with the status of the one who vows;

       F.   and the estimate of the years of age is made in accord with the status of the one whose Valuation is vowed.

    G.   And when this is according to the Valuations spelled out in the
            Torah, it is in accord with the status, as to age and sex, of the one
            whose Valuation is pledged.
    H.   And the Valuation is paid in accordance with the rate prescribed
            at the time of the pledge of Valuation [M. Ar. 4:1A-D].
I.21 A.   "The priest shall value him":
      B.   This serves as the generative analogy covering all cases of
            Valuations, indicating that the priest should be in charge.

The program of the Mishnah and the Tosefta predominates
throughout, for example, Nos. 1, 12, 13, 14-15. The second methodical
inquiry characteristic of our authorship, involving exclusion and
inclusion, accounts for pretty much the rest of this well-crafted
discussion. Now we see a coherent and cogent discussion of a topic in
accord with a program applicable to all topics, that trait of our document
which so won our admiration. Thus Nos. 2-11, 17-20, involve inclusion,
exclusion, or extension by analogy. I should offer this excellent
composition as an example of the best our authorship has to give us, and
a very impressive intellectual gift at that. The point throughout is
simple. We know how the compilers of canonical writings produced
treatments of the Mishnah. The one thing that they did not do was to
create a scriptural commentary to the Mishnah. That is not the only type
of writing lacking all correspondence to documents we have or can
imagine, but it is a striking example.

IX. The Three Stages of Literary Formation

Now to return to my starting point, namely, those sizable selections
of materials that circulated from one document to another and why I
tend to think they were formed earlier than the writings particular to
documents. The documentary hypothesis affects our reading of the
itinerant compositions, for it identifies what writings are
extradocumentary and nondocumentary and imposes upon the
hermeneutics and history of these writings a set of distinctive
considerations. The reason is that these writings serve the purposes not
of compilers (or authors or authorships) of distinct compilations, but the
interests of a another type of authorship entirely: one that thought
making up stories (whether or not for collections) itself an important
activity; or making up exercises on Mishnah Scripture relationships; or
other such writings as lie beyond the imagination of the compilers of the
score of documents that comprise the canon. When writings work well
for two or more documents therefore they must be assumed to have a
literary history different from those that serve only one writing or one
type of writing, and, also, demand a different hermeneutic.

My "three stages" in ordinal sequence correspond, as a matter of fact, to a taxic structure, that is, three types of writing. The first – and last in assumed temporal order – is writing carried out in the context of the making, or compilation, of a classic. That writing responds to the redactional program and plan of the authorship of a classic. The second, penultimate in order, is writing that can appear in a given document but better serves a document other than the one in which it (singularly) occurs. This kind of writing seems to me not to fall within the same period of redaction as the first. For while it is a type of writing under the identical conditions, it also is writing that presupposes redactional programs in no way in play in the ultimate, and definitive, period of the formation of the canon: when people did things this way, and not in some other. That is why I think it is a kind of writing that was done prior to the period in which people limited their redactional work and associated labor of composition to the program that yielded the books we now have.

The upshot is simple: whether the classification of writing be given a temporal or merely taxonomic valence, the issue is the same: Have these writers done their work with documentary considerations in mind? I believe I have shown that they have not. Then where did they expect their work to makes its way? Anywhere it might, because, so they assumed, fitting in nowhere in particular, it found a suitable locus everywhere it turned up. But I think temporal, not merely taxonomic, considerations pertain.

The third kind of writing seems to me to originate in a period prior to the other two. It is carried on in a manner independent of all redactional considerations such as are known to us. Then it should derive from a time when redactional considerations played no paramount role in the making of compositions. A brief essay, rather than a sustained composition, was then the dominant mode of writing. My hypothesis is that people can have written both long and short compositions – compositions and composites, in my language – at one and the same time. But writing that does not presuppose a secondary labor of redaction, for example, in a composite, probably originated when authors or authorships did not anticipate any fate for their writing beyond their labor of composition itself.

Along these same lines of argument, this writing may or may not travel from one document to another. What that means is that the author or authorship does not imagine a future for his writing. What fits anywhere is composed to go nowhere in particular. Accordingly, what matters is not whether a writing fits one document or another, but whether, as the author or authorship has composed a piece of writing, that writing meets the requirements of any document we now have or can even imagine. If it does not, then we deal with a literary period in which the main kind of writing was ad hoc and episodic, not sustained and documentary.

Now extra and nondocumentary kinds of writing seem to me to derive from either [1] a period prior to the work of the making of Midrash compilations and the two Talmuds alike; or [2] a labor of composition not subject to the rules and considerations that operated in the work of the making of Midrash compilations and the two Talmuds. As a matter of hypothesis, I should guess that nondocumentary writing comes prior to making any kind of documents of consequence, and extradocumentary writing comes prior to the period in which the specificities of the documents we now have were defined. That is to say, writing that can fit anywhere or nowhere is prior to writing that can fit somewhere but does not fit anywhere now accessible to us, and both kinds of writing are prior to the kind that fits only in documents in which it is now located.

And given the documentary propositions and theses that we can locate in all of our compilations, we can only assume that the nondocumentary writings enjoyed, and were assumed to enjoy, ecumenical acceptance. That means, very simply, when we wish to know the consensus of the entire textual (or canonical) community[3] – I mean simply the people, anywhere and any time, responsible for everything we now have – we turn not to the distinctive perspective of documents, but the (apparently universally acceptable) perspective of the extradocumentary compositions. That is the point at which we should look for the propositions everywhere accepted but nowhere advanced in a distinctive way, the "Judaism beyond the texts" – or behind them. Now on to the issue at hand: compositions and even composites in the Bavli that clearly have been worked out to create an analytical critical exegesis for some document other than the Bavli: the *talmuds* that never survived.

X. The Unrealized Talmud of Sifra Cases in
Bavli Menahot Chapters Six, Seven, and Eight

What we now shall see is a set of examples of how the analysis, in the Bavli, of a passage in the Sifra follows precisely the same rhetorical and logical rules that govern the analysis in the Bavli of a passage of the Mishnah. That fact by itself shows that the same way framers of passages of analysis and criticism of the Mishnah that found their way into the Bavli's commentary to the Mishnah characterized the work of

---

[3]I prefer Brian Stock's "textual community," see his *Implications of Literacy* (Princeton, 1986: Princeton University Press).

framers of a passage of the Sifra that the Bavli has preserved for us. It would seem to me that the prevalence of the same literary conventions in the reading of two distinct documents, each with its own indicative traits, strongly suggests the work was done more or less within the same period of literary formulation and among people responsive to the same conventions of analysis. Then a further fact will prove exceedingly suggestive. It is that the analysis of the Sifra's passage proceeds wholly in terms required by that passage and ignores the setting, within the composite of the Bavli, in which the Sifra's passage has been preserved. That seems to me to mean that the framers of the commentary on the Sifra's passage had in mind a document that would be devoted to not the Mishnah but Sifra. Then the framers of the critical analysis of the Sifra's materials proposed to produce a commentary to the Sifra, parallel to what was being accomplished for the Mishnah. But that commentary to the Sifra, that is, that *talmud to Sifra*, did not survive, except in bits and pieces in the Bavli itself.

To begin with, let me give an example of how a passage of the Sifra, left without exposition in its own terms and framework, is introduced in the clarification of the Mishnah. It will be the contrast between this simple utilization of the Sifra and the secondary exposition, in Sifra's terms and framework, of Sifra's materials, that will point us toward the conclusion that, alongside a *talmud* for the Mishnah, a *talmud* for the Sifra was under way.

Menahot 6:4A-L

	A.	They reaped it,
	B.	and they put it into baskets,
	C.	They brought it to the court [of the Temple].
	D.	"They did parch it in fire, "so as to carry out the requirement that it be parched with fire (Lev.2:14)," the words of R. Meir.
	E.	And sages say, "With reeds and with stems of plants do they [first] beat it [to thresh it], so that it not be crushed.
	F.	"And they put it into a tube.
	G.	"And the tube was perforated, so that the fire affects all of it."
	H.	They spread it out in the court, and the breeze blows over it.
	I.	They put it into a grist mill and took out therefrom a tenth-ephah, which is sifted through thirteen sieves [M. 6:7].
	J.	And the residue is redeemed and eaten by anyone.
	K.	And it is liable for the dough-offering, but exempt from tithes.
	L.	R. Aqiba declares it liable for both dough-offering and tithes.
I.1	A.	*Our rabbis have taught on Tannaite authority:*
	B.	"... new ears parched with fire" (Lev. 2:14) – this refers to fresh ears of grain.
	C.	This teaches the following:
	D.	"They parched it in fire, so as to carry out the requirement that it be parched with fire," the words of R. Meir.

E.   And sages say, [66B] "The language at hand does not bear the meaning of parching, but it bears a different meaning. [On the problems of the text here, see Finkelstein, *Sifra*, p. 95, ns. to lines 31-34].

F.   "With reeds and with stems of plants they beat it first, so that it is not crushed. And they put it into a tube, and the tube was perforated, so that the fire affects all of it" [Sifra XXVI:IV.1].

I.2   A.   "... new ears parched with fire":

B.   I do not know whether the fresh ears of grain must be parched, or crushed grain must be parched. It is to be as grits, in such a way that the ear itself is parched.

C.   Scripture says, "with fire," and that breaks off the subject [Cashdan: hence it cannot refer to the subsequent expression but only to the one preceding, so the fresh ears of grain must be parched.]

I.3   A.   "Grits of the fresh grain":

B.   Tender, yet brittle [Jastrow, s.v., ML, p. 785b].

C.   And so Scripture says, "A man came from Baalshalishah, bringing the man of God bread of the first fruits, twenty loaves of barley, and fresh ears of grain in his sack" (2 Kgs. 4:42).

D.   "Fresh ears of grain" means that they were tender, yet brittle.

E.   "In his sack":

F.   He came and poured out for us and we ate and it was fine.

G.   And likewise we find the following: "Let us solace ourselves with love" (Prov. 7:18).

H.   That is, Let us talk together and then let us go up on the couch and rejoice and revel in caresses.

I.   And so, too, "The wing of the ostrich beats joyously," (Job 39:13), meaning, it carries the egg, flies upwards with it, and deposits it in the nest.

J.   And so Scripture says, "Because your way is perverse before me" (Num. 22:32):

K.   The ass feared when she saw the angel and she turned aside [Sifra XXVI:V.1-2].

I.4   A.   The Tannaite authority of the household of R. Ishmael: "'Karmel' means 'rounded and full.'"

This passage is simply parachuted down, an entirely routine amplification of materials that the Mishnah introduces. It is not expounded, either in relationship to the Mishnah or otherwise. In my second example, we see how the Sifra's materials are articulated in relationship to the Mishnah.

Menahot 6:6

A.   The offering of the first sheaf of barley rendered [the produce of the new crop] permitted in the country, and the two loaves [of Pentecost/Shabuot, Lev. 23:16, rendered new produce permitted for the meal-offering] in the sanctuary.

B.   Before the offering of the first sheaf of barley, they do not bring [from new produce, grain that is to be used for] meal-offerings,

first fruits, and the meal-offering which accompanies [drink-]
offerings along with beasts.

C. And if one brought [grain for any of these before the offering of
the first sheaf of barley], it is invalid.

D. [As to bringing grain for any of these items of B] before the two
loaves – one should not do so (Lev. 23:16).

E. And if one brought grain from the new crop for use in preparing
them, it is valid.

I.3 A. *Rami bar Hama raised this question:* "If the two loaves are presented
not in the proper order, what is the law on their permitting what is
forbidden before that time?" [Cashdan: In the ordinary course
grain is sown sometime before the offering of the sheaf of new
barley, so that before the grain is permitted for use as meal-
offerings, that is, after the offering of the two loaves, the two
periods affecting grain have passed in normal sequence; first the
offering of the sheaf of barley, second, the offering of the two
loaves. What if the grain is always permitted for meal-offerings
after these two points have passed, without regard to the
sequence?]

B. *What sort of case is contemplated by this question?*

C. *For instance, grain was sown in the spell between the offering of the sheaf
of first barley and the offering of the two loaves, and then the time for
offering the two loaves and the next sheaf of barley passed. Do we say that
the two loaves permit use of the new crop only when the offerings follow
the usual order but not when they do not follow the usual order, or do they
permit the use of the new grain for the meal-offerings even when not in the
usual order?*

D. Said Rabbah, *"Come and take note"*:

E. "If you bring a meal-offering of first fruits to the Lord, [you shall
bring new ears parched with fire, grits of the fresh grain, as your
meal-offering of first fruits]":

F. This refers to the meal-offering that is the sheaf of first grain.

G. And whence does it derive? From barley.

H. You say that it derives from barley. Might one suppose that it
derives from wheat?

I. R. Eliezer says, "Here the word 'new ears' is used here and also
with reference to the events in Egypt.

J. "Just as, with reference to the events in Egypt, the word 'new ears'
refers to barley, so here it refers to barley. [So we find at Ex. 9:31:
'The flax and the barley were ruined, for the barley was in the ear
and the flax was in bud. But the wheat and the spelt were not
ruined, for they are late in coming up.']"

K. R. Aqiba says, "In regard to a communal offering the bringing of
first fruits at Passover is noted, and the bringing of first fruits at
Pentecost as well. Of the species of grain from which the
individual person brings her obligatory offering [that is, the wife
accused of adultery], the community brings its offering of first
fruits at Passover, and so, too, from the species of grain from
which the individual brings her obligatory offering, the
community likewise should bring its first fruits at Pentecost.

L. "Now what is the species from which the individual brings his obligatory offering? It is barley [that is, the barley-offering of the wife accused of adultery], and so, too, the community should present its offering from barley.

M. "And do not object by appealing to the analogy to the obligatory offering of the community in connection with the two loaves of bread [which form a meal-offering, and which is obligatory, and which derives from wheat], for the two loaves of bread do not fall into the category of first fruits [and so do not present a relevant analogy]" [Sifra XXVI:III.1-2].

N. *[Rabbah now continues:] "Now if it were the fact that the two loaves permit use of the new crop even when not in the usual order, then how can you claim that the two loaves are not classified as first fruits at all* [for the **two loaves of bread do not fall into the category of first fruits**]? *For it can come about that the sheaf of first barley is presented out of the grain that took root before the presentation of the two loaves but after the presentation of the sheaf of first barley for the prior year, and the grain used for the two loaves of the grain that had taken root prior to the presentation of this year's sheaf of first barley but after last year's two loaves."*

O. *But do you really suppose that* **[69A]** *we require the two loaves to derive from first fruits of any particular fruit [Cashdan: and therefore as long as no grain of any particular sowing has been used in the Temple, the two loaves may serve as first fruits]? That is not the case. We require them to be first fruits of the altar* [that is, first fruits of the year's produce to be offered on the altar (Cashdan)], *and in this case the altar has consumed this year's produce* [Cashdan: for wheat used for the sheaf of barley was of this year's produce, even though of an earlier sowing].

What is important is the character of Rabbah's continuation of the abstract from the Sifra. He spells out the implications of that abstract for the issue raised at the outset. So we cannot regard N as a comment on the foregoing; the talmud here focuses upon the question raised by Rami bar Hami, which is an investigation of how the principles of the law pertain to interstitial matters. What follows, in context, is a long set of equivalent theoretical issues, typical of one standard type of Talmudic amplification of the Mishnah's law. The abstract from Sifra has contributed only an illustrative fact; the Sifra has not been given a sustained reading, in its own terms, like that accord to the Mishnah and to the issues raised by the Mishnah's principles of law.

Let us now turn to a passage that illustrates my contention that the Sifra, like the Mishnah, is read in its own terms, and not solely in relationship to some other, principal document (in the case of the Bavli, the Mishnah). In my first example, we shall see how the Bavli to M. Menahot 6:3 reads the Mishnah paragraph. Then Sifra's contribution in its own terms follows. The important side will be what follows that passage.

Mishnah-Tractate Menahot and Its Bavli
6:3

A. How did they do it?

B. Agents of the court go forth on the eve of [the afternoon before] the festival [of Passover].

C. And they make it into sheaves while it is still attached to the ground, so that it will be easy to reap.

D. And all the villagers nearby gather together there [on the night after the first day of Passover], so that it will be reaped with great pomp.

E. Once it gets dark [on the night of the sixteenth of Nisan], he says to them, "Has the sun set?"

F. They say, "Yes."

G. "Has the sun set?"

H. They say, "Yes."

I. "[With] this sickle?"

J. They say, "Yes."

K. "[With] this sickle?"

L. They say, "Yes."

M. "[With] this basket?"

N. They say, "Yes."

O. "[With] this basket?"

P. They say, "Yes."

Q. On the Sabbath, he says to them, "[Shall I reap on] this Sabbath?"

R. They say, "Yes."

S. "[Shall I reap on] this Sabbath?"

T. They say, "Yes."

U. "Shall I reap?"

V. They say, "Reap."

W. "Shall I reap?"

X. They say, "Reap" –

Y. three times for each and every matter.

Z. And they say to him, "Yes, yes, yes."

AA. All of this [pomp] for what purpose?

BB. Because of the Boethusians, for they maintain, "The reaping of the [barley for] the offering of the first sheaf of barley is not [done] at the conclusion of the festival."

I.1 A. *Our rabbis have taught on Tannaite authority:*

B. *These are the days on which there is to be no fasting, and on some of them also, mourning is forbidden as well:*

C. *from the first until the eighth day of Nisan, during which the daily whole-offering was set up, mourning is forbidden;*

D. *from the eighth of Nisan until the close of the festival of Passover, during which time the date for the festival of Pentecost was reestablished, fasting is forbidden.*

The Tannaite complement, when amplified, will tell us the meaning of the references to specific parties or facts that the Mishnah contains. It is now amplified to the point.

I.2   A.   *from the first until the eighth day of Nisan, during which the daily whole-offering was set up, mourning is forbidden:*
       B.   For the Sadducees said, "A private person may voluntarily present a daily whole-offering."
       C.   *What was the exegesis of Scripture that supported their claim?*
       D.   "The one lamb you shall offer in the morning and the other lamb you shall offer at dusk" (Num. 28:4) [the "you" is singular, hence an individual may provide the daily whole-offering].
       E.   *And what did the other side answer?*
       F.   "My food which is presented to me for offerings made by fire, of a sweet savor to me, you shall observe" (Num. 28:2) [and the "you" here is plural].
       G.   This indicates that all of them should derive from funds taken up from the public funds in the chamber.

I.3   A.   *From the eighth of Nisan until the close of the festival of Passover, during which time the date for the festival of Pentecost was reestablished, fasting is forbidden:*
       B.   For the Boethusians say, "The festival of Pentecost must always coincide with a Sunday [seven full weeks after the offering of the first sheaf of barley grain, which in their view was offered only on a Sunday].
       C.   Rabban Yohanan ben Zakkai engaged with them and said to them, "You total and complete schmucks! How do you know it?"
       D.   Not a single one of them could answer, except a doddering old fool, who stumbled and mumbled against him, saying, "Our lord, Moses, loved Israel and knew that Pentecost lasted for only one day, so he therefore made sure to place it on a Sunday, so that Israel would have a two-day vacation."
       E.   He recited in this regard the following verse: "It is an eleven-day journey from Horeb to Kadesh Barnea by way of Mount Seir" (Deut. 1:2)."
       F.   [65B] "Now if our lord, Moses, really loved Israel all that much, why did he delay them in the wilderness for forty years!"
       G.   He said to him, "My lord, do you think you can get rid of me with that kind of garbage?"
       H.   He said to him, "You total schmuck! Are you going to treat the complete Torah that is ours like the idle nattering and chattering that is all you can throw up? One verse of Scripture says, 'You shall count for yourself fifty days' (Lev. 23:16), and another verse states, 'Seven weeks shall be complete' (Lev. 23:15). So how about that? The one verse refers to a case in which the festival day coincides with the Sabbath, the other, when a festival day coincides with a week day." [Pentecost may coincide with any day of the week.]

I.4   A.   R. Eliezer says, "That proof is not necessary. Lo, Scripture says, 'You shall count for yourself fifty days' (Lev. 23:16) – the counting depends upon the court, [the court fixed the days of the festivals, so they tell the community the time from which to commence counting the days of the waving of the sheaf of barley], and, it follows, the meaning of 'Sabbath' cannot be the Sabbath that commemorates creation, for then the counting would be in the hands of just anybody [and not the court in particular. Everybody could do it.]" [Cashdan: If the counting starting on Sunday, after the Sabbath that commemorates creation, everybody could do it just as well.]

I.5   A.   R. Joshua says, "The Torah has said, 'count a month of days (Num. 11:20), and [after counting twenty-nine days, the thirtieth day] is to be sanctified as the new moon, and, further, 'sanctify the festival of Pentecost' (Lev. 23:15-16). Just as on the occasion of the new moon, something new takes place at the beginning of the counting" [Cashdan: namely, the new moon, for the twenty-nine days are counted from the first day of the new month], so with Pentecost something new takes place [Cashdan: namely, the festival of Passover. Now if the counting always commenced on Sunday, nothing new would take place.]

I.6   A.   R. Ishmael says, "The Torah has said, 'Present the sheaf of first barley on Passover and the two loaves on the festival of Pentecost. Just as the latter are offered on the festival, at the start of the festival, so the former is presented on the festival, at the start of the festival [and that is not always on a Sunday]."

I.7   A.   R. Judah b. Betera says, "Here we find a reference to the Sabbath [in regard to Pentecost, 'unto the morrow of the seventh Sabbath (Lev. 23:16)] and we find a reference to the Sabbath there as well [with reference to the sheaf of barley, 'on the morrow after the Sabbath' (Lev. 23:11)]. Just as in the first instance, the festival day, indeed the commencement thereof, is near the Sabbath [starting as it does immediately after the Sabbath, meaning, the week], so the festival in the latter case must commence near the offering of the barley sheaf, indeed at the beginning of the festival." [Cashdan: Thus the festival of Passover is immediately to precede the offering of the sheaf of barley; Sabbath in context clearly means the festival day.]

Now comes Sifra's treatment of the same theme. The issue is precisely the one that has been treated: proof that "after the Sabbath" refers not to Sunday but to the day following the first festival day of Passover. The proof is worked out in its own terms, but the issue is identical. The purpose of inserting what follows then is clear: further proof of the same proposition, an anthology of such proofs, all of them equally to the point of the amplification of the Mishnah. So Sifra's composition on its own terms has been inserted as an aspect of Mishnah commentary: information required to make sense of what the Mishnah says – not for the purpose of expounding a passage of the Sifra in terms of the requirements of its statements, their logic, their cogency.

I.8   A.   *Our rabbis have taught on Tannaite authority:*

      B.   "And you shall count for yourself" (Lev. 23:15) – the duty of counting is incumbent on every person.

      C.   "On the morrow after the Sabbath" (Lev. 23:16) – that is, on the day after the festival [of Passover].

      D.   But perhaps that refers to the day after the Sabbath that commemorates creation?

E. R. Yosé bar Judah says, "Lo, Scripture says, 'You shall count fifty days' (Lev. 23:16) – every time you make a count, it shall not be for more than fifty days. Now if you maintain that the cited verse speaks of the day after the Sabbath, meaning, after the Sabbath of creation, then sometimes the count might reach fifty-one, or fifty-two, or fifty-three, or fifty-four, or fifty-five, or fifty-six!"

F. R. Judah b. Batera says, "That proof is hardly required. [66A] Lo, Scripture says, 'And you shall count for yourself' (Lev. 23:15) – the duty of counting is incumbent on every person. So the counting depends upon the decision of the court, and the meaning cannot be the Sabbath that commemorates creation, in which case the counting would be in everybody's hands."

G. R. Yosé says, "'On the morrow after the Sabbath' (Lev. 23:16) – that is, on the day after the festival [of Passover]. You say that it is on the day after the festival [of Passover]. But perhaps that refers to the day after the Sabbath that commemorates creation?

H. "Can you really say so? Now does Scripture say, 'From the morrow after the Sabbath with respect to Passover'? And is not 'from the morrow after the Sabbath' stated without further explanation?

I. "Now is not the entire year filled with Sabbaths? Then go and reckon what Sabbath is under discussion?

J. "And, furthermore, here we find a reference to 'from the morrow after the Sabbath,' and elsewhere we find the same language ['counting fifty days to the morrow after the seventh Sabbath'].

K. "Just as 'from the morrow after the Sabbath' refers to a festival day and the beginning of the festival day [specifically, Pentecost, to which reference is made here],

L. "so 'on the morrow after the Sabbath' used here refers to the festival and the beginning of the festival [hence, the morrow after the Sabbath that is the first day of Passover]."

M. R. Simeon b. Eleazar says, "One verse of Scripture says, 'Six days you will eat unleavened bread' (Deut. 16:8), and another verse says, 'Seven days you will eat unleavened bread' (Ex. 12:15).

N. "How are these two verses of Scripture to be sustained despite their contradiction?

O. "It must be unleavened bread that you cannot prepare and eat from new grain all seven days but only for six days, which is to say, unleavened bread made from grain of the new growing season may be eaten [only from the second day of the festival of Passover onward].

P. "Then how am I to interpret 'on the morrow of the Sabbath'?

Q. "'on the morrow' after the festival day."

R. "from the day that you brought the sheaf of the wave-offering; seven full weeks shall they be, counting":

S. Might one suppose that one may harvest, bring the sheaf of first grain, and count, whenever one wants to do so?

T. Scripture says, "You shall count seven weeks; begin to count the seven weeks from the time you first put the sickle to the standing grain [then you shall keep the feast of weeks to the Lord your

God with the tribute of a freewill-offering from your hand" (Deut. 16:9-10).

U. If "from the time you first put the sickle to the standing grain," might one suppose that one should indeed reap the sheaf and do the counting, but make the presentation whenever he wants to do so?

V. Scripture says, "From the day that you brought the sheaf of the wave-offering; seven full weeks shall they be, counting fifty days to the morrow after the seventh Sabbath; then you shall present a cereal-offering of new grain to the Lord."

W. Might one suppose that one reaps, counts, and makes the presentation by day?

X. Scripture says, "Seven full weeks shall they be."

Y. When are they full? When one begins in the [prior] evening.

Z. Then might one suppose one should reap by night, count by night, and make the presentation by night also?

AA. Scripture says, "From *the day* that you brought...."

BB. The presentation takes place only by day.

CC. How so?

DD. The reaping and the counting are by night, and the presentation by day [Sifra CCXXXII:I.1-6].

I.9 A. *Said Raba, "All of the proposed proofs are subject to refutation except for the last two named authorities of the first, and the last two named authorities of the second formulation [Yosé's second contribution and Simeon b. Eleazar's], which cannot be refuted.*

 B. *"Now as to the demonstration of Rabban Yohanan ben Zakkai, here is the refutation: perhaps the harmonization of the conflicting verses is in line with what Abbayye said, for said Abbayye, "The religious duty is to count the days and also the weeks." [Cashdan: One verse speaks of counting days, the other, weeks.]*

 C. *"As to the demonstration of R. Eliezer and R. Joshua, "How do you know that when reference is made to the festival day, it is to the first day of the festival? It could speak of the last day of the festival."*

 D. *"As to the proof of R. Ishmael and R. Judah b. Batera, these are beyond refutation. For if it is from R. Yosé bar Judah's reading, there is this refutation: Perhaps the fifty days excludes the six days you list. And if from the view of R. Judah b. Batera, here is the refutation: How do we know that reference is made to the first day of the festival, perhaps it is to the last day of the festival. So R. Yosé himself perceived the same problem, which is why he added the second interpretation, 'and furthermore.'"*

No. 9 focuses upon the exposition of the Sifra's proofs. It is a tertiary formation, but it can be classified as a gloss upon a gloss upon the Mishnah. What follows cannot:

I.10 A. *Reverting to the body of the foregoing:*

 B. *Said Abbayye, "The religious duty is to count the days and also the weeks":*

 C. *the rabbis of the household of R. Ashi counted the days and also the weeks.*

 D. *Amemar counted the days but not the weeks, saying, "This is a memorial to the sanctuary."*

No. 10 serves not the Mishnah, nor yet the gloss upon the gloss of the Mishnah, but only the requirement of expounding the clarification of Sifra's clarification – in its own terms. This is not a stunning example of the besought writing, but it suggests what we may expect: a commentary to the Sifra that is not required for the purposes of Mishnah exegesis or amplification of Mishnah exegesis.

In the following, the Sifra's materials are introduced simply to show that a verse adduced in evidence for one proposition serves some other altogether. Any discussion then of the Sifra's passage is irrelevant to the purpose for which the Bavli requires the passage – a mere probative fact, not a dialectical argument – and in fact is joined to the Sifra, in terms of the Sifra, and only then carried over, entire and complete, into the Bavli, where it serves no coherent purpose at all.

Menahot 7:1

A. And these are meal-offerings [from which] the handful is taken, and the residue of which belongs to the priests (Lev. 7:7-9):

B. (1) the meal-offering of fine flour (Lev. 2:21),

C. and (2) [the meal-offering prepared in] a baking pan (Lev. 2:9, 7:8),

D. and (3) [the meal-offering prepared in] a frying pan,

E. and (4) the loaves,

F. and (5) the wafers (Lev. 2:9-10),

G. and (6) the meal-offering of gentiles,

H. and (7) the meal-offering of women,

I. and (8) the meal-offering of the offering of the first sheaf of barley (Lev. 2:16),

J. and (9) the meal-offering of a sinner (Lev. 5:12),

K. and (10) the meal-offering of a woman accused of adultery (Num. 5:26).

L. R. Simeon says, "[From] the meal-offering of a priest who was a sinner (Lev. 7:16), the handful is taken [even though the whole of it in any case is offered on the altar], and the handful is offered by itself, and the residue [thereof] is offered by itself."

III.1 A. [And these are meal-offerings [from which] the handful is taken, and the residue of which belongs to the priests (Lev. 7:7-9): and (6) the meal-offering of gentiles:] Said R. Huna, [73B] "Peace-offerings of gentiles are to be classified as burnt-offerings." [Cashdan: No part may be eaten, they are wholly burned; their meal-offerings also must be wholly burned.]

 B. "If you wish, I shall prove this on the basis of reasoning, and if you wish, I shall prove it on the basis of a verse of Scripture:

 C. "If you wish, I shall prove this on the basis of reasoning: the gentile in his heart has only Heaven in mind [and does not possess the intentionality of planning to eat part of the offering himself or have the priest eat any of it; he does not know that such distinctions are feasible].

 D. "And if you wish, I shall prove it on the basis of a verse of Scripture: 'Which they will offer to the Lord for a burnt-offering'

(Lev. 22:18) – whatever they present shall be classified as a burnt-offering."

E.   Objected R. Hama bar Guria: **"A gentile who volunteered to present peace-offerings, if he gave them to an Israelite, the Israelite eats them. If he gave them to a priest, the priest eats them [T. Sheq. 3:11A-C]."**

F.   *Said Raba, "This is the sense of the statement: 'If it was on the* stipulation that an Israelite might achieve atonement through them, then the Israelite eats them; if it was on the stipulation that a priest may achieve atonement through them, then the priest eats them."

G.   Objected R. Shizbi, **"And these are meal-offerings [from which] the handful is taken, and the residue of which belongs to the priests (Lev. 7:7-9): and (6) the meal-offering of gentiles."** [Cashdan: So it is not entirely burned, and the same is the case with his peace-offerings.]

H.   *Said R. Yohanan, "That really is no contradiction, for the one statement represents the position of R. Yosé the Galilean, the other, of R. Aqiba, as has been taught on Tannaite authority":*

I.   **["And the Lord said to Moses, Say to Aaron and his sons and all the people of Israel, When any one of the house of Israel or of the sojourners in Israel presents his offering, whether in payment of a vow or as a freewill-offering which is offered to the Lord as a burnt-offering to be accepted you shall offer a male without blemish, of the bulls or the sheep or the goats. You shall not offer anything that has a blemish, for it will not be acceptable for you. And when any one offers a sacrifice of peace-offerings to the Lord, to fulfil a vow or as a freewill-offering, from the herd or from the flock, to be accepted it must be perfect; there shall be no blemish in it" (Lev. 22:17-21).]**

J.   **"Israel":**

K.   These are Israelites.

L.   **"Sojourners":**

M.   This refers to proselytes.

N.   **"The sojourners":**

O.   This encompasses wives of proselytes.

P.   **"In Israel":**

Q.   This includes women and slaves.

R.   **"Then why does Scripture refer to 'any one'?**

S.   **"That encompasses gentiles who may give sacrifices through making vows or as freewill-offerings ["whether in payment of a vow or as a freewill-offering"] like Israelites.**

T.   **"'Whether in payment of a vow or as a freewill-offering which is offered to the Lord as a burnt-offering':**

U.   **"I know that the law at hand applies only to a burnt-offering. How do I know that peace-offerings also are subject to the same rule?**

V.   **"Scripture says, 'in payment of a vow' [which may be for a peace-offering].**

W.   **"How do I know that the law covers a thanksgiving-offering?**

X.   **"Scripture says, 'or as a freewill-offering.'**

Y. "How do I know that the law encompasses birds, meal-offerings, libations, frankincense, and wood for the fire?

Z. "Scripture says, 'in payment of a vow,' covering all the vows that people may make to contribute to the Temple, 'or as a freewill-offering,' covering all the things that they may contribute as freewill-offerings.

AA. "If so, why does Scripture make explicit reference to the burnt-offering: 'Which is offered to the Lord as a burnt-offering'?

BB. "This excludes offerings brought by Nazirites," the words of R. Yosé the Galilean [Sifra: Aqiba].

CC. Said to him R. Aqiba [Sifra: Yosé], "Even if you spend the whole day adding to the arguments, still, here we have a reference only to burnt-offerings alone. '...which they will offer to the Lord for a burnt-offering' means that gentiles may present only burnt-offerings" [Sifra CCXXIII:I.1-2].

III.2 A. *But does the rule that a gentile may not present a Nazirite offering derive from the stated source? Surely it derives from the following:*

B. "Speak to the children of Israel and say to them, When either man or woman shall clearly utter a vow, the vow of a Nazirite, to consecrate himself to the Lord" (Num. 6:2) – Israelites take a vow, and gentiles do not take such a vow.

C. *If the proof had derived from that source, I might have concluded that it is an offering that he may not present, but that the Nazirite vow does apply. So the passage before us teaches us that that is not the case.*

III.3 A. *In accord with which authority is the following, which we have learned in the Mishnah:* Said R. Simeon, "Seven rules did the court ordain, and this (1) [foregoing one] is one of them. A gentile who sent his burnt-offering from overseas and sent drink-offerings with it – they are offered from what he has sent. But if not, they are offered from public funds. And so, too, a proselyte who died and left animals designated for sacrifices – if it has drink-offerings, they are offered from his estate. And if not, they are offered from public funds. And it is a condition imposed by the court on a high priest who died, that his meal-offering (Lev. 6:13) should derive from public funds" [M. Sheq. 7:6].

B. *May we then say this rule [which allows gentiles to present drink-offerings] is in accord with the position of R. Yosé the Galilean, not with R. Aqiba?*

C. *You may even maintain that it represents the position of R. Aqiba, for the sense is,* burnt-offerings plus everything that goes along with them.

III.4 A. *In accord with which Tannaite authority is the following, which our rabbis have taught as a Tannaite statement:*

B. "All who are native shall do these things in this way, in offering an offering by fire, a pleasing odor to the Lord" (Num. 15:13) – but then a gentile does not present drink-offerings.

C. Might one suppose that his burnt-offering will not require drink-offerings?

D. Scripture states, "...in this way...."

E. *Now in accord with whom is that formulation? For it cannot be either R. Yosé the Galilean or R. Aqiba!*

F.   *It cannot be R. Yosé the Galilean, for lo, he has said, even wine a gentile may not present, nor can it stand for R. Aqiba, for lo, he has said that a gentile may present a burnt-offering but nothing else!*

G.   *If you like, I shall tell you that it accords with the position of R. Yosé the Galilean, and if you like, I shall tell you that it accords with the position of R. Aqiba.*

H.   *If you like, I shall tell you that it accords with the position of R. Yosé the Galilean: Just remove from the formulation reference to wine.*

I.   *And if you like, I shall tell you that it accords with the position of R. Aqiba: He holds that the gentile may present not only a burnt-offering, but* burnt-offerings plus everything that goes along with them.

The Sifra's passage is introduced, to begin with, to show that there are two distinct positions on the issue at hand. All that is needed from the Sifra, therefore, is evidence of that fact. Then No. 2 addresses the claim of the Sifra's passage to show the source for the rule from the cited passage, rather than from some other; here is a fine example of how a passage of the Sifra is subjected to an analysis entirely congruent to analyses of passages of the Mishnah ("What is the source...it is from this verse...but is that the real source? Is not the source the following verse...?"). Not only so, but No. 3, again a mode of analysis entirely familiar from the Mishnah, appeals to the Sifra as its focus. We want to know which of the two of Sifra's authorities stands behind the cited passage of the Mishnah, and No. 4 continues this analysis of how the Sifra's statements relate to other Tannaite statements. None of this is required for the purposes of Mishnah exegesis, but all of it is quite natural to a document that wishes to read the Sifra in the way in which the Mishnah is read.

What follows provides a first-class example of how the treatment of the Sifra's passage will highlight what the Sifra wishes to show, not what the Bavli's frame of a Mishnah commentary cites the Sifra's passage to prove; the two propositions are complementary, but they are distinct. Then the further discussion of the passage at hand concerns not what is proved by the Sifra that is relevant to the Mishnah, but what is proved by the Sifra in terms important to its own framers. The distinction here is critical. The one passage wants to know how come "[From] the meal-offering of a priest who was a sinner (Lev. 7:16), the handful is taken [even though the whole of it in any case is offered on the altar], and the handful is offered by itself, and the residue [thereof] is offered by itself." The Sifra's author is going to prove that "the performance of the meal-offering rite of a priest [who has inadvertently sinned] is assigned to that priest [so that he may perform his own rite and retain possession of the residue of the meal-offering that he himself has presented]." Now as a matter of fact these propositions are entirely complementary. But the one is not the other. And the appended analysis, Nos. 2ff. below, is formulated wholly in terms of the Sifra's issue. That is, then, a talmud to the Sifra, not to the Mishnah.

IV.1   A.   R. Simeon says, "[From] the meal-offering of a priest who was a sinner (Lev. 7:16), the handful is taken [even though the whole of it in any case is offered on the altar], and the handful is offered by itself, and the residue [thereof] is offered by itself":

       B.   *What is the scriptural basis for this position?*

       C.   *It is in line with that which our rabbis have taught on Tannaite authority:*

       D.   "It shall belong to the priest, like the meal-offering" (Lev. 5:13) –

       E.   The meaning is that the performance of the meal-offering rite of a priest [who has inadvertently sinned] is assigned to that priest [so that he may perform his own rite and retain possession of the residue of the meal-offering that he himself has presented].

       F.   Or might the intent not be to declare permitted [to the priesthood the residue] of the tenth-ephah of fine flour that has been brought by a priest? [Cashdan: The verse then tells us that a priest's obligatory meal-offering is like the meal-offering of an Israelite that is eaten by the priests after the handful has been taken out.]

       G.   How then shall I interpret the statement, "Every meal-offering of a priest shall be wholly burned, it shall not be eaten" (Lev. 6:23, Heb. 6:16)?

       H.   This then would refer to a meal-offering that the priest has brought as a free will-offering, and as to the tenth-ephah that he has presented, that may be eaten.

       I.   But [contrary to that line of argument] Scripture states, "It shall belong to the priest, like the meal-offering":

       J.   Lo, it is in the status of the meal-offering that he presents as a freewill-offering, with the result that just as the freewill-offering of meal that he presents does not yield a residue that may be eaten, so the tenth-ephah of fine flour that he presents may not be eaten.

       K.   Said R. Simeon, "And is it written, 'and it shall be the priest's as his meal-offering'? What it says is, 'It shall belong to the priest, like the meal-offering':

       L.   [73B] "lo, the tenth-ephah of fine flour that a priest has brought is in the classification of the tenth-ephah of fine flour that an Israelite presents.

       M.   "Just as the tenth-ephah of fine flour that an Israelite presents yields a handful, so a handful is taken up from this offering as well.

       N.   "But might one then say, just as the handful is taken from the meal-offering presented by the poor sinner who is an Israelite, and the remainder may be eaten, so when the handful is taken from the poor sinner's meal-offering presented by a priest, the residue may be eaten?

       O.   "Scripture states, 'the priest's as the meal-offering': In what regards the priest, it is like the meal-offering of a sinner who is of the Israelite caste, but in respect to what concerns the fire on the altar, it is not like that meal-offering.

	P.	**"The handful that is taken up is presented by itself, and the residue is presented by itself" [Sifra LXII.I.16].**
IV.2	A.	*But is the rule that the rites of the priest's meal-offering may be carried out by the priest drawn from that exposition? Surely it derives from the following:*
	B.	How on the basis of Scripture do we know that a priest may come to present his offerings at any occasion and at any time that he wants?
	C.	Scripture states, "And come with all the desire of his soul...and minister" (Deut. 18:6).
	D.	*Had I derived the ruling from that verse, I might have suppose that reference is made to something that is not presented by reason of sin, but as to something that is presented by reason of sin, I might have said that that is not the case.*
IV.3	A.	*But is the rule that the rites of the priest's meal-offering may be carried out by the priest drawn from that exposition? Surely it derives from the following:*
	B.	"And the priest shall make atonement for the soul that errs, when he sins through error" (Num. 15:28) – this teaches that a priest may make atonement for himself through his own act of service.
	C.	*Had I derived the ruling from that verse, I might have suppose that that rule pertains only to offerings that are presented for a sin committed in error, but not for offerings presented for a sin committed deliberately; so we are informed that that is the case as well.*
	D.	*So are there really offerings that are presented for sins committed deliberately?*
	E.	*Yup: deliberately taking a false oath [Lev. 5:1].*

As we proceed to IV.1, we find ourselves on familiar ground. A passage of the Sifra is introduced to prove a rule set forth in the Mishnah rests on scriptural foundations. But what that passage proves is distinct, though related: not that the handful of the meal-offering of a priest who has sinned is burned on the altar, along with the residue, but that the priest may present his own meal-offering under the specific circumstances. Then No. 2 raises a question pertinent not to the issue that has required the framer of No. 1 to introduce the abstract of the Sifra, but to the passage of the Sifra itself. And No. 3 goes forward along the same lines. That is important, because the now run-on quality of the composite is entirely routine in the Bavli; here we see that precisely the principles of agglutination that govern in the Bavli's exposition of the Mishnah are in place in the exposition of the Sifra's claims.

Our next example in sequence has a sizable abstract from the Sifra, obviously entirely directed toward the amplification of the Mishnah's statements. But then when the Sifra's passage is complete, the discussion will focus on the Sifra's passage, without reverting to the Mishnah.

Menahot 7:3

A.   All meal-offerings that are prepared in a utensil [a baking pan or a frying pan] require three applications of oil:

B.   (1) pouring [oil into the utensil],

C.   (2) stirring [the meal into the oil],

D.   and [then again], (3) putting oil into the utensil prior to their preparation.

E.   "And as to the loaves [baked in an oven], one stirs them [with oil]," the words of Rabbi.

F.   And sages say, "The fine flour [alone] was mixed with oil."

G.   The loaves require stirring.

H.   The wafers are anointed.

I.   How does one anoint them?

J.   In the form of a chi [an X] [that is, in the form of a cross].

K.   And the remainder of the oil is eaten by the priests.

I.2   A.   *Our rabbis have taught on Tannaite authority:*

B.   "If your offering is a meal-offering on a griddle, [it shall be of choice flour with oil mixed in, unleavened. Break it into bits and pour oil on it; it is a meal-offering:]"

C.   This teaches that the offering requires the use of a utensil [for its preparation and presentation].

D.   [75A] Reference is made twice to the word "your offering" ["If your offering is a meal-offering on a griddle, it shall be of choice flour with oil mixed in, unleavened. Break it into bits and pour oil on it; it is a meal-offering. If your offering is a meal-offering in a pan, it shall be made of choice flour in oil."] This serves to establish an analogy.

E.   Here "your offering" forms the basis for a classification. Just as 'your offering" here involves adding oil and saturating the meal with oil, so "your offering," used later invokes the requirement of adding oil and saturating the meal with oil.

F.   And, further, just as the classification of "your offering" noted below involves putting oil in a utensil prior to the preparation of the offering, so "your offering" in the present instance also involves putting oil in a utensil prior to the preparation of the offering [Sifra XXI:I.1-2].

II.1   A.   "And as to the loaves [baked in an oven], one stirs them [with oil]," the words of Rabbi. And sages say, "The fine flour [alone] was mixed with oil":

B.   *Our rabbis have taught on Tannaite authority:*

C.   "It shall be of choice flour with oil mixed in":

D.   This teaches that one mixes the oil into the fine flour.

E.   Rabbi says, "And as to the loaves [baked in an oven, one stirs them with oil (M. Men. 6:3C)]. ["In the case of loaves, they stir oil into them...as it is said, 'Loaves mixed with oil'" (Lev. 7:12) [= T. Men. 8:7B-C]."

F.   They said to him, "But in connection with the cakes that accompany the thank-offering, is it not said, 'Flour mixed with oil' (Lev. 23:13)" [= T. 8:7C]?

G. "And it is possible to stir in only with flour. [B. Men. 75a: It was not possible to mingle the cakes with oil but only the flour.]

H. "How does one do this? One puts oil into the flour and stirs it in, then oil into a utensil and prepares it, and stirs it, and mixes [the flour] with oil." [Tosefta's version: "How does one do this? He puts oil into the utensil and fries it. Then he puts oil into the flour and stirs it and breaks it up. And he then pours oil on it as one pours oil on pounded beans" [T. Men. 8:5C-D].

I. Rabbi says, "One puts oil into a utensil and prepares it, and stirs it, and then mixes the flour with oil, and then goes and pours oil on it" [Sifra XXI:I.1].

J. "How does one do this? To begin with one puts in oil into the utensil, then puts in flour, kneads it, bakes it, breaks it into pieces, adds oil to it, mixes the two together, adds more oil on it, and then takes the handful from it."

All of this is simply a large abstract from the Sifra inserted whole for the entirely routine purposes of Mishnah amplification. But what follows comments on the Sifra's materials in their own framework, and the amplification of the Mishnah is in no way advanced:

II.2 A. *[Following Cashdan's version of the text:] That was a good argument that sages addressed to Rabbi.*

B. *What was it?*

C. Said R. Samuel bar R. Isaac, "Since there was only a quarter log of oil, how was it possible to spread it among so many cakes?"

III.1 A. The loaves require stirring. The wafers are anointed:

B. *Our rabbis have taught on Tannaite authority:*

C. "Unleavened cakes with oil mixed in":

D. But wafers are not saturated in oil.

E. Now is the contrary to that proposition not a matter of logic?

F. If cakes, which do not require to be spread with oil, do require saturation in oil, wafers, which do require to be spread with oil, should surely require saturation in oil!

G. [Accordingly, it is necessary for] Scripture [to make the point explicit, when it says,] "unleavened cakes with oil mixed in":

H. But wafers are not saturated in oil.

I. "Unleavened wafers spread with oil":

J. But cakes do not have to be spread with oil.

K. Now is the contrary to that proposition not a matter of logic?

L. If wafers, which do not have to be saturated in oil, do have to be spread with oil, cakes, which do require saturation in oil, surely should have also to be spread with oil.

M. [Accordingly, it is necessary for] Scripture [to make the point explicit, when it says,] "unleavened wafers spread with oil":

N. But cakes do not have to be spread with oil [Sifra XX:III.2-5].

Once more, in what follows, we are told what we need to know to understand what Sifra has just now stated, not what the Mishnah demands.

III.2　A.　*What is the exegetical reasoning that yields this conclusion?*
　　　B.　*Said Raba, "Scripture should not have left out at least one time the phrase "cakes anointed with oil and wafers mixed with oil"* [Cashdan: The fact that Scripture always speaks of cakes mingled with oil and wafers anointed with oil indicates that the manner of applying the oil is exclusive in each case.]

The next passage follows suit.　What makes this especially interesting is that it is very common in sequences of Mishnah exegeses in the Bavli to find a recurrent pattern, so that a question asked once will be asked over and over again.　Here we see that a question asked of one Sifra passage, integral to the exposition of that passage but hardly required for the amplification of the Mishnah, is repeated in the very next.

Menahot 7:4A

　　　A.　**All meal-offerings that are prepared in a utensil require breaking up [for the taking of the handful].**

I.2　A.　*Our rabbis have taught on Tannaite authority:*
　　　B.　"Break it into bits and pour oil on it; it is a meal-offering":
　　　C.　This serves to extend the rule of breaking up to all meal-offerings.
　　　D.　Might one suppose that that same rule extends also to the two loaves and the show bread?
　　　E.　Scripture says, "it...."
　　　F.　How come you encompass all meal-offerings but exclude the two loaves and the show bread?
　　　G.　[Sifra adds:] After Scripture has used inclusionary language, it has then made an exclusion.
　　　H.　Just as these are distinguished in that part of the offering is placed on the altar fires, so excluded are the two loaves of bread and the show bread, none of which is put on the altar fire [but all of which is given to the priests to eat].
　　　I.　"Break it into bits and pour oil on it; it is a meal-offering":
　　　J.　This serves to extend the rule of pouring oil on the offering to all meal-offerings.
　　　K.　Might one suppose that that rule extends also to a meal-offering that is baked?
　　　L.　Scripture says, "on it."
　　　M.　I shall then exclude the loaves, but not the wafers?
　　　N.　Scripture says, "it is [a meal-offering]," [encompassing wafers under the rule of applying oil] [Sifra XXI:IV.1-2].
I.3　A.　*What is the exegetical reasoning that yields this conclusion?*
　　　B.　*Ought I not exclude the meal-offering of the priests?*
　　　C.　[75B] Said Rabbah, "Which is the offering that has to be excluded by two distinct formulations?　You have to say it is the meal-offering baked in the oven" [Cashdan: for it consists of two kinds, cakes and wafers, so two exclusionary expressions are required to exclude it].

The recurrent pattern shows us, once more, that the way people were reading the Mishnah guided their reading of the Sifra, so that the talmud to the one bears conceptual and also rhetorical resemblance to the talmud for the other. Further pertinent examples of the same pattern follow:

Menahot 7:7

A. The [meal-offering of the] offering of the first sheaf of barley was sifted through thirteen sieves [each finer than the former].

B. And the two loaves (Lev. 23:17) [were sifted through] twelve sieves.

C. And the showbread [was sifted through] eleven sieves,

D. R. Simeon says, "There is no prescribed limit to the matter [of C].

E. "But flour that was sifted as much as necessary did one bring,

F. "as it is said, And [in the case of showbread] you will take fine flour and bake it (Lev. 24:5) – that it should be sifted as much as necessary."

II.1 A. R. Simeon says, "There is no prescribed limit to the matter [of C]. But flour that was sifted as much as necessary did one bring, as it is said, 'And [in the case of showbread] you will take fine flour and bake it' (Lev. 24:5) – that it should be sifted as much as necessary":

B. *Our rabbis have taught on Tannaite authority:*

C. "And you shall take fine flour and bake it into twelve loaves of it; two-tenths of an ephah shall be in each loaf. And you shall set them in two rows, six in a row, upon the table of pure gold. And you shall put pure frankincense with each row, that it may go with the bread as a memorial portion to be offered by fire to the Lord. Every Sabbath day Aaron shall set it in order before the Lord continually on behalf of the people of Israel as a covenant for ever. And it shall be for Aaron and his sons, and they shall eat it in a holy place, since it is for him a most holy portion out of the offerings by fire to the Lord, a perpetual due" (Lev. 24:5-9):

D. "Fine flour and bake it":

E. How do we know that one may also take wheat [for baking the twelve loaves of bread under discussion here]?

F. Scripture says, "You shall take fine flour."

G. Might one suppose that other meal-offerings also may derive from wheat [not barley, the usual grain for that purpose]?

H. Scripture says, "It."

I. This derives from wheat, but other meal-offerings do not derive from wheat [Sifra CCXLI:I.1].

J. That is on account of the excessive expense.

K. *What is the meaning of,* That is on account of the excessive expense?

L. Said R. Eleazar, "The Torah took into consideration the Israelites' capital [here: their cattle]. *And where is this shown?* 'And you shall give the congregation and their cattle something to drink' (Num. 20:8)."

The only reason for K-L to be added is to explain J, which the Bavli understands to be continuous with the foregoing; but if J be seen as a gloss on the Sifra, than K-L gloss a gloss to the Sifra; it comes down to the same thing. Sifra's complement to the following Mishnah paragraph amplifies the Mishnah paragraph's own scriptural demonstration. What is important to us will be whether the further extension of discussion concerns the Mishnah's or the Sifra's formulations of matters, and, as we shall see, it is with the latter.

Menahot 8:2D-I

D.   [77B] And from all of them did one take one [loaf of each kind] out of ten as heave-offering, as it is said, "And he shall offer one out of each offering as a heave-offering to the Lord" (Lev. 8:14) –

E.   "One" – that he should not take a broken one;

F.   "Out of each offering" – (l) that all the offerings should be equivalent [ten loaves for each kind of animal],

G.   and (2) that he should not take [two loaves] from one offering [and none at all] for its fellow [that is, he should take one loaf of each kind].

H.   "To the priest who tosses the blood of the peace-offerings it shall belong" (Lev. 8:14) –

I.   And the remainder [of the bread] is eaten by the owner.

I.1   A.   *Our rabbis have taught on Tannaite authority:*

B.   "[And of such he shall offer one cake from each offering, as an offering that is raised up to the Lord;] it shall belong to the priest who throws the blood of the peace-offerings":

C.   [The one cake is to be taken] from the mass [of cakes that are] joined together.

D.   "One":

E.   Meaning that one should not take half a loaf [of five, but rather, a whole loaf of ten. [That is, one should not prepare five loaves of each required type and take of the five loaves a half of a loaf, which would then yield the requisite one of ten in proposition. Rather, there must be ten loaves of each type, and one takes one loaf of each type, for the requisite tenth.]

F.   "From each offering":

G.   This teaches that all of the offerings should be equal in size [so that one is not large, another small]. [Or: That all should be treated in one and the same manner.]

H.   [Further,] that one should not take a loaf from one offering in behalf of what is owing from its fellow, [that is, four loaves of a single variety in behalf of all of the loaves of the three sorts.]

I.   "as an offering that is raised up to the Lord":

J.   I do not know how many are required.

K.   Lo, I reason as follows:

L.   We find here reference to "an offering that is raised up," and we find the same usage with regard to the offering that is raised up out of the tithe. Just as the latter usage involves one-tenth, so here, too, the requirement is one-tenth. [The offering to the Lord is one-tenth of the number of cakes and wafers of various sorts, for example, four out of forty, and the residue is left for the priesthood.]

M.   Or take this route:

N.   We find here reference to "an offering that is raised up," and we find the same usage with regard to the first fruits.

O.   Just as when we find the usage, "An offering that is raised up" in regard to first fruits, there is no fixed volume that is required, so when we find that same usage here, there is no fixed volume that is required.

P.   Let us then determine the correct analogy:

Q.   Let us draw an analogy for "an offering that is raised up" in which there is no further offering to be made, [namely, the offering of the cakes and wafers] from a case of "an offering that is raised up" in which there is no further offering to be made [namely, the offering raised up from the tithe itself, from which no further offerings are exacted],

R.   but let not the case of the offering of first fruits serve as the generative analogy, from which a further offering thereafter is raised up [specifically, the heave-offering that is raised up and also the offering that is raised up out of the tithe].

S.   Or take this route:

T.   We draw an analogy for a case of an offering that is raised up and then eaten in the place in which the offering is made [that is, the offering of the loaves] from the case of an offering that is raised up and then eaten in the place in which the offering is made, [namely, the offering of first fruits, both of them being eaten in Jerusalem],

U.   but the offering that is raised up from tithe, which is not eaten in the place in which the offering is made, should not give testimony [since it may be eaten even in the provinces, and not only in Jerusalem].

V.   Accordingly, Scripture settles the issue when it says, "As an offering that is raised up to the Lord,"

W.   for the use of the language, "raised up," serves to establish an analogy [between offerings in which exactly that language is used:]

X.   We find here reference to "an offering that is raised up," and we find the same usage with regard to the offering that is raised up out of the tithe. Just as the latter usage involves one-tenth, so here, too, the requirement is one-tenth. [The offering to the Lord is one-tenth of the number of cakes and wafers of various sorts, and the residue is left for the priesthood.]

Y.   Now we have learned that in the case of an offering that is raised up, the requisite proportion is one out of ten.

Z.   But I do not know how large a loaf is involved.

AA.   Lo, I reason in this way:

BB.   Here we find a reference to "leavened bread" ["This offering, with cakes of leavened bread added, he shall offer along with his thanksgiving sacrifice of well-being" (Lev. 7:13)], and elsewhere, with reference to the two loaves, we find the same ["You shall bake choice flour and bake of it twelve loaves (Lev. 24:5)].

CC.   Just as leavened bread with reference to the two loaves involves a tenth-ephah per loaf, so leavened bread here involves a tenth-ephah for each loaf.

DD.   Or take this route:

EE.   We find reference to loaves here and likewise with reference to the showbread.

FF.   Just as when we find a reference to loaf in regard to the showbread, two-tenths of an ephah are required per loaf, so here, too, two-tenths of an ephah are required for each loaf.

GG.   Let us then determine the correct analogy:

HH.   Let us derive an appropriate analogy for a meal-offering which is presented leavened and is presented along with a sacrifice from a meal-offering which is offered leavened and is presented with a sacrifice, but let the showbread not serve, for it is not offered leavened [but only as unleavened bread] and it also is not presented with a sacrifice.

II.   Or take this route:

JJ.   Let us draw an analogy for a meal-offering which derives from grain grown both in the land and abroad, grain that is of the new season along with grain of the old, from a meal-offering the grain of which may derive from the land or from abroad, and from grain grown in the new season or grain of the old.

KK.   But let the case of the two loaves not provide an analogy, for these derive only from grain grown in the land, and they are presented only from loaves back from grain grown in the new growing season.

LL.   Scripture states [with references to the two loaves], "You shall bring from your settlements two loaves of bread as an elevation-offering; [each one made of two-tenths of a measure of choice flour, baked after leavening, as first fruits to the Lord. With the bread you shall present as burnt-offerings to the Lord seven yearling lambs without blemish....The priest shall elevate these – the two lambs – together with the bread of first fruits as an elevation-offering before the Lord...]" (Lev. 23:17-18).

MM.   Now Scripture's reference to "you shall bring" can only mean that you must bring the offering which is analogous to one that is specified in another passage [hence the analogy is between the showbread and the bread-offering that goes along with a thanksgiving-offering (following the commentary of Rabbenu Hillel)].

NN.   Lo, the one is like the other.

OO.   Just as the one involves a tenth-ephah of fine flour per loaf, so what you bring that is analogous but in another connection involves a single tenth-ephah of fine flour per loaf. [That would prove that the two loaves of the showbread are made each of a tenth of a measure of choice flour!]

PP.   Or take this route:

QQ.   Just as these [namely, the two loaves of Lev. 23:17-18] have to be made of two-tenths of an ephah of fine flour, so those must be two two-tenths of an ephah of fine flour.

RR.   [These conflicting results require attention to the language before us.]   Scripture states, "will be...," and the use of the plural indicates that two-tenths of an ephah of fine flour are required here.

SS.   We have learned in regard to the leavened bread that it is to be ten-tenths [in all, for the required loaves].

TT.   How do we know that the unleavened bread also is to be made of ten-tenths of an ephah of fine flour in all?

UU.   Scripture states, "This offering, with cakes of leavened bread added, he shall offer along with his thanksgiving sacrifice of well-being" (Lev. 7:13).

VV.   As a counterpart to the leavened bread, bring unleavened bread.

WW.   Just as the leavened bread involves ten-tenths, so the unleavened bread should involve ten-tenths of an ephah.

XX.   Might one suppose that the ten-tenths of an ephah of fine flour involved in the unleavened bread should form a single offering?

YY.   Scripture states explicitly, "Then he shall offer with the thank-offering unleavened cakes mixed with oil, unleavened wafers spread with oil, and cakes of fine flour well mixed with oil."

ZZ.   And then: "And of such he shall offer one cake from each offering, [as an offering to the Lord]."

AAA. The upshot is a third of a tenth from each species and so three loaves per tenth, and, further, the upshot is that the bread of a thanksgiving-offering is made up of forty loaves. One takes one of them for each species, thus four loaves, and gives them to the priest,

BBB.   "it shall belong to the priest who throws the blood of the peace-offerings":

CCC.   And the remainder is eaten by the owner [Sifra LXXXVI:I.1-7].

I.2   A.   A master has said, "'[And of such he shall offer one cake from each offering, as an offering that is raised up to the Lord;] it shall belong to the priest who throws the blood of the peace-offerings': [The one cake is to be taken] from the mass [of cakes that are] joined together":

       B.   *But what about the following:* "And all the fat thereof shall he take off from it" (Lev. 4:19) – *How here can we carry out the rule of taking the offering from the mass that is joined together?*

       C.   *The answer accords with what R. Hisda said Abimi said, for* said R. Hisda said Abimi, "The meat may not be cut up before the portions that are presented as a sacrifice have been removed." [Cashdan: When the fat is taken off, the animal therefore is all connected in a mass.]

I.3   A.   A master has said, "We find here reference to 'an offering that is raised up,' and we find the same usage with regard to the offering that is raised up out of the tithe. Just as the latter usage involves one-tenth, so here, too, the requirement is one-tenth. [The offering to the Lord is one-tenth of the number of cakes and

        wafers of various sorts, and the residue is left for the priesthood]":

B.   *But why not derive the appropriate rule from the analogy of the heave-offering at Midian* [the portion of the spoil at Num. 31:28-29, which was a five-hundredth part given to the priest, Eleazar (Cashdan)]?

C.   We adopt as our governing analogy for heave-offering that is given throughout all generations the law applying to heave-offering that is given throughout all generations, but let not the case of heave-offering presented at the episode of Midian decide matters, for it does not apply for all generations to come.

D.   *But how about inferring the rule from the analogy of the heave-offering in the matter of dough-offering [Num. 15:19, a twenty-fourth]?*

E.   A Tannaite authority of the household of R. Ishmael [stated], "We adopt as our governing analogy for heave-offering concerning which the language 'of it...as heave-offering unto the Lord' (Lev. 7:14) the rule that pertains to heave-offering concerning which the language 'of it...as heave-offering unto the Lord' (Num. 18:26, the heave-offering of the tithe) is used, *and that eliminates the heave-offering of dough, concerning which the language 'of it...as heave-offering unto the Lord' is not used.*"

I.4   A.   *Raba raised this question:* "As to the heave-offering taken up from the cakes of thank-offering, are people liable on that account [should nonpriests eat this offering deliberately] to the death penalty or [if the act was inadvertent] to the sanction of paying the added fifth of the value, or is that not the case? Since an analogy is drawn to heave-offering of tithe, then in this matter, too, the analogy applies, or perhaps the All-Merciful has excluded this type of heave-offering, otherwise analogous to the other, when it uses the language 'therein' (Lev. 22:9) and 'from it' (Lev. 22:14) [which pertain only to heave-offering of produce, not any other kind of heave-offering]?

B.   "If it falls into ordinary food, does it impose upon that food the status of heave-offering or not [as would be the case of heave-offering of ordinary food that was mixed with other produce]?"

C.   *The questions stand.*

I.5   A.   A master has said, "[These conflicting results require attention to the language before us]. Scripture states, "will be...," and the use of the plural indicates that two-tenths of an ephah of fine flour are required here":

B.   *What is the exegesis that pertains here?*

C.   [78A] Said R. Isaac bar Abdimi, "'Will be' in the plural is used here" [and the word is written with two Ys, each bearing the numerical value of ten, so ten-tenths, which can refer not to the two loaves, which are said explicitly to be made up of two-tenths, can refer only to the leavened cakes of the thank-offering (Cashdan)].

D.   *But maybe it means ten qapizas [ten half-qabs]?*

E.   Said Raba, "In context, Scripture is speaking of tenth-ephahs."

I.6   A.   **We have learned in regard to the leavened bread that it is to be ten-tenths [in all, for the required loaves]. How do we know that the unleavened bread also is to be made of ten-tenths of an ephah of fine flour in all? Scripture states, "This offering, with cakes of**

> leavened bread added, he shall offer along with his thanksgiving sacrifice of well-being" (Lev. 7:13). As a counterpart to the leavened bread, bring unleavened bread. Just as the leavened bread involves ten-tenths, so the unleavened bread should involve ten-tenths of an ephah:

B. But can a rule that is derived by analogy based on the congruence of other shared traits [but not verbal ones in context] turn around and teach a lesson through an analogy based on on the congruence of other shared traits [but not verbal ones in context]?

C. It is a case in which the original rule was derived on a polythetic basis ["from itself and something else"]. [Cashdan: The original inference that the leavened cakes of the thank-offering shall consist of ten-tenths, a tenth for every cake, was not entirely drawn from the case of the two loaves, inasmuch as the number of cakes, ten, is deemed to be expressly stated in connection with the leavened cakes of the thank-offering by virtue of the expression 'they shall be.' Accordingly, the leavened cakes supplied the rule that there must be ten cakes, and the two loaves supplied the rule that there must be a tenth for each cake]. And any case of polythetic congruence is not classified as an argument that is basically one from congruence.

D. *That poses no problem to him who takes the view that it indeed is not classified as an argument from congruence. But from the perspective of him who maintains that it is indeed an argument from congruence, what is to be said?*

E. The language "you shall bring" is augmentative. [Scripture states explicitly, "Then he shall offer with the thank-offering unleavened cakes mixed with oil, unleavened wafers spread with oil, and cakes of fine flour well mixed with oil." And then: "And of such he shall offer one cake from each offering, [as an offering to the Lord]." The upshot is a third of a tenth from each species and so three loaves per tenth, and, further, the upshot is that the bread of a thanksgiving-offering is made up of forty loaves.]

There can be no doubt that in this enormous and successful dialectical argument, Sifra's vast complement and restatement is expounded in its own framework. In context, the Mishnah's brief version looks like a summary; or Sifra's like a vast expansion. But in actuality, Sifra's authorship states this matter the way it commonly works matters out, the modes of argument being routine for that document, the rhetoric being standard. So there is no settling the question. It is clear that Nos. 2, 3-4, 5, 6 form a *talmud* to the Sifra's text. It was this passage that first alerted me to the phenomenon which we now see is routine. The next instance shows that we deal with what is routine and not an isolated instance.

Menahot 8:4A-C

A. For the [bread brought with] consecration [offering, Lev. 8:22-28] they brought [the offerings] like the unleavened [bread of the meal-offering] which goes with the thank-offering: (1) loaves and (2) wafers and (3) [oil-] soaked cakes.

B. The [wafers of the] Nazirite's [meal-offering] consisted of two-thirds of the unleavened [cakes] of the thank-offering: [ten unleavened] loaves and [ten unleavened] wafers. But soaked cakes are not [brought along] with it.

C. They [the Nazirite's offering] turns out to be ten Jerusalem qabs [five for unleavened loaves, five for unleavened wafers] which are six-tenths [of an ephah]; and something left over [six and two-thirds tenths].

II.1 A. They [the Nazirite's offering] turn out to be ten Jerusalem qabs [five for unleavened loaves, five for unleavened wafers] which are six-tenths [of an ephah]; and something left over [six and two-thirds tenths]:

B. *Our rabbis have taught on Tannaite authority:*

C. "His peace-offerings":

D. This serves to encompass the peace-offerings brought by a Nazirite, indicating that [Sifra lacks:] they [the Nazirite's offering] turns out to be ten Jerusalem qabs [five for unleavened loaves, five for unleavened wafers] which are six-tenths [of an ephah]; and something left over [six and two-thirds tenths].

E. Might that involve everything that is stated in the present context?

F. Scripture says, "with cakes of unleavened bread," [Bavli lacks:] [following Elijah of Vilna's emendation:] and it is not presented saturated in oil. How then am I to interpret the meaning of "his peace-offerings," so far as that phrase encompasses the peace-offerings of a Nazirite? It means that the peace-offerings of the Nazirite are subject to the rule requiring ten [cakes made of] Jerusalem qabs [of flour] for a quarter of a log of oil] [Sifra LXXXV:I.13].

II.2 A. *What is the exegesis behind this reading?*

B. Said R. Pappa, "['His peace-offerings' encompasses within the Nazirite's offering] only those species that are covered by the language 'unleavened,' *excluding soaked cakes, that are not covered by the term 'unleavened."* [Cashdan: This term describes the cakes and wafers prescribed for the thank-offering, Lev. 7:12; accordingly the unleavened cakes spoken of in the Nazirite offering signify these same cakes.]

C. A Tannaite authority of the household of R. Ishmael [stated], "'A basket of unleavened bread' (Num. 5:16) forms an encompassing generalization; 'cakes' and wafers' then represent particularizations of the foregoing. So we have an encompassing generalization followed by a particularization, and whenever we have an encompassing generalization followed by a particularization, then what is covered under the encompassing generalization is only what is explicitly stated in the particularization: *Only cakes and wafers, nothing more.*"

II.1 provides a routine clarification, borrowed from Sifra, and No. 2 presents an amplification of the foregoing.

Let me conclude with a somewhat ambiguous case, in which a well-crafted analysis of language and its sense, I.2, may be read as a talmud to either the Mishnah or the Sifra. As we shall now see, the Sifra's initial question, I.1.B, presupposes that we have been given a variety of cases, as is made explicit at M. Hence clauses I.1.K, L, M of the Mishnah precipitate the Sifra's formulation. But, as we see, in its own framework, Sifra cites the Mishnah and its corresponding Toseftan complement more or less verbatim at I.1.D. So in the balance I think that No. 2 forms a *talmud* to the Sifra, and not to the Mishnah, though the contrary possibility is not decisively excluded.

8:4D-M

D.   (1) The offspring of a thank-offering
E.   and (2) a beast designated as its substitute [in line with Lev. 27:10] –
F.   and (3) he who sets aside his thank-offering,
G.   and it was lost, and he separated another in its place [and thereafter the lost one was found] –
H.   [When they are offered, as they must be,] they do not require bread,
I.   as it is said, "And he shall offer up with the sacrifice of the thank-offering" (Lev. 8:12) –
J.   The [one which is offered as a] thank-offering requires bread,
K.   but (1) its offspring,
L.   and (3) that which is brought in its place,
M.   and (2) its substitute do not require bread.

I.1   A.   *Our rabbis have taught on Tannaite authority:*
        B.   What is the purpose of the statement, "If he offers it for a thanksgiving-offering"?
        C.   How do you know the basis for the following ruling:
        D.   He who designated a beast for his thanksgiving-offering, which was lost, and who then designated another in its stead, and did not suffice to offer it before the first was found, so that lo, both of them are available [cf. M. Men. 7:4E, T. Men. 8:20C-E] –
        E.   How do we know that he brings whichever one of them he prefers, and brings with it the requisite bread-offering,
        F.   and that as to the second, he presents it without the bread-offering?
        G.   Scripture says, "If he offers it for a thanksgiving-offering."
        H.   Might one suppose that both of the beasts require a bread-offering?
        I.   Scripture says, "...offers it...," meaning, one requires a bread-offering, but the two of them do not require a bread-offering.
        J.   And how do I know that the law encompasses the offspring of such beasts and the beasts are declared substitutes for them?
        K.   Scripture says, "If he offers it for a thanksgiving-offering."
        L.   Might one think that all of them require a bread-offering?

M.   Scripture refers to "the thanksgiving-offering," meaning, it is the thanksgiving-offering that requires a bread-offering, but its offspring does not require a bread-offering, nor does a beast given in exchange for it, nor does a beast declared to be its substitute, require a bread-offering [Sifra LXXXV:I.1-2]

I.2   A.   [Now in this connection] R. Hanina sent word in the name of R. Yohanan, "They repeated this rule only in connection with the case after atonement had been carried out [with the offering of the mother animal], but if it was before atonement had been carried out, it would have required the bread-offering." [Cashdan: If both animals are available, whichever is offered, whether the original thank-offering or the offspring or substitute, requires a bread-offering.]

B.   R. Amram considered this statement: "To which case does this ruling pertain? If I should propose that it pertains to what has been presented in place of the thank-offering that was obligatory [that is, one has vowed such an offering, designated an animal, and then the animal was lost, so another was presented instead], then we already have in hand the Tannaite rule governing the case in which it was offered prior to making atonement and we also have the Tannaite rule governing the case in which it was offered afterward! [Scripture refers to "the thanksgiving-offering," meaning, it is the thanksgiving-offering that requires a bread-offering, but its offspring does not require a bread-offering, nor does a beast given in exchange for it, nor does a beast declared to be its substitute, require a bread-offering. Thus whichever one is offered requires the bread-offering, and once the offering has been made, the others do not require a bread-offering.] [80A] *But then should I imagine that at issue is the beast presented in place of a thank-offering presented not out of obligation but as a freewill donation? Then surely, whether it is offered prior to, or after, atonement, there must be a bread-offering, since this is simply an additional thank-offering.* [Cashdan: Since the original is a freewill thank-offering, there is no obligation to replace it if lost, so what is brought in replacement is simply another thank-offering and does require the bread-offering.] Then does the rule pertain to the offspring of an animal designated as a thank-offering? Then whether offered before atonement or afterward it does not require a bread-offering, since it represents merely the surplus of a thank-offering! [Cashdan: Any accretion to the original thank-offering is treated as surplus, and like the surplus of money used for the purchase of a thank-offering, it does not require a bread-offering.] Rather, it refers to the offspring of a thank-offering that is obligatory. If this is presented prior to atonement, it requires a bread-offering, if afterward, it does not require a bread-offering."

C.   *But that is so obvious that we must wonder what the cited passage proposes to tell us that we do not already know?*

D.   R. Yohanan takes the position that someone may attain atonement through using the increase of what is already consecrated [namely, the offspring in this case]. [Cashdan: As the offspring may be used

> for the atonement, it is deemed a thank-offering just as is the
> mother and therefore requires a bread-offering.]
>
> E.   *Abbayye reflected on the matter in precisely the same way.*

We have now to ask ourselves, to which of the prior components of the
composite, the Mishnah's rule or Sifra's restatement, does No. 2 pertain?
The answer is clear, when we realize that the passage in the Sifra has
cited the language of the Mishnah through the Tosefta's complement, so
the operative distinction, important at I.1.M, which derives from the
Mishnah, is in literary terms intrinsic to Sifra's statement. That is to say,
from the language before us we cannot imagine that the framer of Sifra
depended upon the language of the Mishnah cited out of the Mishnah,
since his own framing of matters has used the language in its own terms.
It must follow that the question raised at **I.2.A** depends solely on **I.1.M**,
and No. 2 has to be classified as a sustained reading of the Sifra's
statement. Put in terms relevant to this monograph, No. 2 serves as a
talmud to the Sifra. The key, so it seems to me, is that the analysis at No.
2 addresses the Sifra's formulation and is continuous with it. What is
decisive is that the question of 2.A is answered at 2.B out of Sifra's
language through an allusion to Sifra.

What are we to make of data of this kind (stipulating that I have not
selected the sole candidates for analysis in the whole of the Bavli)? Now
everybody knows that the compilers of the Bavli and even the authors of
some of its compositions will adduce important passages of the Sifra for
their own purposes. What is important for our purpose is how these
abstracts are treated when they have served the Bavli's framers' purpose.
Are they then left unexamined, as inert facts? Yes indeed, in our sample
we found that that was sometimes the case (for example B. Men. to 6:4A-
L). Are they examined in relationship to the exegesis of the Mishnah?
Yes, that is quite so, and in our sample we have seen some such instances
(for example, B. Men. to 6:6). But are the Sifra passages read in terms of
their own interests, program, foci, points of cogency, and coherent
discourse? Indeed they are, and for the present purpose, that is the key.
For what I have aimed to show in this chapter is not that there certainly
was a *talmud* to the Sifra equivalent to the Talmud of Babylonia to the
Mishnah. Nor do I mean to suggest that a sizable proportion of what we
find in the Sifra has been subjected to that program of critical analysis
that the Bavli brings to the Mishnah. Those propositions do not pertain
to the thesis I here set forth. All I wish to show is two facts.

[1]   The way in which the framers of the Bavli read the Mishnah is
        the way in which the framers of passages, in the Bavli, on the
        Sifra read the Sifra. In the sample examined here, the following

show that that is the fact: B. to Men. 6:3, No. 9; and the items listed below follow suit and exemplify the same fact.

[2]   Passages in the Sifra that are subjected to exegesis may be read not for purposes of Mishnah exegesis but for purposes of Sifra exegesis. In the sample examined here, the following show that that is the fact: B. to Men. 6:3 No. 10; B. to Men. 7:1 III.1-4; IV.1-2; B. to Men. 7:3 II.1-2; III.1-2; B. to Men. 7:4 I.2; B. to Men. 7:7 II.1; B. to Men. 8:2D-I I.1-6; B. to Men. 8:2A-C I:1-2.

What we have learned is one simple fact. There could have been a *talmud* to the Sifra, and, if there were, it would have looked remarkably like "The Talmud," that is, the Bavli. So the Bavli to the Mishnah ought to have equalled the preserved and recorded composition and set of compositions, the composite of critical analysis to the Sifra. But if there was such a *talmud* to the Sifra, it has not survived. There could have been such a document; we do not have it.

Why not? Maybe there was such a *talmud*, but it did not survive. But what if we can show that materials for a talmud to the Tosefta also were fully in hand? On the one side, that, too, may yield only two accidents of circumstance. After all, our sample for Sifra shows what might have been, for the sample is too much a sequence of brief episodes, and out of such, no *talmud* could have come. But what if we see that, in point of fact, the Talmud that we do have in fact for large stretches serves *not* the Mishnah but the Tosefta? Then it would follow that, if there was a talmud to the Tosefta, it has been absorbed into the Talmud to the Mishnah. In that case a very different picture emerges. It is then a fact that will make sense of my question about how the Bavli has shaped rabbinic discourse. So onward to the Tosefta, with a new question: not only whether we find evidences of a talmud to a document other than the Mishnah, but how important such a *talmud* can have been in its own context.

XI. How the Bavli Shaped Rabbinic Discourse

I have shown that we may classify certain passages now preserved in the Bavli as *talmud* to not the Mishnah but Sifra or Tosefta or baraita compositions and compilations. These writings clearly took shape in response to the documentary requirements of a writing other than the Bavli, and I think that they took shape not in the time of the closure of the Bavli but at some prior time. Let me explain why. For two reasons, one general, the other specific, I am inclined to suppose that nondocumentary compositions took shape not only separated from, but in time before, the documentary ones did. The specific reason, for the present study, is the very simple one that the Yerushalmi shows us that the Bavli's treatment of the Tosefta's amplification of the Mishnah's materials in Mishnah-tractate Berakhot Chapter Eight took shape prior to the closure of the Bavli. That is documentary evidence of a very solid order indeed. The more general reason derives from *Making the Classics in Judaism: The Three Stages of Literary Formation.*

Three classifications of writing, all assigned Tannaite standing, all formed after the time of the Mishnah, were read precisely as the Mishnah was read: the Sifra, the Tosefta, and compositions and compositions bearing Tannaite marking known as baraitot. We know that fact because in the pages of the Talmud of Babylonia, substantial passages of all three types are preserved, not solely for the purposes of the compositions concerning the Mishnah or propositions deriving from Mishnah exegesis that the framers of the Bavli formulated. They were preserved along with sustained discussions of their own statements, whether those discussions were required for the purposes of the framers of the passages in which they occur. In point of fact, where we find a sustained analysis of a passage of the Sifra or Tosefta, it is clear, that analysis concerns itself with the requirements of the Sifra or the Tosefta and its meanings in its context; we cannot account for the analytical program by appeal to the interests of Mishnah exegesis and its amplification, but only, to the concerns of Sifra or Tosefta or baraita exegesis. That means that the critical analytical reading of passages, sometimes sizable, of the Sifra, the Tosefta, and the baraita corpus, was undertaken in its own terms. This leads to three conclusions.

[1]   Because the modes of thought and analysis concerning the Sifra, the Tosefta, and the baraita corpus in no way diverged from those that guided inquiry into the Mishnah, I claim that the work that was done falls into the category of *talmud*, as defined earlier.

[2]   And because some of these passages are sustained, I allege that, in addition to The Talmud, the one that imposes meaning upon the Mishnah, there not only can have been, but almost certainly were, other talmuds, in progress for the Sifra, the Tosefta, and components of the baraita compositions and even compilations.

[3]   Where a *talmud* was taking shape around the Tosefta, the Talmud to the Mishnah would consist of the Tosefta's talmud, itself amplified and revised in relationship to the Mishnah's statements, thus, Mishnah paragraph, Tosefta amplification through restatement, in the Mishnah's language, of what the Mishnah was supposed to mean, and, third, further analysis of the Tosefta's judgment of the Mishnah's meaning and the Mishnah's unresolved issues.

These facts, set forth here as foundations for a hypothesis to be tested against a variety of other passages of the Talmud of Babylonia, yield a rather unanticipated conclusion, which is that the framers of the Bavli not only set forth a statement of their own, out of a sizable corpus of received materials. That point I have maintained in prior monographs and requires no amplification here.[4] The framers of the Bavli also took control of, and closed off, prior discourse. They not only chose what would form the systemic statement that defined what we should call "Judaism" and what their apologists would call "the one whole Torah of Moses, our rabbi." They also privileged one document of choice, making its exegesis critical, and set in the background other documents that in earlier times, were subjected to exactly the same engaged exegesis as the Mishnah had long enjoyed. Alongside the Talmuds to the Mishnah (the Yerushalmi and the Bavli as we know them), there might have been a variety of *talmuds* – the *talmud* to Sifra, the *talmud* to Tosefta; the Talmud that we do have, had it emerged only as a secondary development of the talmud to Tosefta, might have been a very different document from what it is. But that is not what we have. And the extant components of such other *talmuds* as have reached us hardly lead us to suppose that somewhere along the line such *talmuds* existed and then were suppressed, though that judgment must be classed as a merely reasonable guess.

Since, it is clear, a variety of received writings were read in one and the same way and even produced writing of a singularly uniform character as to both rhetoric and logic, we must conclude that the *talmud* to the Sifra and the *talmud* to the Tosefta as well as the Talmuds to the Mishnah were taking shape among pretty much the same sorts of persons and at the same time. That proposition, ignoring the document's own allegations concerning the names of the authorities cited therein, which in fact are the same names as those who dominate Mishnah exegesis,[5] seems to me a plausible way of explaining the facts in our

---

[4]*The Bavli and its Sources: The Question of Tradition in the Case of Tractate Sukkah* (Atlanta, 1987: Scholars Press for Brown Judaic Studies); *Tradition as Selectivity: Scripture, Mishnah, Tosefta, and Midrash in the Talmud of Babylonia. The Case of Tractate Arakhin* (Atlanta, 1990: Scholars Press for South Florida Studies in the History of Judaism); *Language as Taxonomy. The Rules for Using Hebrew and Aramaic in the Babylonian Talmud* (Atlanta, 1990: Scholars Press for South Florida Studies in the History of Judaism); *The Rules of Composition of the Talmud of Babylonia. The Cogency of the Bavli's Composite* (Atlanta, 1991: Scholars Press for South Florida Studies in the History of Judaism); *The Bavli's One Voice: Types and Forms of Analytical Discourse and their Fixed Order of Appearance* (Atlanta, 1991: Scholars Press for South Florida Studies in the History of Judaism).

[5]We cannot verify the attributions, so we cannot use them as historical facts or indicators. That the same names occur in a variety of passages can form a

hands about the uniformity of the exegetical discourse on the variety of documents. That seems to me that at a given point, a variety of writings were read in the same way, so that documentary lines played no important role. But then the other fact, that the results of the exegesis of one document were formed into a massive and authoritative writing, the Talmud (of Babylonia, of the Land of Israel), while the results of the exegesis of the other documents, as well as of received materials not formed into a sustained document at all, comes into play. And that other fact tells me that at some point the received program of exegesis, and the forms that that exegesis was to take for preservation and transmission to the future, were radically redefined. At that point, as I have now suggested, the Mishnah assumed a position of priority; all other (potential) talmuds were moved off-stage, and their contents would form a part of the background scenery for the principal drama: the reading of the Mishnah.

How then did the Talmud shape rabbinic discourse? The answer to this question is in two parts. The first concerns the first of the two Talmuds, the Yerushalmi. That document clearly found its definition in the work of Mishnah exegesis. The brief passage we examined showed that it defined the program that the Bavli later on would bring to bear upon precisely the same passage of the Mishnah. What the earlier exegetes found important in relationship to that passage derived from the Tosefta, and the later exegetes followed suit; each set of exegetes, to be sure, put forth its own message, the latter in no way depending upon the former for their agendum. So the framers of the Yerushalmi, with their principal interest in the problem of Mishnah exegesis (in relationship to the Tosefta, in our passage, not so in many, many more passages), will not have provoked much astonishment among the framers of the Sifra, or, indeed, of the Tosefta, or of compositions and even composites of exegesis of baraita sayings. We do not know whether the work of forming a talmud to Sifra or the Tosefta or the baraita compositions and composites went forward after the formation of the Yerushalmi. I should be surprised if it ceased with the Yerushalmi, but I cannot think of any compelling reasons to take one position or the other.

But the work of making a *talmud* to the other documents certainly did come to an end prior to the closure of the Bavli, since, it is obvious, nothing like a sustained talmud to them has come down, and that fact brings us to the latter of the two Talmuds, the Bavli. Whether or not systematic work on the Sifra, Tosefta, or baraita compositions went forward, each in its own documentary setting, after the closure of the

---

convention of later pseudepigraphic authors, so by themselves, names that recur prove nothing.

Yerushalmi, the authorities behind the Bavli clearly had decided that the Mishnah, and the Mishnah alone, would define the structure and order of discourse, and the Mishnah, through the Bavli, did just that. All other writings from the Mishnah forward or assigned the same Tannaite standing as the Mishnah together with received amplifications thereof would be recast into the framework of Mishnah commentary – amplification, complement or thematic supplement – within the pages of the Bavli. Whatever sizable exegeses those materials had already received – once again, amplification, complement or thematic supplement – would follow in the wake of the passages of the primary documents that were selected, and that is why we have them. But there are no grounds for doubting that everything was made to say one thing, which is, the Mishnah is primary, its program paramount, its formation of the Torah authoritative. All other writings, whether the Written Torah or its amplification in the Sifra and parallel compilations, whether the secondary expansion of the Mishnah in its framework, were made to acknowledge this privileged and entitled position accorded to the Mishnah.

If I had to choose a single document, the subordination of which strikes me as remarkable, however, it is not the Sifra but the Tosefta. For the Tosefta can have defined the path that would lead to the talmud to the Mishnah, but in the Talmud as we have it, the Tosefta is merely another source of Tannaite sayings, no more important than any other. I have already set forth, in *The Bavli That Might Have Been: The Tosefta's Theory of Mishnah Commentary Compared with That of the Babylonian Talmud,*[6] a sustained account of what might have been, as against what was. In that work I showed that, while the Tosefta forms a commentary to the Mishnah, and so, too, does the Talmud of Babylonia or the Bavli, the latter document differs from the former in its conception of what is to be done with the Mishnah. By comparing the Tosefta's with the Bavli's treatment of the Mishnah, I demonstrated not only that the Bavli's approach to Mishnah commentary differs from the Tosefta's (which is hardly surprising), *but that the differences in the aggregate are uniform and predictable.* I proved beyond doubt, on the basis of a substantial sample, the fact that the comparison yields a fixed and coherent set of contrasts. So what? In that monograph what I thought important was that, as I had shown to be the case for the Tosefta's authorship in my *The Tosefta: Its Structure and Its Sources* (Atlanta, 1986: Scholars Press for Brown Judaic Studies), so, too, the Bavli's authorship referred to a coherent and cogent program of exegetical principles when they turned to the Mishnah. That is why I attach such weight to the fact that the differences between the

---

[6]Atlanta, 1990: Scholars Press for South Florida Studies in the History of Judaism.

two documents are fixed and predictable. When we compare one document's reading of the original source to the other document's reading of that same source, therefore, we are able to show by the persistence of a fixed set of differences that the latter document is a well-crafted and thoughtfully composed statement, not a mere compilation of this and that: a composition, not a compilation. Since the Bavli is commonly represented as a mere conglomeration of whatever people happened to have received – a sedimentary piece of writing, not a planned and considered one, the result of many centuries of accumulation, not the work of a generation or two of thoughtful writers – these results provide a detailed argument against one proposition and in favor of another.

But in this monograph the same results point our attention elsewhere. What is important is not only difference, but a pattern of difference: the Bavli's framers differ in their theory of Mishnah commentary from the Tosefta's framers, and the differences are consistent throughout. Ordinarily, for example, at any given passage of the Bavli, we begin with the clarification of the Mishnah paragraph, turn then to the examination of the principles of law implicit in the Mishnah paragraph, and then broaden the discussion to introduce what I called analogies from case to law and law to case. These are the three stages of our discussion. It would be very easy to outline a given Talmudic discussion, beginning to end, and to produce a reasoned account of the position and order of every completed composition and the ordering of the several compositions into a composite. But this tripartite program in no way characterizes the Tosefta's reading of the same passage of the Mishnah. That outline has told the framers of the Bavli's passage what comes first – the simplest matters of language, then the more complex matters of analysis of content, then secondary development of analogous principles and cases. Steinsaltz is wrong: we do move from simple criticism of language to weighty analysis of parallels. True, we invoke facts treated elsewhere; but reference is always verbatim, so, with a modicum of information, we can follow the discussion. True, the Talmud is not an elementary primer of the law, but it does not pretend to be. It claims to discuss the Mishnah paragraph that it cites, and it discusses that Mishnah paragraph. So the Bavli's framers had their own ideas of how to read the Mishnah, and they imposed these ideas upon the entire received corpus. This they did by using what they found pertinent. Their silence on the rest tells the story. They wanted the Mishnah to be read first – and not Scripture, as the Sifra's framers maintained. They wanted the Mishnah to be read in its own terms – and not in terms of the Tosefta, as the framers of the talmud to the Tosefta proposed. And they wanted to read the Mishnah themselves, in their own terms, and not only third in line after the framers of the Tosefta and of other Mishnah exegetes, for example, those who worked over the Mishnah in response to Scripture, represented by the Sifra.

So in the manner in which they disposed of the received heritage – not only the heritage of exegesis, received from their masters and their masters from theirs, but the heritage of sacred writ, of Torah, encompassing not only the written but also the oral part preserved in the Mishnah and in other statements bearing Tannaite standing – they defined the discourse of Judaism, always precipitated by the Bavli as was the case, from then to now. Discourse in Judaism would commence with the Mishnah, circle around back to Scripture, proceed outward in every possible direction, always ending where it began: with the oral component of the one whole Torah of Moses, our rabbi.

Index

South Florida Studies in the History of Judaism